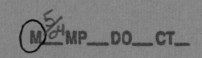

THE WAY THEY GO TO CALIFORNIA.

**WHEN I HEAR THE IRON HORSE MAKE THE HILLS ECHO ... IT SEEMS AS IF THE EARTH HAD GOT A RACE NOW WORTHY TO INHABIT IT.**

*— Henry David Thoreau, Walden, 1854*

SOUTHERN

1401

*Above: Southern Railway steam locomotive*
*Number 1401, built 1926.*
*Previous page: Cartoon laughs at 1850s gold rush fever.*

**MY FAVORITE THING IS TO
GO WHERE I'VE NEVER BEEN.**

*– Diane Arbus, 1971*

*Model of the S.S.* Leviathan *as refitted in 1923.*

*Dodge school bus, used in Martinsburg, Indiana, 1940s.*

WHEN I DECLINED TO GIVE UP
MY SEAT, IT WAS NOT THAT DAY,
OR BUS, IN PARTICULAR.
I JUST WANTED TO BE FREE
LIKE EVERYBODY ELSE.

—*Rosa Parks, 2000*

Smithsonian
*National Museum of American History*
*Behring Center*

# ON THE MOVE

## TRANSPORTATION AND THE AMERICAN STORY

### BY JANET F. DAVIDSON & MICHAEL S. SWEENEY

NATIONAL GEOGRAPHIC

WASHINGTON, D.C.

*Above: Faceplate from an automobile turn signal, made by hand and patented in 1929.*
*Previous page: O. Winston Link photograph captures America on the move at a drive-in theater in Iaeger, West Virginia, 1956.*

# CONTENTS

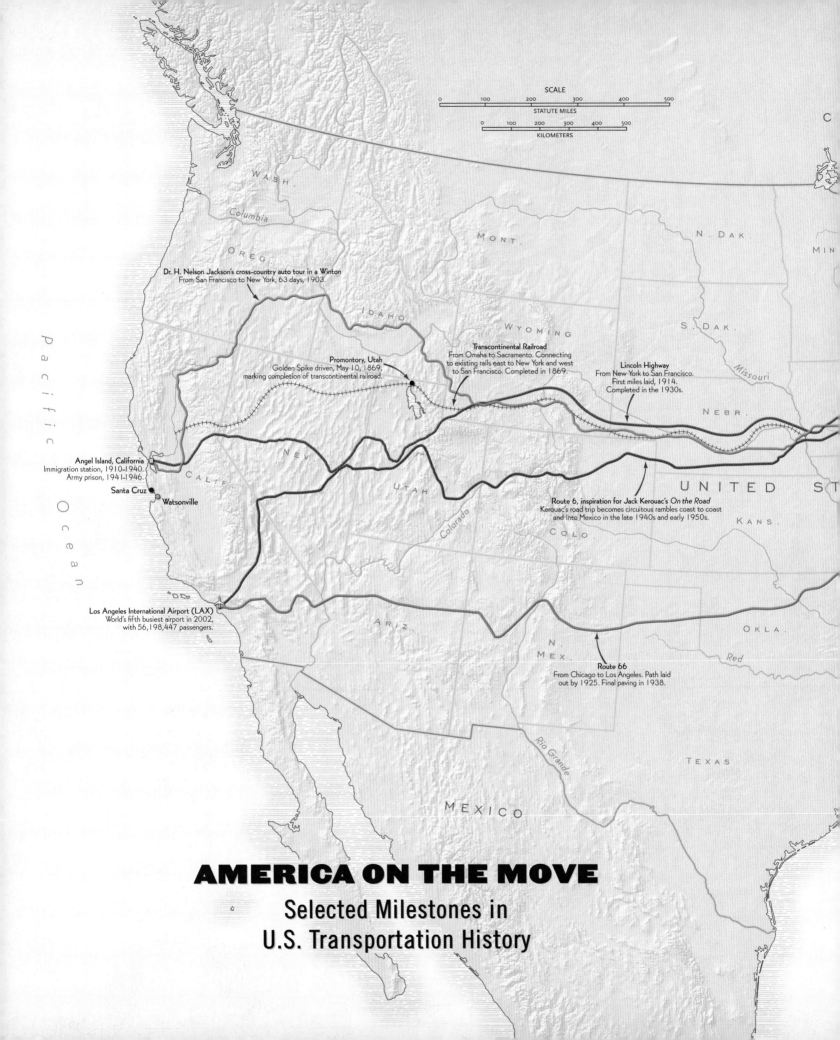

Dr. H. Nelson Jackson's cross-country auto tour in a Winton
From San Francisco to New York, 63 days, 1903.

Promontory, Utah
Golden Spike driven, May 10, 1869,
marking completion of transcontinental railroad.

Transcontinental Railroad
From Omaha to Sacramento. Connecting
to existing rails east to New York and west
to San Francisco. Completed in 1869.

Lincoln Highway
From New York to San Francisco.
First miles laid, 1914.
Completed in the 1930s.

Angel Island, California
Immigration station, 1910–1940.
Army prison, 1941–1946.

Santa Cruz

Watsonville

Route 6, inspiration for Jack Kerouac's *On the Road*
Kerouac's road trip becomes circuitous rambles coast to coast
and into Mexico in the late 1940s and early 1950s.

Los Angeles International Airport (LAX)
World's fifth busiest airport in 2002,
with 56,198,447 passengers.

Route 66
From Chicago to Los Angeles. Path laid
out by 1925. Final paving in 1938.

SCALE

100   200   300   400   500
STATUTE MILES

100   200   300   400   500
KILOMETERS

Pacific Ocean

Columbia

WASH.

OREG.

IDAHO

MONT.

N. DAK.

WYOMING

S. DAK.

NEBR.

NEV.

CALIF.

UTAH

Colorado

COLO.

UNITED    ST

KANS.

ARIZ.

N.
MEX.

OKLA.

Red

Rio Grande

TEXAS

MEXICO

Missouri

# AMERICA ON THE MOVE
## Selected Milestones in
## U.S. Transportation History

Erie Canal
From Lake Erie, near Buffalo, to the Hudson River and on to New York City. Completed in 1825.

Rochester

Buffalo

Detroit
Ford Model T introduced, 1908. First assembly line in nearby Highland Park, 1913.

Chicago-O'Hare International Airport (ORD)
World's second busiest in 2002, with 66,501,496 passengers.

Levittown, New York
First house sold, 1949. Population 60,000 by 1960.

New York

New York John F. Kennedy International Airport (JFK)
World's 25th busiest airport in 2002, with 28,888,686 passengers.

Park Forest
8,000 houses sold by 1950. Population 30,000 by 1960.

Ellis Island, New York
Immigration station, 1892–1954.

Washington, D.C.

Atlanta Hartsfield International Airport (ATL)
World's busiest airport in 2002, with 76,876,128 passengers.

CANADA

Lake Superior

Lake Michigan

Lake Huron

WIS.

MICH.

L. Ontario

L. Erie

IOWA

ILL.

IND.

OHIO

MO.

KY.

TENN.

ARK.

MISS.

ALA.

GA.

Mississippi

Ohio

W. VA.

VA.

N.C.

S.C.

LA.

FLA.

Gulf of Mexico

Atlantic

Ocean

CUBA

---

KEY to CHAPTER HIGHLIGHTS

**CHAPTER 1: 1780s–1869**
╪╪╪╪╪ Transcontinental Railroad
╫╫╫╫╫ Erie Canal, New York

**CHAPTER 2: 1870s–1900s**
● Santa Cruz, California
● Watsonville, California

**CHAPTER 3: 1870s–1920s**
── Lincoln Highway

**CHAPTER 4: 1880s–1930s**
── Jackson's cross-country auto tour

**CHAPTER 5: 1890s–1930s**
▣ Ellis Island, New York
▣ Angel Island, California

**CHAPTER 6: 1900s–1940s**
● Detroit, Michigan

**CHAPTER 7: 1920s–1950s**
── Route 66

**CHAPTER 8: 1940s–1950s**
● Levittown, New York
● Park Forest, Illinois

**CHAPTER 9: 1930s–1970s**
── Jack Kerouac's Route 6

**CHAPTER 10: 1950s–2000s**
✈ Los Angeles LAX airport
✈ Chicago O'Hare airport
✈ Atlanta Hartsfield airport
✈ New York JFK airport

# FOREWORD
# AN AMERICAN STORY

Each of us has a powerful journey story deep in our personal heritage. It may be a story of a family uprooting itself in order to stay together, or of a family sending sons and daughters to far-off places, or of a distant ancestor, perhaps unknown. For those living in North America, the story may be of people who came to the continent millennia ago, or people who came voluntarily as immigrants, or people who came in chains.

For Native Americans, journey stories are central to culture. For all of us, our identities are built partly upon where our families came from and where we've moved since, mixing the culture we've brought with us each time with the conflicts and cultural intersections that further shape identity.

Travel today is fast and cheap. Ancestral travel seems irrelevant. Although some are not so lucky, most of us commute with ease, travel for fun or business, and pull up stakes to move on to fresh opportunity with little trouble. Thus, in the developed world, societies are marked by their mobility. In the United States, each person older than five years made an average of 4.3 trips per day and traveled over 15,500 miles during 2001. Growth in travel also has been phenomenal. Since 1970, vehicle-miles by auto in the United States leaped 77 percent, to over 1.6 trillion in 2001. In the ten years since 1991, the number of passengers annually departing from the country's top 20 airports on major airlines jumped 39 percent, to 327 million.

This frenetic activity is matched in intensity by the movement of goods and raw materials. Measured in tons loaded times miles carried, intercity freight by truck more than doubled in the United States from 1980 to 2000. At the same time, rail freight grew 60 percent. For every person in the country in 2000, the nation's highways, railways, domestic waterways, pipelines, and airways carried 13,800 ton-miles of goods and materials.

We take this way of life for granted. Transportation is like plumbing: We notice it only when it's

*Balancing on Glacier Point at Yosemite National Park, in California, vactioners in 1923 attest to the versatility of the fledgling automobile.*

backed up. In many undeveloped countries, the mobility and commerce of the wealthy may rival Western measures, but for the poor, such measures are still stuck at 18th-century levels. We pause to wonder if the resources of the planet can possibly sustain the standards we are used to, if they were to be applied worldwide.

But does our culture create our transport systems, or is it, at least in part, the other way around? Transportation interconnects every other economic and cultural activity, and thus the ways of transport are interwoven profoundly into every culture. Some would say that with the invention of the train in the 19th century, the advent of the affordable automobile in the early 20th, and then the coming of viable commercial aircraft a few decades later, people just naturally took to these new vehicles. But what of the cultural and economic conditions that were the essential contexts for those inventions and their wide adoption?

A couple of thoughts about culture are worth pondering. The framers of our Constitution and Bill of Rights didn't specifically enumerate a "right of travel." That right comes indirectly, as in the right of free assembly. In a nation made of and by immigrants, the right of personal movement, free from political hindrance, seemed intrinsic—except among its slaves. But slaves, too, took that right to heart: hence, the Underground Railroad. Culture sets conditions for technology and its uses, such as travel.

Or think of other migrations within the United States. After the completion of a national network of railroads in the 1870s, movements of families seeking better lives became common, and such movements went everywhere: not only east to west, but west to east, south to north, and in every direction. As a consequence, the old "Westward!" notion atrophied, the insular sectionalism of our old politics eroded, and intercultural conflicts increased. Before the 1860s, however, a family trekking west was on a one-way trip, across The Great Desert (as it was marked on maps in those days) west of Nebraska to California or Oregon. The family was rending asunder its ties to its former home and friends in a way that we, in the age of the interstate highway and the jet airplane, cannot comprehend. So here, technology changes culture.

In our present age, physical mobility is a precondition of social mobility. And so we come full circle. The older journeys of ancestors seeking better lives are ingrained within us.

The story of transportation is the story of ourselves.

— *Bill Withuhn*
*Curator of Transportation, National Museum of American History*
*Smithsonian Institution*

NOT I, NOT ANY ONE ELSE
CAN TRAVEL THAT ROAD FOR YOU,
YOU MUST TRAVEL IT FOR YOURSELF.

IT IS NOT FAR, IT IS WITHIN REACH,
PERHAPS YOU HAVE BEEN
ON IT SINCE YOU WERE BORN
AND DID NOT KNOW,
PERHAPS IT IS EVERYWHERE
ON WATER AND ON LAND.

— *Walt Whitman, "Song of Myself," 1881*

# TRANSPORTATION AND THE MAKING OF A **CONTINENTAL NATION**

*From the 1860s on, thousands built railroads across the continent. Opposite, clockwise from upper left: A Central Pacific construction gang, April 1869; a Northern Pacific work crew, 1885; a rail car hangs out over a damaged trestle; workers cart dirt near Secrettown, California, 1867. Telegraph keys and lanterns, above, conveyed messages along the tracks.*

On May 10th, 1869, in Promontory, Utah, workers and officials celebrated the completion of the nation's first transcontinental rail link. The ceremony was the culmination of more than two decades of work. A battalion of dreamers, surveyors, engineers, financiers, and politicians, plus an army of thousands of Chinese, Irish, Mormons, and other workers, had turned the idea of a railroad across the North American continent into a reality.

The news sped through the nation: "By a connection of the telegraph with the last spike (a gold one, from California), the last blow given announced to the world the completion of the grand enterprise," reported *Harpers New Monthly Magazine*. When the news reached cities and towns throughout the nation, cannons fired, church bells rang, locomotive whistles sounded, and fire alarms blared in celebration of the new continental connection. Chicago residents held a spontaneous parade that was, as the *Chicago Tribune* put it, "free from the atmosphere of warlike energy and the suggestions of suffering, danger, and death which threw their oppressive shadow over the celebrations of our victories during the war for the Union." New York churches held special services. Trinity Church's bells rang to commemorate the event, and inside Reverend Vinton told his congregation that the railroad would bestow blessings on the nation: "It will populate our vast territory, and be the great highway of the nations; their merchants will cross it to trade with us. But there is another aspect in which we view it as a blessing, and in connection with which we esteem it of still greater import. It will preserve the union of these States."

The completion of the transcontinental railroad was a great technological and engineering feat. More than that, it was a symbolic moment in history. Political will, technological prowess, sheer hard work, and the impulse toward westward expansion came together in a triumphant moment. Progress was writ visible onto the landscape.

Over time, the new transcontinental railroad lost its original luster amidst accusations of corruption and scandal; but its symbolic importance did not fade. In 1876, when Americans looked back at their first century as a nation, many orators used the railroad as a metaphor for the country's progress. Speaking to an ardent Santa Cruz, California, crowd on July 4th, 1876, a town elder proclaimed, "Civilization has reached out over the whole land; the busy hum of trade is heard where the wilderness once stood in undisturbed solitude; the hunting grounds of the savage are covered with waving crops and thrifty homes; the bowels of the earth have been searched, and yield inexhaustible supplies of mineral wealth; distance has been almost annihilated by the locomotive and the telegraph.... Twenty-five years ago a trip across the continent consumed months of travel attended with many hardships and dangers. Now it is accomplished, from ocean to ocean, a distance of over 3,000 miles, in less than four days, with comfort and pleasure."

. . .

Seventy years earlier, the idea of a four-day trip across the country, let alone a transcontinental railroad, was beyond most people's wildest imaginings. Inventors in 1800 were trying to harness the power of steam,

*A shake of the hands, above, celebrated the completion of the first transcontinental line on May 10, 1869. Railroad companies soon began advertising for customers, right. Following pages: As railroads cut across the continent, Native Americans were pushed off their lands and onto reservations. Many resisted but still gathered near reservations like South Dakota's Pine Ridge, site of the 1890 massacre at Wounded Knee.*

but the commercially viable use of steam power lay in the future, and travel remained difficult. The United States was a smaller nation than it is today—16 states, all located east of the Appalachians—and the vast extent of the American continent was yet unexplored by its newest group of inhabitants. Many speculated about a transcontinental water passage, but at the end of the 18th and the beginning of the 19th centuries, the mysterious expanse of land that spread westward seemed formidable yet full of promise to citizens of the United States.

J. Hector St. John de Crèvecoeur, a Frenchman living in New York in the 1790s, believed that the "many ages will not see the... unknown bounds of North America entirely peopled. Who can tell how far it [the continent] extends? Who can tell the millions of men whom it will feed and contain? For no European foot has as yet traveled half the extent of this mighty continent!" Crèvecoeur expressed the optimism and hope—for many, a hope tinged with fear—that people in the nascent nation felt as they turned their gazes westward. Knowing very little about the rest of the continent, most citizens assumed that continental expansion would carry on into the distant future. But at the same time they believed it inevitable, and necessary, that the vast landmass—from the Atlantic to the Pacific—come under the domain of a single government.

In 1801, President Thomas Jefferson certainly held those views. In a letter to James Monroe, then governor of Virginia, Jefferson wrote, "However our present interests may restrain us within our own limits, it is impossible not to look forward to distant

times, when our rapid multiplication will expand itself beyond those limits, and cover the whole northern, if not the southern continent, with a people speaking the same language, governed in similar forms, & by similar laws." Although the landmass was already peopled by a richly diverse set of inhabitants—Native Americans, Africans, African Americans, and the residents of New Spain—Jefferson envisioned a homogeneous continental nation, peopled by independent white yeoman farmers. Fierce political battles may have wracked the early Republic, but Jefferson's opponents shared his vision. The New York *Evening Post*, a Federalist paper, announced in 1802 that "It belongs of *right* to the United States to regulate the future destiny of *North America*. The country is *ours*; ours is the right to its rivers and to all the sources of future opulence, power and happiness."

It was an amazing act of bravado to imagine the United States as a continental nation, even if those visions were tempered with caveats that it would happen in "distant times" or "many ages" hence. America had won the War of Independence and survived the constitutional crisis of the 1780s, but the country was small, poor, weak, and scarcely populated. Its territories stretched to the Mississippi River, but most settlers lived within 50 miles of the Atlantic.

The United States was also surrounded by other sovereignties. While in the East many Native American populations had been decimated by European diseases and pushed off their lands by Anglo-American settlers, they still inhabited the West. Comanche, Mandan, Pawnee, Navajo, Arapaho, Shawnee, Klamath, and other Native American groups still maintained tribal integrity in the western half of the continent. Some had called North America home for thousands of years.

European empires also laid claim to great chunks of the continent in 1800. In residence the longest, the Spanish owned Florida and New Spain, which stretched from today's American Southwest to Panama, and the vast Louisiana Territory, although they were in the process of ceding that to the French. Britain controlled North American lands to the north and held an interest in Oregon. Russia owned Alaska. The United States, internationally recognized only after the 1783 Treaty of Paris, was a young upstart nation whose official region stretched no farther than the eastern banks of the Mississippi River.

Over the next 50 years, the size and scope of the United States changed dramatically. In one fell swoop, Jefferson's 1803 Louisiana Purchase doubled the size of the country. Doubters questioned the deal—and the very idea of a continental nation. They argued it was misguided, financially irresponsible, and unconstitutional. Even Jefferson himself was concerned about overstepping the bounds of his constitutional authority. But he put those doubts aside and declared, in the face of his critics, "The larger our association, the less will it be shaken by local passions; and in any view, is it not better that the opposite bank of the Mississippi should be settled by our own brethren and children, than by strangers of another family? With which shall we be most likely to live in harmony and friendly intercourse?"

Although deeply rooted in his native Virginia, Jefferson was fascinated with what lay to the west.

Mrs. Frances Trollope,

## AN ENGLISH LADY VISITS

**JOURNEY BY STEAMBOAT**

FRANCES TROLLOPE'S SNOBBISH ANTI-AMERICANISM MADE HER THE TARGET OF CARICATURE, ABOVE. SOME LIKENESSES SHOWED A BRAWNY, PIPE-SMOKING HARRIDAN. THIS CARICATURE WAS CLIPPED AND PASTED INTO A 19TH-CENTURY SCRAPBOOK.

WHEN FRANCES TROLLOPE'S BOOK, *Domestic Manners of the Americans,* was published in 1832, it became an instant sensation, both in Europe and the United States, but for very different reasons.

Her prose infuriated many Americans, because she frankly declared that she didn't like the United States. Trollope's portrait of American life was often very unflattering to the residents of the young Republic. "The total and universal want of manners, both in males and females, is so remarkable, that I was constantly endeavouring to account for it," wrote Mrs. Trollope, mother of the Victorian novelist, Anthony Trollope. "I very seldom during my whole stay in the country heard a sentence elegantly turned, and correctly pronounced, from the lips of an American. There is always something either in the expression or the accents that jars the feelings and shocks the taste."

Trollope complained of being unable to hire good servants and criticized the poor manners and habits of Americans. She was especially disgusted by Americans' propensity for "loathsome spitting" and the public's "total want of all the usual courtesies of the table."

Trollope connected these habits to democracy: She disdained what she called "the leveling effects on the manners of the people," produced, she believed, by America's political system. European readers seem to have enjoyed Trollope's domestic portraits, though, full of rich, sharply drawn anecdotes of the daily trials of an "English Lady" in the New World. She was at once a critical ogre and an elegant journalist, as her two very different portraits suggest.

Trollope didn't set out to write a book on America. She set out to escape the indignities of her family's ever increasing poverty. In 1827, Frances and three of her five children left England in the company of a family friend, Frances Wright, an English radical and feminist who had set up a utopian community in Tennessee. As Trollope wrote to a friend, "some pecuniary claims which came upon us quite unexpectedly, made it very necessary that we should leave our pretty place and large establishment for a year or two at least." For an aristocratically inclined Englishwoman, even a utopian community in Tennessee seemed preferable to suffering the public ignominy of having to live frugally in England. And so Frances and her family began what turned out to be a long sojourn in the United States.

Nothing seemed to turn out as planned. The Trollopes, Wright, and a French painter, Auguste Hervieu, who had joined the Trollope coterie, landed in New Orleans on Christmas Day, 1827. By New Year's Day, the party was on the move once more, as they boarded a steamboat bound for Memphis. Two weeks later, they arrived in that Tennessee city and went to Wright's utopian community, Nashoba. Horrified by the conditions, the Trollope party spent only ten days in Tennessee before they decided to leave.

After a five-day wait in Memphis, the Trollope party boarded the steamboat *Criterion* and set off for Cincinnati. They arrived at their destination on February 10, 1828. The 1,500-mile trip up the Mississippi River took just over a month and was fairly uneventful.

To modern travelers, this monthlong trip might seem interminable. But to travelers of the time, steamboats were amazingly fast conveyances. Frances Trollope's journey would have been unthinkable before 1815, the year steamboats began to ply their trade up and down Western rivers. One 1820s traveler described going upriver as traveling "like a comet, at the rate of twelve knots an hour." Finally boats could move against the river's current as well as with it, thanks to newly developed steam power.

OTHER IMAGES CONVEYED FRANCES TROLLOPE AS A LOVELY GENTLEWOMAN, BELOW RIGHT. HER TRAVEL NARRATIVE WAS PUBLISHED IN BOTH ENGLAND AND THE UNITED STATES, BELOW LEFT. MANY EUROPEANS, INCLUDING ALEXIS DE TOCQUEVILLE, CAME TO THE UNITED STATES IN THE EARLY 19TH CENTURY TO SEE THE NEW DEMOCRATIC EXPERIMENT IN ACTION. THEIR OBSERVATIONS INTERESTED READERS ON BOTH CONTINENTS.

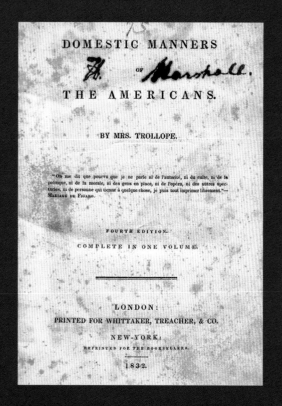

Three exploratory ventures into the interior of the continent had already failed. In January 1803, President Jefferson sent a confidential message to Congress, proposing an expedition to establish trade and diplomatic links with Native Americans in the continent's interior. Jefferson claimed that "An intelligent officer, with ten or twelve chosen men, fit for the enterprise, and willing to undertake it... might explore the whole line, even to the Western ocean." He asked Congress to appropriate $2,500 for the journey and named as its captain his personal secretary, 28-year-old Meriwether Lewis.

Lewis, William Clark, and their Corps of Discovery set off westward with the charge to explore the continent, both the new territory just acquired from the French and the land past its boundaries, through to Oregon and the Pacific Ocean. On June 20, 1803, Thomas Jefferson wrote to Lewis, "The Object of your mission is to explore the Missouri river & such principal stream of it as by it's course and communication with the waters of the Pacific ocean, whether the Columbia, Oregon, Colorado or any other river may offer the most direct & practicable water communication across this continent for the purpose of commerce." Jefferson also wanted the men—for the sake of science, diplomacy, commerce, and posterity—to record what they saw, to collect plant and animal specimens, and to document the geography of the land they crossed.

With a band of nearly four dozen men, and Seaman, Lewis's large Newfoundland dog, Lewis and Clark set off up the Missouri River in May 1804. In October, they had not yet reached the river's source.

Stopping "at the edge of the unknown," the company wintered with the Mandan Indians in modern-day McLean County, North Dakota, where Toussaint Charbonneau and his wife, Sacagawea, a Shoshone Indian, joined them as interpreters. Over the winter Sacagawea bore a son, Jean Baptiste, who joined the expedition. Clark nicknamed him "Pomp."

The expedition crossed the Continental Divide in August 1805. By autumn, the Corps reached the Pacific Ocean. They wintered over in Fort Clatsop, Oregon, then returned eastward, splitting up so that they could document more of the land. At the mercy of the elements, the existing inhabitants, and the very land itself, the Corps was the first group of United States citizens to see and travel through the formidable Rocky Mountains. While Jefferson had dreamed of a navigable water passage to the Pacific, those hopes faded under the height of the Rockies. The map William Clark made in the winter of 1806, using data he collected with his compass and from informants along the route, portrayed a more realistic vision of the continent.

The Louisiana Purchase and the Lewis and Clark expedition were just the beginning of expansions in the 19th century. Spain sold East Florida to the United States in 1819. The United States annexed the independent state of Texas, won victory in the Mexican American War, and made deals with England over the Oregon Territory, thereby adding over one million square miles to the country in the 1840s. By 1850, the nation stretched from sea to shining sea. Amazingly, Jefferson's vision of a continental nation was fulfilled within 25 years of his

death, rather than in the distant future, as he and others had predicted.

Political control does not make a landmass into a nation. Connections and relationships do. Those connections can be idealistic, commercial, cultural, political, or social, but they are also—on an equally profound if more mundane level—physical. Once explorers determined that there was no east-to-west, coast-to-coast waterway, it became clear that only transportation networks could turn the United States into a continental whole. The transcontinental railroad may have been delayed by congressional squabbles over the route, concerns about finances, and engineering challenges. Still, by revolutionizing transportation systems throughout the first half of the 19th century, Americans created connections that made the continent into a nation.

. . .

Transportation systems transformed the nation's commerce. In 1800, most business traveled along America's natural highways: navigable lakes and rivers and the Atlantic Ocean. Waterways worked well for carrying goods to and from some regions, but most of the country remained out of reach. Commerce depended heavily on trade with other nations into the 1800s. As one historian put it,

*At the beginning of the 19th century, the economies of the West and the South were interconnected by trade and transport, opposite. Southern plantation owners bought western grain to feed their slaves, which allowed them to concentrate on cash crops. By 1825, the South produced much of the world's cotton. Millions of African Americans, inset, served King Cotton.*

"Merchants in Boston and New York had more contact with their counterparts in London and the West Indies than with farmers a few miles away."

Through the course of the 19th century, that outward orientation changed. Dreamers, inventors, politicians, and entrepreneurs began to imagine—and pay for—new transportation systems. They exploited natural rivers and waterways, built new waterways, or eased travel over the land itself. By 1860, new transportation systems interlocked and sometimes even competed, forming uneven webs of connection between regions. Wagon roads and railroads, steamboats and canals changed the flow of commerce, shaping a new United States.

Most Americans were still farmers. With new transportation opportunities, farming was becoming part of a larger market economy. In the Northeast, more people were moving into cities and finding work in industry. The South's economy remained primarily agricultural. Slave-grown cotton was king, and the South shipped raw material to Europe and, increasingly, to northeastern textile mill towns like Lowell, Massachusetts. Farmers in states like Illinois and Ohio shipped wheat, corn, and pork to other parts of the country by floating their products down the great Mississippi. Their production levels eclipsed the output of small, rocky New England farms. Midwestern goods helped feed the slaveholding South and the expanding urban populations in the Northeast, linking the newly settled areas of what was then the West to the rest of the country.

Water—the lifeblood of American trade and travel for centuries—remained a profoundly important link between regions, but river and lake travel underwent a dramatic transformation in the 19th century. America's first commercially successful steamboat traveled up the Hudson River to Albany in 1807. By 1815, steamboats were chugging along on the Mississippi. "A steamboat, coming from New Orleans, brings to the remotest villages of our streams, and the very doors of the cabins, a little Paris, a section of Broadway, or a slice of Philadelphia, to ferment in the minds of our young people, the innate propensity for fashions and finery," one observer commented in 1827. By 1840, more than 500 steamboats worked the rivers of the West. Even after the railroads were up and running, steamboats continued to tie together people and places.

Before steamboats, the route down the Mississippi and into New Orleans was the most important commercial link between the Southern and Western parts of the country, but trade could only move downriver. Keelboats could negotiate the passage back up, but it was just too difficult and expensive. To travel from New Orleans to Louisville, for example, could take three months. So bulk goods floated down the Mississippi on wooden flatboats. Arriving downriver, a flatboat was broken up for lumber, and the man who steered it embarked on a months-long northward walk home. Goods reached New Orleans and then were shipped out, either up the coast to seaboard ports or to foreign destinations. Otherwise goods moved overland. But freighting costs were so high to move products overland for long distances that it was rarely attempted.

Distinctively American, the river steamboat changed the flow of traffic in the United States. Eastern steamboats mainly carried passengers on deep rivers like the Hudson. With low-pressure engines, they were designed to go fast. Boats in the West carried more freight and plied shallow, rocky waters, so they differed in design. Tall piloting cabins towered above wide, broad hulls, and flat bottoms provided the shallow draft needed to manage the Western rivers. High-pressure engines and lightweight construction meant that the average western steamboat only paddled the waters for about five years. They were prone to running aground or exploding, so some didn't even make it that long. One observer wrote that they seemed to be "built of wood, tin, shingles, canvas and twine" and "look like a bride of Babylon. If a steamboat should go to sea, the ocean would take one playful slap at it, and people would be picking up kindling on the beach for the next eleven years."

Despite their flimsiness, steamboats made two-way river traffic feasible and reordered the flow of commerce. Goods moved through New Orleans and up the Mississippi, building connections between the plantation South and the newly settled West. New Orleans of the 1820s became a port of commercial and strategic importance. As one observer remarked, it was "the point of union between the North and the South. The production of all climes find their way hither, and for fruits and vegetables it appears [to me] to be unrivalled." Flatboats still carried goods through Louisiana: Four times as many arrived in New Orleans in 1846-47 as had done so in 1814. Upriver steamboats made it easier for the flatboat drivers to get back home.

## THE WEST BEFORE LEWIS AND CLARK

**LITTLE WAS KNOWN OF THE WESTERN TWO-THIRDS OF THE CONTINENT BEFORE THE CORPS OF DISCOVERY EXPEDITION IN 1803-06.**

WHEN MERIWETHER LEWIS, WILLIAM CLARK, AND THE CORPS OF DISCOVERY SET OFF IN 1803, THEY DEPENDED ON THIS MAP BY AARON ARROWSMITH—CONSIDERED THE BEST OF THE DAY—TO CHART THEIR COURSE ON THE EARLY PART OF THE JOURNEY. AS THEY PROGRESSED, THEY HAD NO MAP: MUCH OF THE WEST WAS A BLANK. ONE OF THEIR MISSIONS WAS TO GENERATE THE INFORMATION NEEDED TO MAKE NEW CONTINENTAL RENDERINGS.

AS THE CORPS TRAVELED UPRIVER, DETAILS ON THIS MAP OF THE UPPER BASIN HELPED THE MEN DECIDE TO STAY ON THE MISSOURI RIVER AND NOT TO DETOUR ONTO THE TEMPTING MARIAS RIVER. AT THE SOURCE OF THE MISSOURI, THEY FOUND NO CONNECTING WATERWAY TO THE COLUMBIA—THEIR PATH TO THE PACIFIC—BUT THEY WERE HEADED IN THE RIGHT DIRECTION: WEST.

TO ADD TO THIS VIEW OF THE WEST, WILLIAM CLARK CHARTED THE CORPS'S PATH ACROSS PLAINS AND MOUNTAINS. HE ASKED FUR TRADERS AND NATIVE AMERICANS FOR DETAILS ABOUT THE LAND AND RIVERS. DREAMS OF A WATER PASSAGE ACROSS THE COUNTRY FADED WHEN—BETWEEN THE MISSOURI AND THE COLUMBIA—THE CORPS RECKONED WITH THE ROCKY MOUNTAINS. CLARK LATER MADE A MORE REALISTIC MAP.

Americans also found ways to move beyond the waterways and farther west. By the middle of the 19th century, driven by collective grit and individual determination, settlers numbering in the hundreds of thousands spread all the way to the Pacific Ocean. Despite dismal roads in the East and worse to none farther west, many took up the challenge of long-distance overland travel in the 1840s and 1850s.

Most emigrants settling the Pacific West traveled over land. Even before California became a U.S. territory in 1848, white settlers made the long, difficult journey into the area. Trails to California over the steep Sierra ranges, with year-round snow atop many a peak, made for rough going. California-bound Addison Crane, cutting through Carson Pass in the Sierra Nevadas, called it "the most wild looking chasm eye ever rested upon, and the worst road the human imagination can conceive."

Despite the harsh terrain and the months it took to trek across the country, people traveled west in droves. In 1841, the first emigrant party successfully traversed the California Sierra Nevadas. That May, 69 men, women, and children set off from Sapling Grove, Kansas. They had some provisions, little money, and even less sense of where they were going.

The choice of what to take was difficult for people making a one-way trip. An early guide, from the 1840s, advised that westward travelers take a gun, powder and lead, along with "two hundred pounds of flour or meal; one hundred and fifty pounds of bacon; ten pounds of coffee; twenty pounds of sugar; and ten pounds of salt." Most people carried extra supplies for the wagon, a pared-down set of cooking utensils, and goods to trade with Indians along the way. John Bidwell, one of the organizers, remembered many years later, "I doubt whether there was one hundred dollars in money in the whole party, but all were enthusiastic and anxious to go."

The number traveling with Bidwell dropped by half when they got to Soda Springs, Idaho, on the Bear River: Some turned north toward Oregon. Those continuing to California became afraid that they would not make it before the snows. They abandoned their wagons so they could travel faster. "We stopped one day and threw away everything we could not carry, made pack saddles, and packed the oxen, mules and horses, and started," said Bidwell. They reached California on November 4, 1841.

Between 1841 and 1857, more than 165,000 people migrated to California by land, and hundreds of thousands more traveled by land to Oregon. Emigrant trails established links between the interior and the Pacific. Roads shaped up through California as more and more people expected to receive mail and goods. By the late 1850s, stagecoach roads crossed the continent, all the way into California.

As citizens moved through and onto western lands, they encountered the peoples already dwelling on them. Manifest Destiny carried prerogatives with it, Americans believed, and early 19th-century federal and state officials took steps to seize lands from Native Americans. They encouraged—or insisted—that all Indians move west of the Mississippi, to consolidate the government grip on the entire continent. Officials acted on the principles that whites were superior and that the United States was destined to control the continent. Some Indians resisted. Congress passed the Indian Removal Act in 1830, and the Cherokee took their legal argument all the way to the Supreme Court, winning their sovereign right to lands in Georgia. At the same time, though, a small group of Cherokee signed a removal treaty, agreeing to vacate the land and providing a legal basis for Indian removal from Georgia, even though the signators represented a tiny proportion of the Cherokee Nation. The Senate ratified the treaty, despite many protests. In 1838, the U.S. Army began forcibly removing the Cherokee, sending them to Indian Territory—present-day Oklahoma—over a thousand miles away. As many as 15,000 Cherokee marched west against their will, with such sorrow and devastating loss of life that their path came to be called the "Trail of Tears." As the Indians left, under threat of law or worse, white settlement expanded.

Hundreds of thousands of people, willing and unwilling, settlers and Indians, moved west, traveling by foot, horse, carriage, or wagon. But roads in the 19th century simply did not, and could not, form the backbone of a practical, year-round, all-weather, national transportation network. The more the country expanded, the more clear it became that one was needed.

. . .

*Following pages: Images like Albert Bierstadt's 1864 "Sunset, California Scenery" helped spread the idea that California was beautiful, empty, and wild. Both popular and prolific, Bierstadt painted numerous sublime landscapes of the American West.*

Canals were America's first attempt to move beyond nature's own waterways. Builders often followed natural contours but still cut a man-made swath, creating new routes that responded to human needs. On July 4, 1817, in fitting recognition of the nation's 41st birthday, the first steps were taken toward an Erie Canal. At dawn that day, a crowd gathered in Rome, New York. Judge John Richardson, who held the contract to build the first section of the canal, turned over the first shovelful of earth.

In 1817, the 28-mile-long Middlesex Canal between Boston and Lowell, Massachusetts, was the nation's longest. The Erie was to extend more than 300 miles and connect the Hudson River with Lake Erie, the East Coast with the frontier, joining a chain of waterways between New York and Toledo, Ohio.

Funded by the State of New York, the Erie was more than an engineering project. It was a symbol of transcendent progress. De Witt Clinton—a past New York City mayor, future New York State governor, and one of the canal's leading proponents—argued that it would be "a work more stupendous, more magnificent, and more beneficial than has hitherto been achieved by the human race." Not everyone agreed. Opponents of the canal argued that New York was funding a 40-foot-wide, 4-foot-deep, 363-mile-long "monument of weakness and folly."

They were wrong. Even before the canal was officially opened in 1825, it began to generate income. By the time it was finished, the state had already collected more than a million dollars in tolls. "Its final completion and junction with Lake Erie was effected, amidst the cheers of thousands, on Wednesday,

Built between 1817 and 1825, the Erie Canal crossed New York State from Lake Erie to the Hudson River. The monumental engineering project required workers to excavate locks, opposite top. Horses and mules trudged along towpaths, hauling boats and barges through the canal, opposite bottom. The new trade route helped New York City become an economic powerhouse in the 19th century. Above, decorative plates celebrated the Erie Canal.

October 26, 1825," one contemporary account read. A relay of cannons boomed the news down the length of the canal. When the packet boat *Seneca Chief,* first craft to travel the entire canal, arrived a few days later, New Yorkers marked the historic "wedding of the waters" by emptying kegs of Lake Erie water into the Atlantic Ocean.

A smashing commercial success, the Erie Canal gave 19th-century New York an edge over other commercial port cities up and down the Atlantic coast. It was so successful that in 1835, just ten years after the canal's completion, New York enlarged it. Its influence continues today, as many of the Empire State's best known cities—Rochester, Albany, Buffalo, Syracuse—grew and prospered along the Erie Canal.

The canal traversed land that was by and large unsettled and uncultivated—but that soon changed. There was no city of Rochester in 1812, but it soon became a flourishing town. The area was blessed with rich land and the Genesee River, with its powerful pair of falls. Grain grown in the hinterlands was milled into flour using the river's power. To ship it east, engineers designed an 802-foot aqueduct across the river, part of the network of the great Erie Canal. The city produced 26,000 barrels of flour in 1818, before the Erie Canal was completed. In 1825, over the first ten days of the canal's opening, 40,000 barrels of flour moved out of Rochester alone. By 1830, with a population of 10,000, Rochester was growing into a crossroads for agriculture and manufacturing. By 1840, the city's 24 flour mills provided a quarter of all the flour shipped east on the canal. The prosperous flour mills and good transportation

*Early American locomotives—like the
John Bull, shown here, which ran on the
Camden & Amboy Railroad—were
often built in Britain, the birthplace of the
railroad. The John Bull carried passengers
between New York and Philadelphia in
the 1830s. Soon, American companies were
building rails and locomotives to suit the
United States' needs.*

connections drew people to the region. Workers in Rochester made everything from shoes to pianos.

"Surely the water of this Canal must be the most fertilizing of all fluid," wrote Nathaniel Hawthorne, not yet famous for his writing, as he traveled the canal in 1830, "for it causes towns with their masses of brick and stone, their churches and theaters, their business and hubbub, their luxury and refinement, their gay dames and polished citizens, to spring up, till in time the wondrous steam may flow between two continuous lines of buildings, through one thronged street, from Buffalo to Albany." New York State had been transformed by the waterway.

The Erie's success inspired other states to build canals. Many were financial disasters, such as New England's New Haven and Northhampton Canal, which opened in 1835 and was abandoned in 1847. But the canal-building boom added miles to existing transportation networks. By the 1840s, more than 3,000 miles of canal traversed America.

The Erie Canal's effect reached into the western interior of the nation, and it shaped patterns of trade and travel significantly for years to come. Not only did it connect to the states that it crossed, but it also represented a way west. "Canal boats filled with emigrants, and covered with goods and furniture, are almost hourly arriving," an observer in Buffalo remarked in 1832. "Several steamboats and vessels daily depart for the far west, literally crammed with masses of living beings to people those regions. Some days, near a thousand thus depart."

Just as the Erie Canal provided a travel route west, it also made trade possible between the North and the West. Goods no longer had to travel down the Mississippi through New Orleans. New York City, the canal's eastern endpoint, became the country's premier city and port. Connected by the Erie Canal, farmers, manufacturers, and merchants in the North and the West forged strong commercial links. Those alliances grew even more important during the bitterly divided decades leading up to the Civil War. They competed with, and eventually superseded, the alliances that had developed between the West and South thanks to trade by steamboats.

City fathers in Boston, Philadelphia, Baltimore, and Charleston watched with envy as the Erie Canal boosted New York City to commercial prominence. In 1826, the Commonwealth of Pennsylvania built a canal to compete for the western trade. Although it cost over ten million dollars to build, it couldn't compete with the Erie Canal or the growing network of railroads in Pennsylvania. Planners in other port cities responded by embracing the prospect of the railroad instead, laying the nation's first tracks. On July 4, 1828, the Baltimore & Ohio Railroad broke ground. In 1830 the B&O opened its first section, running from Baltimore to Ellicott's Mills (now Ellicott City), although a horse drew the railroad cars along the track. In Charleston, the South Carolina Railroad opened in 1831, using steam. Soon Philadelphia connected with Pittsburgh in an enterprise that made Pennsylvania one of the nation's preeminent railroad-building states.

With hindsight, the many advantages of the "Iron Horse" are easy to see. Canals were expensive to build. Canal traffic moved slowly. And canals froze when the temperature dropped, making them impassable. Even though Erie Canal traffic peaked after the transcontinental railroad was built, early railroads quickly became a significant part of the nation's growing transportation systems. As one historian has put it, "Within a little more than a decade the railroad had grown from an infant to a giant."

British men built the first steam locomotives and started the first railroads. In 1804, Cornish inventor Richard Trevithick proudly watched his second locomotive pull ten tons of iron and five wagons, loaded with 70 men, nearly ten miles, traveling at almost five miles per hour. Just over 20 years later, in 1825, a railway line opened, connecting the towns of Stockton and Darlington, Yorkshire. On the world's first public passenger train trip, a locomotive designed by British engineer George Stephenson hauled 600 passengers. Some of America's earliest locomotives—such as the *John Bull,* built in 1831 and operating on the Camden & Amboy Railroad in New Jersey by 1833—were built in Britain and shipped across the ocean. But Americans quickly adopted and adapted the railroad and made it over in their own image.

Not everyone thought that railroads were an improvement over canals, steamboats, stagecoaches, and wagons. In 1830, competing forces in the area of Baltimore and Washington began building the Chesapeake & Ohio Canal and the Baltimore & Ohio Railroad. Washington's *National Intelligencer* derided the railroad as "an experiment wholly untried in any country" and asserted that "the idea

*Most early 19th century roads, made to serve local purposes, were dreadful. As Americans started traveling longer distances in stagecoaches, like the brightly colored Concord Coach above, they began to need better roads.*

of its successfully competing with a canal of the same length, over a rough and comparatively wild country, passed the bounds of probability." To the doubters—and to those with vested interests in other transportation networks—railroads were an unproven entity.

Despite the skeptics, railroads soon dominated land transportation in the United States, holding a powerful symbolic sway over Americans' lives and imaginations. Ralph Waldo Emerson, Henry David Thoreau, Nathaniel Hawthorne, Emily Dickinson, and Walt Whitman all explored the meaning of the railroad in 19th-century American society. "But, hark! there is the whistle of the locomotive," wrote Hawthorne a few short years after railroads first forged through the New England landscape. Hawthorne noted the train's "long shriek, harsh, above all other harshness, for the space of a mile cannot mollify it into harmony. It tells a story of busy men, citizens, from the hot street, who have come to spend a day in a country village, men of business; in short of all unquietness; and no wonder that it gives such a startling shriek, since it brings the noisy world into the midst of our slumbrous peace."

While the railroad was disturbing Hawthorne's bucolic reflections, for other writers it was growing into an overwhelming metaphor for progress. "And the Iron Horse, the earth-shaker, the fire-breather, which tramples down the hills, which outruns the laggard winds, which leaps over the rivers, which grinds the rocks to powder and breaks down the gates of the mountains," intoned a writer in 1853, waxing nearly biblical, "he too shall build an empire and an epic. Shall not solitudes and waste places cry for gladness at his coming?" For all such rhetoric, early railroads began not by inspiring new growth in "solitudes and waste places" but instead, like most new transportation networks, by connecting places that were already significant. It was not until the 1850s that railroads spread to the Midwest, and not until after the Civil War did they have the effect of opening up land for new settlement.

Journeys on antebellum railroads were neither comfortable nor speedy. Accounts of railroad travel published by *Harpers* in the 1850s were often uncomplimentary. Stephen Sharply, the protagonist of "Two Days on the Erie Road," traveled by rail from Cleveland to New York on a journey expected to take 12 hours or less. It took two days. Sharply described the trip in a sardonic tone, suggesting that the passengers were mannerless, that railroad stations were hubs of confusion, and that no railroad workers actually expected the trains to run on schedule. He stayed a night in a Binghamton hotel, where the host "swore badly" and dinner was "a little hard nubbin of steak, whether beef, or venison, or mutton I cannot say." He got up at 6 a.m. and arrived at the train station "in the company of four or five others... where we were startled by the announcement, on the telegraphic blackboard of the establishment, that the 'Cincinnati train was six hours behind time.'

*By the 1850s, railroads like the Baltimore & Ohio, right, linked northeastern communities. The United States already had more miles of rails than any other nation, and railroads were reaching their iron tentacles into Iowa and Missouri.*

"And what amazed me most," Sharply continued, "was that nobody, from the ticket-seller down to the hackmen, seemed at all surprised. 'Lauck suds!' said one of the men I consulted, 'that's nothing. She ain't up to time any day these three weeks.'"

Others responded to the railroad experience even more pointedly. An anonymous three-page rant in an 1855 *Harpers* demanded, "Suppose you are an American citizen, and belong to the biggest and most braggadochio country in the world, does that give you any right to assail my boots with your saliva, my ears with your howling and oaths, and my sense of decency with general disgust? Because you are an American citizen must you cease to be a gentleman? Because you are an American citizen must you fling apple parings against a hot iron stove, and fill a small close car with horrid odors?"

The railroad's intermittent and confusing service provoked ambivalence in some travelers. But as the system grew and expanded, it exerted a profound effect on the nation and its people. Railroads boldly entered the worlds even of people who preferred to stay put, such as Emily Dickinson, the New England poet famous for her reclusiveness. She made her home in Amherst, Massachusetts, and although she rarely ventured from there, she recognized the railroad as an agent of change and wrote a poem of praise for the Iron Horse:

> *I like to see it lap the Miles,*
> *And lick the Valleys up,*
> *And stop to feed itself at Tanks;*
> *And then prodigious, step*

*Operating only in 1860 and 1861, the Pony Express traveled between St. Joseph, Missouri, and California. Settlers traveling overland took 4 to 6 months to complete the journey, but Pony Express riders reached the West in 8 to 15 days.*

*Around a Pile of Mountains,*
*And, supercilious, peer*
*In Shanties, by the sides of roads—*
*And then a Quarry pare*

*To fit its sides, and crawl between,*
*Complaining all the while*
*In horrid hooting stanza;*
*Then chase itself down Hill*

*And neigh like Boanerges;*
*Then, prompter than a Star,*
*Stop—docile and Omnipotent—*
*At its own stable door.*

Emily Dickinson's hometown of Amherst was established well before the invention of railroads. Once tracks began to be laid, though, the people of Amherst fought to be connected into the new national transportation system. Fearful for their economic future without a railroad link, leading citizens including Edward Dickinson, Emily's father, put forth huge efforts to bring the railroad to Amherst. They offered bonds to raise money for their railroad. They founded a newspaper, the *Hampshire and Franklin Express,* to advertise their cause. Their efforts paid off in 1851, when the General Court of Massachusetts incorporated the Amherst & Belchertown Railroad Company. Edward Dickinson was on the board of trustees.

Much of the backbreaking work of building the nation's railroads was performed by immigrants. Amherst was near Boston and New London, both major ports of entry for mid-century Irish people who fled famine conditions at home. In 1852, Irish workers began to build the roadbed for the Amherst and Belchertown train. At the groundbreaking ceremony in Belchertown, about ten miles southeast of Amherst, Reverend Wolcott rejoiced, "in a few months hence the snorting of the Iron Horse will be heard among these valleys, and his tramp will reverberate among the hills!" By June 1853, the first Amherst and Belchertown passenger train took to the lines. Residents of towns along the line celebrated their newly forged connection by parading through Amherst. As her father joined the festivities, Emily observed from a nearby wood.

Less than ten years later, at about the time Emily Dickinson was writing her famous poem, the local railway company was already struggling financially. Like so many other small railroads, the Amherst & Belchertown Railroad ended up being swallowed up by a larger railroad company. In the meantime, though, Emily Dickinson's Amherst—like many other towns in the nation—had connected into the country's transportation network. The train linked Amherst to Boston and other major cities in New England. Goods and people could flow between those places in new and more affordable ways. Merchants and manufacturers who once had a corner on the local market now found that they had to compete with businesses in other towns, near and far.

In many ways, railroads changed the communities they entered. Despite the positive notes in her poem, Emily Dickinson didn't see it as an unalloyed change for the good. With easier access, new

people were coming to Amherst. "Our house is crowded daily with the members of this world, the high and the low, the bond and the free, the 'poor in this world's goods,' and the 'almighty dollar,' and 'what in the world they are after' continues to be unknown," she wrote. "But I hope they will pass away."

Even those who resisted had to accommodate to the change, and artistic works like Emily Dickinson's poem or George Inness's 1855 painting, "The Lackawanna Valley," which also incorporates the railroad into a pastoral landscape, showed how artists of all stripes were trying to make the new steam locomotive fit into the fabric of American life.

. . .

American railroads came of age at a time when that fabric was unraveling. They soon became a tool for military operations in the Civil War. Confederate and Union soldiers battled against one another in what one historian has called "the first railroad war." Battles were fought over railroad lines. One railroad company in particular, the Baltimore & Ohio—its line running from Baltimore to Washington, then through Harpers Ferry, Martinsburg, and on to Wheeling in the West—traversed both Confederate and Union strongholds. "The terminus at one end [Baltimore] is among the mobocracy," a West Vir-

*All forms of transportation were put to use during the nation's bloody, fratricidal Civil War, 1861-65. Clockwise from top left: Union troops use railroad tracks to move a mortar; Union troops arrive by steamboat in Kentucky, 1861; former slaves test sabotage techniques near Alexandria, Virginia; Union troops board a train in New Jersey, bound for Washington, D.C.*

ginia newpaper editor wrote in April 1861, while "the other end, here in Wheeling, [is] among good, order-loving Union men." Early on in the war, Confederate troops led by Gen. Stonewall Jackson gained control of part of the B&O line, trapping more than 50 locomotives and hundreds of railroad cars near Martinsburg, West Virginia. In June 1861, troops "kindled huge fires" around the rolling stock and, as a reporter for the pro-Union *National Intelligencer* put it, "We counted the line of locomotives that had been burnt (forty-one or forty-two in all) red and blistered with heat. The destruction is fearful to contemplate."

Railroads, used to move troops and supplies to battles, were considered so important that both sides exempted some railroad workers from the draft. With more miles of track in its territory, the North used the railroad more strategically than the South and thereby gained an edge. In battles in Tennessee in 1863, for example, the railroad line was a critical part of the equation.

Suffering a defeat at Chickamauga, Union troops retreated to Chattanooga and were cut off from supplies. Put in command, Gen. George Thomas declared he would "hold the town till we starve," but it didn't come to that, thanks to the railroad. A force of 23,000 soldiers and all their supplies advanced by rail from Alexandria, Virginia, through Ohio and Indiana, toward Tennessee. "The railroad stations along our route were crowded with cheering men, women, and children," one of the traveling soldiers wrote in his diary.

As the trains continued into Kentucky and Tennessee, the Union soldiers found themselves less welcome. Still, they reached Chattanooga and helped General Thomas secure it. Joining 15,000 other Union soldiers, led by Gen. William Tecumseh Sherman, they marched toward Atlanta in May 1864. The victories that followed won the war for the Union side.

By war's end, the railroad was embedded in the American psyche. It was a key feature in some of the decade's most memorable moments. Abraham Lincoln rode in a train from Illinois to his Presidential Inauguration, stopping along the way to meet citizens and drum up their support. Amidst the war to preserve the Union, Lincoln still found time to sign the bill that made the transcontinental railroad a reality. And after Lincoln was assassinated at Ford's Theatre in Washington, D.C., in 1865, a railroad car carried his body from the capital city back to his hometown.

Leaving Washington on April 21, the casket traveled first to Harrisburg, then to Philadelphia, and then on to New York. "Early in the morning crowds of people gathered in the City Hall Park, and waited there for hours in order to obtain a view of the features of their departed hero," reported *Harpers*. "This scene was only exceeded in solemnity by the procession of the following day—the largest that ever thronged the streets of the great metropolis."

After New York, the train stopped in Chicago, where "an escort of torches" accompanied the casket as it left the train, and "thirty-six young ladies in white placed wreathes upon the coffin" for public viewing. The President's body was finally laid to rest in Springfield, Illinois, on May 4, 1865.

. . .

The politics of the Civil War had both helped and hindered the transcontinental railroad. Congressmen had been arguing for decades about whether it should take a northern or southern route. When the South seceded from the Union, the issue no longer faced opposition. Congress passed the legislation needed to make the transcontinental railroad a reality. On January 8, 1863, just days after President Lincoln signed the Emancipation Proclamation that freed slaves in the Confederate states, Central Pacific workers began in Sacramento, California, laying track that would eventually meet track laid from the East.

Despite the bill's easy passage in Congress, material supplies grew more expensive and capital supplies all but dried up because of the war. Men who might have invested in railroads invested in war industries instead, considering them a less risky prospect. It took six years to complete the transcontinental railroad, and by that time, the world had changed. President Lincoln had been assassinated. Congress had passed constitutional amendments intended to banish the specter of slavery and make African Americans eligible for citizenship. The Union had triumphed over the Confederacy.

Amidst all these changes, railroads spanned the country. They exerted a more and more powerful influence. They helped shape American culture, society, and politics. And they strengthened the connections among regions, states, and territories, making the vast continent into one nation.

IN TRAVERSING THE WILDS
IT IS CUSTOMARY
FOR A PARTY EITHER OF HORSE OR FOOT
TO FOLLOW EACH OTHER
IN SINGLE FILE LIKE THE INDIANS;
SO THAT THE LEADERS BREAK THE WAY
FOR THOSE WHO FOLLOW,
AND LESSEN THEIR LABOR AND FATIGUE.

— *Washington Irving*, **A Tour on the Prairies**, *1835*

# COMMUNITY BUILDING
## IN THE RAILROAD AGE

**THE WAY THEY GO TO CALIFORNIA.**

*Many scrambled to California, above, stricken by gold rush fever in the 1850s. Opposite, clockwise from upper left: In the 1850s, sailors abandoned ships in San Francisco harbor, fleeing inland for gold; Minnesota teacher George W. Northrup posed as a miner but never got to California; starting in 1852, Wells, Fargo & Co. transported freight, including gold, from California; and gold seekers developed mechanized techniques, such as this washing trough.*

James Marshall was building a sawmill near Coloma, California. He had been hired to do so by John A. Sutter, an immigrant adventurer from Switzerland. Sutter had moved to California in 1839, when it was still owned by Mexico, and had been granted a huge tract of land by the Mexican governor of Monterey.

On January 24, 1848, Marshall suddenly showed up on Sutter's doorstep, 45 miles from the sawmill site. Already rich and powerful, Sutter was about to find his fortunes changing dramatically. "I was sitting one afternoon, just after my siesta, engaged, by the bye, in writing a letter to a relation of mine at Lucern," he recalled years later, "when I was interrupted by Mr. Marshall.... From the unusual agitation in his manner I imagined that something serious had occurred, and, as we involuntarily do in this part of the world, I at once glanced to see if my rifle was in its proper place." The worker was so agitated that Sutter "thought something has touched Marshall's brain, when suddenly all my misgivings were put at an end to by his flinging on the table a handful of scales of pure virgin gold."

News of Marshall's discovery spread slowly, and gold fever didn't reach San Francisco until after May 12, when Sam Brannan, a Mormon who had been in California two years, brought the glittering evidence into town. By May 29, *The Californian*, a weekly, reported that "the whole country from San Francisco to Los Angeles, and from the sea shore to the base of the Sierra Nevadas, resounds with the sordid cry of gold, GOLD! GOLD! While the field is left half-planted, the house half-built, and everything neglected but the manufacture of shovels and pickaxes."

It took even longer for the news of gold to reach the East Coast. A small article appeared in the *New York Herald* in August. In that same month, Col. Richard B. Mason wrote a military report to Washington, stating that "the discovery of these vast deposits of gold has entirely changed the character of Upper California. Its people, before engaged in cultivating their small patches of ground, and guarding their herds of cattle and horses, have all gone to the mines, or are on their way thither."

On the basis of this report, when President James K. Polk gave his State of the Union Address on December 5, 1848, he said that although "accounts of the abundance of gold in that territory... scarcely command belief," the findings were real. "Nearly the whole of the male population of the country [California] have gone to the gold districts. Ships arriving on the coast are deserted by their crews and their voyages suspended for want of sailors.... This abundance of gold and the all-engrossing pursuit of it have already caused in California an unprecedented rise in the price of all the necessaries of life."

As the news spread outward from California, men from all over the world—Latin America, Australia, China, Europe—flocked to California in search of a fortune. First residents of the California territory headed to the mines, then gold rushers came from nearby Oregon and Mexico and places like Hawaii, Chile, and Peru, from which you could sail to San Francisco. It took American East Coasters longer. To reach California by sea, they had to take a four- to six-month trip around Cape Horn or a quicker but more dangerous voyage through the disease-plagued

RESIDENCE OF HON. F. A. HIHN. SANTA CRUZ. CAL.

*German immigrant Frederick Hihn, right, moved to Santa Cruz in the 1850s. An entrepreneur with wide interests, in 1872 he built a stately mansion for his family, above. Hihn became a land speculator, state assemblyman, and railroad builder. He founded the resort town of Capitola. His mansion later became Santa Cruz's city hall.*

Isthmus of Panama. Or they could trek overland, a journey that took four to six months from Missouri. With all these transportation challenges, large numbers of Americans struck by gold fever did not arrive in California until a year and a half after James Marshall burst in on Sutter. Few men fulfilled their dreams of riches by mining gold, but California did prove to be one of the world's largest gold producers during the last half of the 19th century. With people from all over the U.S. and the world rushing to the West Coast, California's communities began to change.

One of those drawn to California during the gold rush was young Frederick Augustus Hihn. Hihn left Germany in the spring and sailed on the ship *Reform* from Bremen to Rio de Janeiro, with a stopover in Valparaiso, Chile, then on to California. The trip took 280 days, so it must have delighted Hihn and his fellow passengers to awake on that October day when, as he wrote in his journal, "This morning we all got up early to look at the coast of California." While still on board ship, Hihn "decided to go to the mines with some other passengers." He and seven other immigrants left San Francisco and took a schooner to Sacramento to search for gold. Together they bought a claim near the Feather River. Disaster struck quickly: The river rose, and the swift current swept their tools away. The men gave up on the site and headed back to Sacramento, where Hihn abandoned the search for gold and instead set up a candy factory with a partner. Two weeks later the elements intervened again, and floods destroyed their business.

Next Hihn tried his hand at hotel ownership, but floods got the best of him again. He headed back to

San Francisco in 1851 and opened a drugstore to serve some of the thousands of people now turning the once-small settlement into a busy city. Gold had lured so many people to the state, some enterprising individuals realized they might make their fortunes by starting other ventures in California. With a fast-growing population that needed to be fed and housed, and poor transportation links to the rest of the country, labor and goods were often in short supply. When merchants had goods to sell, they got high prices for them. In December 1849, for example, San Francisco grocers could sell a "rather ordinary" head of cabbage for three dollars—more than a day's wages even in the tight California labor market.

Despite this promise, Hihn's drugstore failed. Two of the many fires that plagued the booming city consumed his worldly goods. In the summer of 1851, Frederick Hihn confided to his diary that he was "Discouraged. Made up my mind to go back to my fatherland. Was on my way to ship as a sailor to work my passage." But a chance meeting on the way to the docks changed everything. His fellow shopkeeper was confidently rebuilding the store after the fire. If someone had to get rich in California, he told Hihn, it might as well be them. He must have been quite a salesman, because Hihn decided to stay.

First he sold soap. Then he and a new business partner bought mules and goods to sell and set off for the countryside near Mission San Antonio, a good hundred miles down the rocky coast from San Francisco. Only 22, Hihn was losing his optimism again. He melancholically reflected that he had been roughing it since he left Germany, and now he was

*After buying a local line on the coast of California and changing the track to standard gauge, the Southern Pacific Railroad company used advertisements like this one in 1885 to attract families and day-trippers to the pretty seaside town of Santa Cruz and to the Monterey area as a whole.*

down to his last three hundred dollars of merchandise. But he and his partner turned a good profit. The plan to sell goods from the city in rural areas seemed to be working. At the end of his second mercantile trip, Hihn ended up in Santa Cruz, between San Francisco and Mission San Antonio, and stayed there for the rest of his life, becoming a leading citizen who owned much of the county's real estate. He also owned lumber mills, founded the resort town of Capitola, served as a state assemblyman, held offices in local banks, and invested in local roads and railroads.

When Frederick Hihn first moved to Santa Cruz in the early 1850s, it was a tiny town in a sparsely populated county, only 650 inhabitants in all. Still, enterprising men had already begun to develop the region's industrial and agricultural potential. Elihu Anthony, for example, a Methodist minister, had left Indiana in 1847 and settled in Santa Cruz in 1848. In the late 1840s, Anthony started a foundry that made plows and mining picks. It quickly became the business center of the town, serving as a general store, post office, and blacksmith shop. Gradually Anthony's interests changed. He saw the need not only to develop the real estate in the town and surrounding countryside but also to connect Santa Cruz to other growing California towns. In 1849, Anthony built a wharf, hoping to stimulate travel and trade along the coastline into Santa Cruz.

Men like Frederick Hihn opened stores that became very successful by serving the growing local population's needs. In Santa Cruz and its nearby mountains, early manufacturing ventures depended on the area's magnificent redwood forests, tanbark oak trees used for tanning, and rich limestone deposits. Lumbering, tanning, and processing lime formed the county's growing industrial base. Other residents tried to make a living from the county's rich soil. In the early 1850s, Eliza Farnham, the spunky widow of an early California freight entrepreneur, moved from Ossining, New York, where she was matron of the women's section of Sing Sing Prison, to El Rancho La Libertád—a plot of land her husband had left her near Santa Cruz. She brought with her a whole household of people, all willing to try their hands at farming.

Santa Cruz was the biggest, but not the only, Anglo settlement in the region. In 1852, Watsonville began life as a small settlement, about 20 miles away from Santa Cruz, on the edge of the county. Although the town was not formally incorporated until 1868, farmers began to exploit the rich soil and good climate that Watsonville and the nearby Pajaro Valley had to offer. The economic fates of these two towns, Santa Cruz and Watsonville, would be determined by whether useful connections between them and the larger world evolved.

While industrial and agricultural activities were beginning in the region, Santa Cruz was poorly connected to markets, including San Francisco, in the 1850s. People and goods traveled there either by boat or by foot or pack animal over mountains. Many deliverymen ignored the new wharf and unloaded their boats directly onto the beach, incurring considerable costs and often considerable losses. Santa Cruz residents could ride on horseback over the mountains to San Francisco, but it was hard going. And sometimes no options were available: Winter storms could crash through the area, trapping residents for weeks at a time. Until a dependable, all-year form of transportation served the area, Santa Cruz's economy would remain small-scale.

In 1850, 9,000 miles of railroad track had been laid in America, but most of it was in the Northeast, clustered near the coast and existing settlements. What became Oklahoma was still Indian Territory. Neither Minnesota, the Dakotas, Montana, Wyoming, Idaho, Colorado, Utah, Washington, Oregon, California, Nevada, Arizona, New Mexico, nor Kansas was a state yet. Overland travel was time-consuming. It took about two months for Chinese gold rushers to travel nearly 7,000 miles by sea from Hong Kong to San Francisco. It took Americans the same amount of time to travel the roughly 600 overland miles there from Salt Lake City.

Some of these limitations were overcome in the second half of the 19th century. Between 1850 and 1860, the number of miles of railroad track in the U.S. tripled to over 30,000. Railroads reached out of Illinois, into Iowa and Missouri. In 1850, Chicago was served by a short rail line that did not connect into a network. In 1860, 11 railroads served Chicago. In that same decade, California's first railroad was completed: In 1856, the Sacramento Valley Railroad ran the 22 miles from Sacramento to Fulton.

The first transcontinental railroad reached from coast to coast by 1869, built simultaneously from the East and the West. On the California end, Leland Stanford, Charles Crocker, Collis P. Huntington, and Mark Hopkins banded together and formed the Central Pacific Company in Sacramento. Already

successful businessmen, these men—who came to be known as "the Big Four"—grew rich off the company they owned, which soon dominated the railroad scene in California. Control of the rails was moving out of local hands and into the hands of large corporations, the likes of which America had never seen.

By the time Santa Cruz residents tried to get a railroad to come to their town, California was dominated by the Central Pacific and its many corporate offspring. Renamed the Southern Pacific Railroad, the company controlled the western part of the original transcontinental connection and operated a line that snaked down California, taking travelers from San Francisco through Los Angeles, then heading east toward El Paso and New Orleans on a cross-country route that opened in 1883.

By 1900, three more major railroad lines crisscrossed the nation, changing how people lived. The Northern Pacific rolled through North Dakota, Montana, and Washington, ending up in Portland, Oregon; the Atchison, Topeka & Santa Fe served the growing town of Los Angeles; and the Great Northern traveled between Minneapolis and Seattle.

As these transportation systems were built, they helped transform communities like Santa Cruz and Watsonville. Local economies became connected to

*By the 1890s Watsonville's freight yards, above right, formed a bustling hub of commercial activity as local farmers delivered their produce for shipping to markets near and far. Meanwhile, the Santa Cruz Union Depot, below right, hummed with activity on summer weekends. Visitors arrived by the Southern Pacific line, via Watsonville, or by the South Pacific Coast Railroad line, through the mountains.*

*Manufactured in Philadelphia in 1876
at the Baldwin Locomotive Works,
the wood-burning steam locomotive named
Jupiter traveled the Santa Cruz Railroad
until 1883, when the track was switched
to standard gauge. Beautifully appointed
and richly decorated, the Jupiter pulled
ornate coaches along the 21.5 miles of track
between Santa Cruz and Watsonville.*

the rest of the country and the wider world. Like Emily Dickinson's father in Amherst, Frederick Hihn and his neighbors actively tried to bring the railroad to their own doorsteps. In the decades between the Amherst and Santa Cruz efforts, though, many railroad corporations had grown in size and strength. By the end of the century, the behemoth Southern Pacific Railroad was "the state's largest corporation, largest landowner, and largest employer." It owned most of the rail lines in California, large and small, and as Southern Pacific tracks crept closer to Watsonville and Santa Cruz, they seemed to promise connections into the growing national rail network.

In 1869, Southern Pacific opened a line between San Jose and Gilroy, only a few miles from Watsonville, so it seemed likely that the Pajaro Valley town would be the next stop on the line. Indeed, in 1871, the broad-gauge line came through on its way to San Francisco. The station was built on the outskirts of town, though, across the Pajaro River from Watsonville. The railroad company did not build a bridge, much to the chagrin of the townspeople, but at least a rail connection was made, linking Watsonville and the Pajaro Valley's rich agricultural region with the rest of California and beyond.

Residents of Santa Cruz, Frederick Hihn among them, wanted a railroad link to their town, too. Santa Cruz was roughly 20 miles northwest of Watsonville, but without further track built, Santa Cruz would gain little benefit from the trains coming through Watsonville. "All agreed," a local newspaper reported, "that a railroad was almost an absolute necessity to keep up the town and advance our local interests."

A group of Santa Cruz citizens formed a Railroad Committee in October 1869. After arguments over the route, the committee finally decided they needed tracks around the mountains to Watsonville, and they would agitate for the county to issue bonds and loans to support the endeavor. On their behalf, Frederick Hihn—now a state assemblyman—"introduced an act to authorize the County of Santa Cruz to aid in the construction of railroads and other roads," as reported in the *Santa Cruz Sentinel* on April 2, 1870.

This first bill was defeated, perhaps because, as Watsonville's newspaper pointed out, it included a branch line to nearby Soquel, where Hihn had lumber interests. C. O. Cummings, editor of the *Watsonville Pajaronian,* continued to denounce the plan for years, complaining that the railroad was one of the "chimerical schemes" designed to benefit speculators. Residents of Watsonville generally suspected Hihn's motives, and in 1872, when the subsidy issue came up again, they voted overwhelmingly against it. But Watsonville's voters were out-numbered by those in the rest of the county, and the railroad subsidy passed. In January 1872, Santa Cruz residents joined together to form the Santa Cruz & Watsonville Railroad Company, with Frederick Hihn as president and Elihu Anthony on the board.

Six months into its formation, the Santa Cruz railroad committee members began to think that a big out-of-state corporation might help them in their crusade. The Atlantic & Pacific Railroad Company (later the Atchison, Topeka & Santa Fe) was trying to get a foothold in California, so that it could complete its own transcontinental line and present new

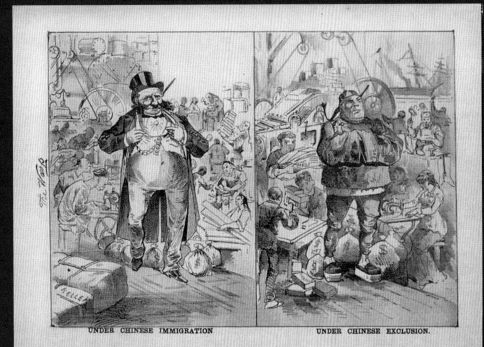

UNDER CHINESE IMMIGRATION · UNDER CHINESE EXCLUSION.

## LEGAL DISCRIMINATION

### THE CHINESE EXCLUSION ACT

EXPRESSING LATE 19TH-CENTURY FEARS ABOUT CHINESE IMMIGRANTS, THIS CARTOON APPEARED IN 1882, THE SAME YEAR THAT CONGRESS PASSED AN EXCLUSION ACT TO FORBID CHINESE WORKERS FROM ENTERING THE UNITED STATES.

DURING THE GOLD RUSH OF THE 1850s, thousands of men from Southern China traveled to California in search of a fortune. They entered an already complex racial equation in the United States. Only whites were allowed by law to be naturalized. Many African Americans were still slaves. California entered the Union in 1850 as a free state, but its citizens did not necessarily live together in racial harmony. Many white Californians of all classes believed that the Chinese people coming to American threatened their nation's values.

Chinese immigrants soon became the victims of legally sanctioned racial discrimination. In the goldfields, the state's Foreign Miners Tax required Chinese mine workers to pay for the privilege of working. White San Franciscans boycotted clothing and shoes made by Chinese workers. An 1873 law prohibited pedestrians from carrying poles on their shoulders, which forced Chinese peddlers and deliverymen out of business. Chinese workers moved into niche economies such as laundries, restaurants, and domestic services.

Most 19th-century Chinese immigrants were males. Many had left wives back in China. The Chinese women who did come often made a living as prostitutes. By the 1870s, strict measures had gone into effect: Federal laws restricted Chinese women's entry and California laws barred marriage between a white and a "negro, mulatto, or Mongolian." Thus in 1900, although Chinese people had been moving to America for more than 50 years, very few were female, and few Chinese families had formed on American soil.

Other laws compounded discimination. In 1854, California's Supreme Court barred Chinese people from testifying. In a state referendum, the vast majority of California voters favored the total exclusion of the Chinese from their state.

Although most of America's Chinese population lived

in California, the "Chinese problem" played itself out on the national political scene. As early as 1855, Hinton Helper, a Republican who was against slavery, called the Chinese "semibarbarians." Henry George, most famous for writing *Poverty and Progress,* called the Chinese "utter heathens, treacherous, sensual, cowardly and cruel."

In 1870, the federal government affirmed citizenship rights for African-American ex-slaves. At the same time, Congress ignored abolitionist Charles Sumner's argument for broader racial equality, made on the Fourth of July: "It is 'all men' and not a race of color that are placed under the protection of the Declaration," Sumner argued. "The word 'white' wherever it occurs as a limitation of rights, must disappear." Still, Congress left Asians off the list of races eligible for citizenship.

In 1877, the U.S. Senate took up the Chinese question. "Their difference in color, dress, manners, and religion have, in my judgement, more to do with this hostility," declared Indiana Senator Oliver P. Morton, "than their alleged vices or any actual injury to the white people of California." But in the end, the committee reported that "there is not sufficient brain capacity in the Chinese race to furnish motive power for self-government. Upon the point of morals there is no Aryan or European race which is not far superior to the Chinese." The committee urged legislation "to restrain the great influx of Asiatics to this country." In 1879, President Rutherford B. Hayes declared, "I would consider with favor any suitable measures to discourage the Chinese from coming to our shores."

Shortly after, in 1882, the nation's legislators overwhelmingly passed the Chinese Exclusion Act and barred Chinese laborers from entering the country—the first U.S. law barring immigration on the basis of race and nationality. The Act was not rescinded until 1943.

THOMAS NAST, PREMIER POLITICAL CARICATURIST, PORTRAYED COLUMBIA, BELOW—THE SYMBOL OF AMERICA—PROTECTING AN EMBATTLED CHINESE MAN FROM AN ANGRY MOB. "AMERICA MEANS FAIR PLAY FOR ALL MEN!" SHE CRIES. *HARPERS* PUBLISHED THIS CARTOON IN 1871 WITH AN ARTICLE CALLING THE IDEA OF A CHINESE INVASION "ALTOGETHER MYTHICAL."

competition to the Southern Pacific. Planners for the Atlantic & Pacific wanted to connect St. Louis to San Francisco with a route going through Santa Cruz. Santa Cruz's local elite put their own plans on hold.

The plan didn't pan out. Southern Pacific (which had by now swallowed its parent company, Central Pacific) fought to keep its monopolistic grip on California's railroads. Its influence on the San Francisco business community made support for the Atlantic & Pacific plan evaporate. In September 1872, Frederick Hihn announced to his fellow Santa Cruzans, "The Atlantic and Pacific R.R. Co having changed their route, and the owners of the Southern Pacific Railroad Co. not complying with their promises to build a wide gauge railroad, from Santa Cruz to Watsonville, we are forced to conclude that if we want a railroad we must build it ourselves." Hihn and other local notables incorporated under the name of the Santa Cruz Railroad Company and planned a narrow-gauge track to Watsonville. It was not the ideal solution—freight and passengers would have to switch trains and board the standard-gauge Southern Pacific near Watsonville—but it seemed the most practical step to take at the time.

When the Southern Pacific announced plans for a standard-gauge connection between Watsonville and Santa Cruz, the plot twisted again. Surveys started in January 1873, but when an economic depression gripped the nation, those plans faded. Back to the local drawing boards. Town notables including Hihn, tannery owner Joseph Kron, and Claus Spreckels, a wealthy German immigrant who owned land in nearby Aptos, bought stock in the Santa Cruz

Railroad Company (SCRR). A local narrow-gauge line would finally become a reality.

Construction commenced in August 1873. Nothing seemed to go easily. Building a local railroad depended on materials from far away—but until the railroad was built, lack of access was a problem. Builders could make railroad ties from redwood cut in the nearby mountains, but they couldn't get rails and other critical supplies locally. After buying four miles of used iron rail from San Francisco, the SCRR waited for more rails to come from the East. First the cargo ship *John Bright*, headed for Santa Cruz with a load of rail, sank off the coast of Brazil. Then a second shipment, coming on the *Whittier*, ran into trouble: On the way to Santa Cruz, the ship caught fire and was laid up for repairs for four months. In desperation, the SCRR ordered more expensive rails from nearby San Francisco, which finally arrived in February 1875. Anxious to claim success, and having ordered a locomotive from San Francisco, the directors jumped the gun. On May 22, 1875, they announced the grand opening of the Santa Cruz Railroad line, even though its tracks reached only eight miles, from Santa Cruz to Aptos.

One year later—and more than ten years after Frederick Hihn began plans to bring the railroad to town—the Santa Cruz Railroad finally connected through Watsonville to the Pajaro station, and from there to the national rail system. "At last our enterprising young city is in full connection with the rest of mankind," boasted the *Santa Cruz Sentinel*. "At last she is free from the rule of the sleepy stage coach. At last she is counted among the shining jewels that the deft fingers of commerce have woven together with threads of iron." Even newspaper editor C. O. Cummings grudgingly admitted in June 1876 that "we were far more favorably impressed with the road than we expected." By the end of the year, though, he was calling the enterprise a "Narrow Gauge Fraud" and printing vituperative attacks on Hihn's character.

The SCRR provided a modest service, offering local transit on narrow-gauge tracks. Mixed trains of passengers and freight traveled the rails. The company made just over $5,000 in profit in its first year. Those profits allowed the company to buy a third locomotive—the *Jupiter,* built at the Baldwin Locomotive Works in Pennsylvania—along with more passenger and freight cars. Now two mixed trains ran each day, plus extra excursion trains on the weekend. What was big business in Santa Cruz was small potatoes elsewhere, though. Railroad tycoon Leland Stanford had made so much money from both the transcontinental railroad and the Southern Pacific, he was stuffing his two-million-dollar mansion on San Francisco's Nob Hill with extravagant treasures, such as a vase he claimed to have belonged to Marie Antoinette.

After modest first-year profits, the SCRR quickly tumbled through a series of losses, going into receivership in 1881 and becoming absorbed by the mighty Southern Pacific in 1883. Another railroad line had actually set the SCRR on the downward spiral toward bankruptcy, though. The South Pacific Coast Railroad, which traveled over and through the mountains to Santa Cruz, opened in June 1880. It took much of the local business and put the SCRR in jeopardy. The local railroad limped along until January 1881, propped up by cash infusions from Frederick Hihn. Then massive rains wreaked havoc on the rights-of-way along the tracks—and worse. "When the bridge across the San Lorenzo went out to sea," as the local paper put it, "it was the death knell of the Santa Cruz Railroad." The SCRR had cost more to build than anticipated. Repairs to the infrastructure cost more than investors could bear, particularly now that an alternate link to the national rail network existed. The company went bankrupt.

But the route did not die. A Southern Pacific subsidiary bought out the railroad, repaired the damage, started running trains again, and soon converted to broad gauge for smoother connections at Pajaro. By 1893, five times a day, people and freight were taking the hour-and-ten-minute trip from Watsonville to Santa Cruz and back. Two trains ran between San Francisco and Santa Cruz, accomplishing the journey in just under four hours. Eleven other narrow-gauge trains ran from Santa Cruz to Felton, nine miles north. Four went on to San Francisco.

Finally, Santa Cruz was connected.

. . .

By the end of the 19th century, growing transportation networks were connecting not only big cities, but smaller, growing towns like Santa Cruz. Local

*As more fresh and canned produce was shipped around the country, growers began to package their wares in boxes with attractively illustrated labels, right. Following pages: Watsonville's apple boom took off in the 1890s, and harvesttime called for an army of workers who hand-picked Yellow Newtown Pippins and Yellow Bellflowers off the branches of the area's growing orchards.*

# Appleton
## BRAND

CONTENTS ONE BUSHEL

GROWN PACKED AND SHIPPED BY

BELLFLOWER

BORGOVICH & DR

WATSONVILLE ~ C

## UNIQUE MAP OF CALIFORNIA, 1888

THE SOUTHERN PACIFIC RAILROAD AND THE STATE BOARD OF TRADE PARTNERED TO MAKE A MAP AND PROMOTIONAL TOOL.

AFTER THE GOLD RUSH LURED WHITE SETTLERS TO CALIFORNIA, THE ECONOMY THERE TOOK AN AGRICULTURAL TURN. AND AFTER RAILROADS CONNECTED THE STATE WITH THE REST OF THE NATION, TOURISM GREW. THIS MAP PROMOTED BOTH, PORTRAYING CALIFORNIA AS A LAND OF GREAT NATURAL BEAUTY AND PRODUCTIVE FARMLANDS.

THE MAP TAUGHT THE GEOGRAPHY OF THE STATE BY DISPLAYING IMAGES AND RELIEF OF NOTEWORTHY FEATURES. IT DESCRIBED RICH SOILS AND MODERATE TEMPERATURES, AND GENERALLY PROMOTED THE IDEA THAT CALIFORNIA HAD "THE GRANDEST SCENERY IN NORTH AMERICA," WHERE THE AIR WAS "DRY, PURE, AND INVIGORATING." IMAGES OF PALM TREES, MOUNTAINS, AND LUXURIOUS HOTELS REINFORCED THE IDEA THAT CALIFORNIA WAS A CULTIVATED GARDEN OF EDEN THAT ALL SHOULD VISIT.

THE MAP ALSO GAVE A SNAPSHOT OF CALIFORNIA'S AGRICULTURAL ECONOMY: BESIDE EACH COUNTY NAME IS A LIST OF ITS ACREAGE, NATURAL RESOURCES, AND PRODUCE GROWN. ORANGES, LUMBER, FIGS, ALMONDS, HONEY, CEREALS, QUICKSILVER, DAIRY PRODUCTS, AND SEMITROPICAL FRUITS MADE CALIFORNIA A LAND OF NATURAL DIVERSITY AND PLENTY.

politics, interrailroad competition, and the vagaries of landscape and weather combined with the forces of national economics to create a different story for each region. When a railroad was bought out, it was no longer under local control. Instead, it became part of the behemoth system. Communities across America were increasingly tied in to the nation's growing industrial machine. The Southern Pacific may have been the first big-business influence on the community of Santa Cruz, but it was not the last. In fact, it paved the way for other sorts of businesses. In the 1900s, the local gunpowder works was taken over by the Wilmington, Delaware–based DuPont Company. As the nation progressed into the 20th century, the citizens of Santa Cruz County— and people all over the country—were more likely to live and work in the shadows of big business.

More than 20,000 people lived in Santa Cruz County in 1900, a quarter of them in the city of Santa Cruz. More than 3,000 lived in Watsonville, the county's second largest town, touted as a "thriving, busy, rustling, hustling pretty town." In towns like these across the nation, ideas about time and distance changed as travel became easier. When Eliza Farnham traveled from Santa Cruz to San Francisco in the 1850s, she had to find an escort, and the trip took two days. In the 1870s, her counterpart could hop on a train and arrive in San Francisco in just under four hours.

Easier trade and travel changed local economic landscapes in unexpected ways. In Watsonville and the Pajaro Valley, people still made their living off the land, but the railroad made life different. Wheat had been the dominant crop of the 1850s and '60s. Grist mills made flour from local wheat, and nearby factories used the wheat straw to make paper. With rail links, both enterprises began to die. In the 1870s, and especially in the 1880s, valley agriculturalists turned to growing fruits and vegetables for farflung markets instead.

Some doors opened; others closed. With access to a larger market, local natural resources like timber flowed out of the region at a faster rate. Once considered inexhaustible, raw materials began to disappear. In 1870, there were nine tanneries in Santa Cruz County. By the 1880s, the county's tanners had stripped and killed many of the area's oak trees. The bark was too difficult to import from elsewhere, and the Santa Cruz tanning industry dwindled.

At the same time, Santa Cruz's commercial fishing industry flourished in new ways. The area's early Chinese population had started a fishing fleet in the 1850s. They sold abalone and other bay delicacies, mainly to Chinese residents in California and abroad. With limited ability to transport their catch, these early fishermen dried it rather than selling it fresh. But once the Santa Cruz Railroad connected the local coastline with big city markets, fishermen could sell fresh seafood in San Francisco.

By 1879, the Santa Cruz fishing fleet was prospering. Italians joined the Chinese as fishermen. Together they shipped 139,000 pounds of fish a year over the new rail lines. Fishermen caught an equal amount of fish off Capitola, nearby. It was all loaded onto railcars and sent to market in San Francisco.

Once travel to Santa Cruz got easier, tourism grew.

"Life at Santa Cruz during the summer is one round of pleasure," one town history declared. People had visited Santa Cruz for health and recreation since the 1850s. Its lovely beach, spectacular redwoods, mild climate, and proximity to the mountains made it a delight, and now the railroad made the journey quicker and easier. Thousands flocked to Santa Cruz in the summertime. Entrepreneurs of the 1890s opened grand family hotels, such as the Sea Beach. Sea Beach proprietor J. T. Sullivan considered Santa Cruz "pre-eminently the fashionable Watering Place of California, the 'Newport' of the Pacific Coast." Santa Cruz competed for the tourists with nearby Monterey, which was developed by the real estate division of Southern Pacific.

Watsonville changed and flourished as well. Throughout the 19th century, with more people moving into cities and the nation's economy becoming industrialized, farmers grew more food to send to market. Early California farmers had grown grain on vast tracts of land, making the state the nation's second biggest wheat producer in those days. Watsonville farmers had grown for the market as early as 1851, selling their potatoes for "enormous prices" in the goldfields and in San Francisco. The bottom fell out of the potato market a year later, but the new rail connections still gave Pajaro Valley farmers hope. By the 1880s they were marketing hops, sugar beets, apples, strawberries, and other crops—locally, regionally, nationally, and internationally.

In the process, the Pajaro Valley landscape changed. "Fields of beans, of potatoes, of sugar beets, and of corn and of strawberries have taken the place of the fields of barley and wheat," one observer noted. "Numerous young orchards, and a few of an older growth, attest the fact that residents of this favored section have been brought to a realization of the adaptability of their soil and climate to horticulture."

Late in the 1890s, orchardists planted symmetrical rows of apple trees, giving the valley a new look. To maximize their yield, farmers planted annual field crops in between the young trees: strawberries for the San Francisco market and beets for the local sugar factory. By 1901, area farmers had planted 156,000 trees on 1,780 acres, and the region's apple boom was in swing. In 1909, the valley shipped out two million boxes of apples. In 1910, Watsonville held a five-day Apple Annual, called on one publicity postcard "The world's greatest apple show." Thirty thousand people attended.

Watsonville's Western Beet Sugar Company processed sugar beets into raw sugar. Claus Spreckels, the German landowner who had joined Frederick Hihn in the effort to bring a railroad line to Santa Cruz, was considered California's "Sugar King." Spreckels had been interested in applying the successes of the European sugar beet industry in the States for decades, and by the late 1880s, he judged that the time was right. In 1887, he bought machinery in Germany for a factory capable of processing 350 tons of beets per day. Localities vied for the factory, and Watsonville won out. To induce him to locate his business in their town, citizens raised money, bought a factory site, and donated it to him. Multimillionaire Spreckels just paid for the factory machinery and the building.

*Anti-Chinese sentiment permeated all levels of society. This children's toy, a cap gun, reflected the widely held 19th century belief that people of Chinese origin should be kicked out of the United States: Pull the trigger, and kick the Chinese man out.*

The sugar industry firmly tied Watsonville into the market economy and helped insulate the town from the worst of the depressions that wracked the country in the 1890s. Ironically, sugar beets also helped Watsonville become an apple-growing center since, as one source put it, "growers found they could get two crops from the same field by planting beets between the orchard rows." As Pajaro Valley farmers planted more orchards, they left less land for beets, since interplanting only worked for the first few years, when the trees were immature.

In 1898, Spreckels closed the Watsonville factory and built a new one just outside Salinas, to the southeast. Some Pajaro Valley residents still grew beets, but the area soon became better known for its orchard crops. Although its sugar beet era lasted only a decade, Watsonville entered the 20th century with a solid, commercially based, agricultural economy.

Watsonville became home to dozens of apple-packing houses, many of them owned by Serbo-Croatian families who immigrated to the valley in the 1870s and 1880s, through to World War I. Seasonal workers sorted fruit and packed it into boxes to be sent to markets in San Francisco, to states farther east, and even to Europe. Workers separated out those apples not good enough for eating and sent them to other factories, including S. Martinelli & Sons, to be made into cider or vinegar. Although smaller than Santa Cruz, Watsonville was a busy town in the 1890s, home to the Pajaro Valley Bank and the Bank of Watsonville, the Mansion House hotel, shops and brothels, its own Chinatown, one public school, the Pajaro Valley Orphan Asylum for

Boys, municipal water and electric works, and numerous churches. Men who reaped profits from the valley's rich soil built grand mansions in the town of Watsonville.

The new products grown in the Pajaro Valley increased the demand for workers. Sugar beets had a long growing season and had to be picked very quickly when they were ripe, to maintain the top sugar level. Strawberries had to be tended and picked by hand, and since the harvesting season ran for nine months of the year, laborers were needed on a more constant basis. In season, apples, too, had to be picked, sorted, and packed by hand, not machine.

In the fields and orchards of the Pajaro Valley, as in so many other work sectors of late 19th-century California, Chinese men formed the backbone of the workforce. Residents of South China began to emigrate to California in large numbers during the gold rush of the 1850s. Through the next few decades, the state's Chinese population—like its population in general—grew quickly. More than 20,000 Chinese immigrants came to the new state in 1852 alone. By 1870, over 60,000 Chinese people, most of them men, lived in California.

Most Chinese immigrants didn't come to California to be field hands, but once their dreams of gold

*Workers of many nationalities did the onerous work of growing, hoeing, weeding, and harvesting fruits and vegetables from the rich California soil. Clockwise from upper left: Only a few Chinese families formed; primarily Chinese males worked in the Pajara Valley in the 1890s; Filipino men immigrated and found agricultural work; and a Japanese family, the Izumakis, work together in the strawberry fields.*

faded, they quickly became an important part of the state's labor force. They helped make California a viable part of the Union. Although foremen were initially resistant to hiring them, thousands of Chinese men laid the Central Pacific tracks that created the overland connection between California and the rest of the nation. After that massive endeavor was complete, Chinese men helped build other railroads throughout California, including the Santa Cruz.

The vectors of feeling toward the Chinese in Santa Cruz County present a microcosm of the entire state. The Santa Cruz Railroad hired Chinese railroad laborers, but the men were not allowed to live inside the Santa Cruz city limits. The California Powder Works hired Chinese coopers for a while, but the company finally gave in to the growing tide of anti-Chinese sentiment and fired that portion of its workforce in 1878.

Despite its fairly small Chinese population, Santa Cruz had a flourishing anti-Chinese party. Residents enthusiastically joined organizations with pseudo-scientific names like the Order of Caucasians. In 1878, over 200 people joined the local branch of the San Francisco–based Workingman's Party, led by the Irish-born, anti-Chinese demagogue, Denis Kearney. Despite the party name, the Workingman's Party drew not-so-working-class people, like Duncan McPherson, the editor of the *Santa Cruz Sentinel*, and Elihu Anthony, the eminent Santa Cruz businessman. McPherson published inflammatory rhetoric in the pages of his paper, stirring up anti-Chinese sentiment by claiming, "The Chinamen are an unmitigated curse to this state. They have done a thousand times more evil than good.... Chinamen are not citizens in any sense of the word." In 1878, the Workingman's Party held four of the six seats on the Santa Cruz town council.

California held a statewide referendum, asking citizens if they would like to exclude the Chinese from the state in 1879. Like the rest of the state, Santa Cruz and Watsonville citizens voted overwhelmingly in favor of exclusion. In 1885 and 1886, Santa Cruz town residents declared themselves ready to ban Chinese people from the county. Watsonville citizens opposed the Santa Cruz campaign. They couldn't as easily afford to drive the Chinese out, because they needed them as workers in the fields. They made the beet sugar industry possible, although they did not work in the factory itself. And it wasn't only sugar beets. Hundreds of Chinese men worked in the Pajaro Valley strawberry fields during the 1880s.

The U.S. Congress passed a federal Chinese Exclusion Act in 1882. Chinese laborers were barred from entering the country for the next ten years. By the 1890s, the Chinese population in California was shrinking, its members aging. Watsonville's Chinatown remained vibrant during that decade, but the days of Chinese labor were numbered. California agriculturalists looked around for a workforce to replace the aging Chinese. They found one in Japanese workers, who began to immigrate to the United States and work in the Pajaro Valley in the 1890s. They established a "vigorous Japantown on South Main Street." Like the Chinese before and the Filipinos after them, Japanese residents at the turn of the century provided much needed labor and at the same time caused great concern among Watsonville's Anglo residents.

. . .

As in this little region of California, so across the nation. In just a half-century, the dream of a transcontinental railroad had grown into the reality of a complex transportation system, its arteries reaching older settlements, creating new towns, opening up and spurring on communities along all its many miles of track. By 1900, nearly 200,000 miles of railroad track crisscrossed the nation and played a vital role in transforming territories into states.

The growth of the railroad system set economic, social, and cultural changes into motion. Whether small and local or large and transcontinental, railroads connected people and places. Transportation networks made distance matter less. They provided skeins of connection that transformed communities like Santa Cruz and Watsonville all over the nation, linking Americans to one another and to a market economy in new ways. Railroad tycoons such as Leland Stanford, local entrepreneurs such as Frederick Hihn, and thousands of anonymous workers all did their parts in laying down the tracks for America's future as a modern economic powerhouse.

COME ALL YOU ROUNDERS, I WANT YOU TO HEAR
THE STORY OF A BRAVE ENGINEER;
CASEY JONES WAS THE ROUNDER'S NAME,
ON A BIG EIGHT-WHEELER OF A MIGHTY FAME.

NOW CASEY SAID, 'BEFORE I DIE
THERE'S ONE MORE TRAIN THAT I WANT TO TRY,
AND I WILL TRY ERE MANY A DAY
THE UNION PACIFIC AND THE SANTA FE.'

AROUND THE CURVE COMES A PASSENGER TRAIN,
HER HEADLIGHT WAS SHINING IN HIS EYES
  THROUGH THE RAIN,
CASEY BLEW THE WHISTLE A MIGHTY BLAST
BUT THE LOCOMOTIVE WAS A-COMIN' FAST.

THE LOCOMOTIVES MET IN THE MIDDLE OF THE HILL,
IN A HEAD-ON TANGLE THAT'S BOUND TO KILL,
HE TRIED TO DO HIS DUTY, THE YARD MEN SAID,
BUT CASEY JONES WAS SCALDED DEAD.

HEADACHES AND HEARTACHES AND ALL KINDS OF PAIN
THEY ALL RIDE ALONG WITH THE RAILROAD TRAIN,
STORIES OF BRAVE MEN, NOBLE AND GRAND,
BELONG TO THE LIFE OF THE RAILROAD MAN.

— *attributed to railroad worker Wallace Saunders, circa 1900*

# THE NATIONAL ECONOMY
## GETS A BACKBONE

*Trains supplied America's lifeblood in the second half of the 19th century. Opposite, clockwise from upper left: Santa Fe locomotives await repairs; crew members check watches to stay on time; President Andrew Johnson exhorts voters at an 1866 whistle-stop; passengers relax in a convertible Pullman sleeper. Above, railroads competed with artful marketing.*

The presidential election hinged on which party could win the recount in Florida and two other states. Nationally, the Democrats had beaten the Republicans by less than 250,000 popular votes. In the crucial electoral college, however, disputed returns in three states left the Democrat one elector short of winning. The Florida vote seemed close but clear—until politicians, the press, and corporate powers threw the election into chaos.

The year was not 2000, but rather 1876. And although the parties were quite different then, the results were the same.

Initial counts in South Carolina had favored Ohio's Republican governor, Rutherford B. Hayes, a gray-bearded, Harvard-educated lawyer and former Civil War colonel. In the other disputed states, Florida and Louisiana, the unofficial vote count favored the Democrat, Samuel Tilden, the governor of New York and a railroad lawyer and investor. Each side claimed victory and demanded endorsement from a partisan slate of electors. Congress created a 15-member electoral commission to sort out the mess. Florida, the first state to be considered, would be the litmus test. On an 8-7 vote along party lines, the commission said Hayes won Florida.

Rumors circulated that a behind-the-scenes compromise had been worked out shortly before the commission's vote on the results in South Carolina. The third and final vote, it would sway the election one way or the other. Reportedly, Southern Democrats would support Hayes for two promises: an end to post–Civil War Reconstruction in the South and, to extend the Texas & Pacific Railway from Fort Worth to California, a federal subsidy. Southern leaders hoped that once the government conceded this first step, federal funds might begin to flow more freely in support of a long list of transportation improvements and building projects they had in mind. The commission ruled Republican, and Hayes won the Presidency by one electoral vote not much more than a week before the Inauguration.

The two candidates represented the debate over federal aid to the railroads. Tilden had earned a reputation as an enemy of railroad subsidies, while Hayes favored a liberal policy toward the South, including "internal improvements of a national character." Hayes never explicitly said that he meant putting federal money toward a railroad, and, once President, he never pursued such an appropriation. Yet perceptions lingered that he owed his office to the influence of Thomas A. Scott, head of both the Texas & Pacific and the Pennsylvania Railroads.

Scott possessed charm, intellect, and frizzy sideburn whiskers as prominent as cowcatchers. Scott served President Abraham Lincoln as assistant secretary of war, and his Civil War duties had included supervising railways for Union use. His efficient administrative talents won Lincoln's respect and boosted his career. Scott developed a reputation for solving difficult problems—and for getting his way. He became so politically influential, states had no power to resist him, orator Wendell Phillips observed. "He need not move at all," said Phillips. "A puff of the waste smoke out of his mouth upsets the legislatures."

Scott became president of the Pennsylvania Railroad in 1874. Two years later, it employed

*Train conductors carried tools of the trade. Above, clockwise from top: A leather case, circa 1860, held tickets and cash; a badge on the cap indicated rank on the railway; pocket watches, this one from 1918, were kept in prime working order; and ticket punches marked customers' tickets with differently shaped holes, each assigned to a different conductor.*

200,000 workers and boasted 6,600 miles of track, making it the nation's largest railroad and largest business. Scott's Texas & Pacific was much smaller. In 1877, it joined the northeastern Texas towns of Sherman, Texarkana, Marshall, and the linked towns of Dallas and Fort Worth. Scott wanted to extend tracks southwest, through El Paso to San Diego. Collis Huntington, of the Central Pacific and the Southern Pacific Railroads, had his eye on the growing southern California market as well. He had been pushing tracks south from San Francisco. When Congress chartered the Texas & Pacific, Huntington's lobbyists won federal approval for tracks east to the Arizona border. If Scott wanted his railroad to reach the Pacific, he either had to rely on Huntington or build hundreds of miles of parallel tracks.

According to some skeptics, Scott acted on behalf of Hayes to woo and win the Dixie Democrats, with the understanding that Hayes, when elected, would return quid pro quo. Hayes did nothing to dispel those rumors. On March 2, 1877, when he received the telegram confirming his election, he was riding to Washington in one of Scott's luxurious private railroad cars. Nor did he work to dispel the impression of an alliance with Scott four months later, when he called out Federal troops to protect railroad property and end the Great Railroad Strike of 1877.

The railroads had coped with four years of economic depression by lowering wages and increasing work hours. Railroad workers fought back, starting strikes in several cities. Some strikes turned bloody. When strikers burned trains and buildings in Pittsburgh, Scott said they should try "a rifle diet for a few days and see how they like that kind of bread." President Hayes restored order at gunpoint, which benefited Scott's railroads in the short run. But the strain of the violent summer so weakened him that in 1880, he sold his Texas & Pacific holdings to Jay Gould, who compromised with Huntington and the Southern Pacific. The two lines joined near El Paso in 1881, giving the South a link to the Pacific.

During the entire 19th century, railroads dominated American politics and economics more than any other industry. They connected cities and countryside, producers and markets, restless people and lands of opportunity. They helped transform the economy from agrarian to industrial. The railroads did the most in the 19th century to make America's disjointed regions—islands of isolated commerce, trapped by poor roads and the seasonal cycle of freeze and thaw—interconnected and interdependent. By the 1880s, a Midwestern farm family could wear Mississippi cotton, eat California fruit, roast Dakota beef, bake with Minnesota flour, and break the earth with an Illinois plow. Trains carried letters, regional newspapers, national magazines, and mail-order merchandise to customers hundreds of miles away from any store. The impact of the railroads on American enterprise was immeasurable.

Poet Walt Whitman wrote of the "fierce-throated beauty" that roared with the "pulse of the continent." But when that pulse skipped an iron beat, the economy stumbled. The failed investments in the Northern Pacific Railroad in 1873 and the collapse of the Philadelphia & Reading Railroad Company in 1893 touched off prolonged economic depressions.

The sheer size of America's railroad companies accounted for much of the power they wielded in national commerce. In 1877, the railroad industry's bonded debt of $2.26 billion overshadowed the concurrent national debt of $2.1 billion. The railroads were so gargantuan that they had to invent new ways of doing business. Their needs helped establish Wall Street as the nation's financial center.

Railroad employees along hundreds of miles of track experienced little face-to-face contact, so their companies were the first to introduce a military-type staff hierarchy into the business world. Railroads required complex management of budgets, customers, and markets. Many followed the lead of the Baltimore & Ohio Railroad and split off separate financial and accounting offices. The Louisville & Nashville Railroad introduced "control through statistics," a business strategy that became the standard for all modern business. Railroads grew so powerful that no individual could hope to challenge the company. Thus as railroads grew, so did labor unions, collective bargaining, and populist politics.

Railroad companies fought for dominance in an era of social Darwinism and laissez-faire free enterprise. Unregulated competitors fought their way to the top, proving themselves the fittest simply by surviving. Survivors in the railroad struggle joined John D. Rockefeller and Andrew Carnegie—survivors in the oil and steel struggles, respectively—and became the nation's mega-capitalist "robber barons." The only force able to restrain the power of the railroads for the public good was the government.

. . .

Railroads followed the path of settlement in the East and stamped the imprint of Euro-American civilization on the West. The location of a rail line could spell doom for one town, bonanza for another. "A railroad in a town is like a mine of gold," declared a promotional guide for the Massachusetts Old Colony Railroad in 1875. "The snorting of the iron horse indicates prosperity." Omaha and Wichita owed their lifeblood to the railroad. Denver's population expanded twentyfold from 1870 to 1890, after the Denver Pacific connected the city to the transcontinental railroad in Cheyenne, Wyoming.

Los Angeles remains the prime example of the power of rail lines to shape a metropolis. Its only natural advantages were climate and a seaport; its only natural resource was the surrounding agricultural fecundity. Yet in the first decade of the 20th century, Henry Edwards Huntington predicted that Los Angeles would soon become the largest city in the West, if not "the center of civilization."

Henry E. Huntington was the nephew of Collis P. Huntington, the Southern Pacific president who had clashed with Scott. The younger Huntington did more than any of his contemporaries to ensure that Los Angeles expanded. A six-foot-tall, 200-pound man with soft gray hair and expressive blue eyes,

*It's no contest in an 1883 cartoon, top, when the monopoly-armored railroad jousts with lowly labor. Workers fought anyway—with the power to strike, symbolized by the hammer, however small. Late-century business tycoons such as Henry E. Huntington and Standard Oil's John D. Rockefeller, bottom, did overpower government. Following pages: Boys in rural Connecticut get a thrill as a steam locomotive passes by, circa 1890.*

Huntington had limitless energy and enthusiasm. Growing up in upstate New York, he visited his successful uncle in 1892. Southern California still lagged behind San Francisco in economic and agricultural development, but the land enchanted Henry Huntington. "You come here, and you are conquered," he wrote. In 1898, encouraged by his uncle, Huntington enlisted investors and bought up most of the Los Angeles street railways.

In the mid-1890s, six major streetcar companies served the city. The largest, the Los Angeles Railway, operated only about 73 miles of track before Huntington and his partners acquired it. In 1901, Huntington incorporated Pacific Electric of California and set about consolidating and expanding the lines. Electric railways were sometimes called "trolleys," named for the overhead device that connected the cars to a power line. One of America's first trolley lines, invented by Frank Sprague, was installed in 1888 in Richmond, Virginia, along 12 miles of track. Trolleys spread rapidly through the nation's cities, but nowhere so swiftly as in Southern California. In Los Angeles, Huntington's Red Car fleet connected outlying communities to the city, where his Yellow Car fleet moved people around. By 1910, 350 miles of trolley tracks crisscrossed Los Angeles and 568 miles stretched out into the surrounding region. Henry E. Huntington had become "the modern Colossus of Roads," according to the *Los Angeles Evening News.*

Huntington's downtown lines aimed to move commuters. His suburban lines promoted real estate along the tracks—owned by the Huntington Land and Improvement Company. Creating a brilliant synergy, Huntington also owned the Pacific Light and Power Company, which supplied electricity to his trolleys and sold the excess throughout Los Angeles County. Following pathways that Huntington personally devised, suburban trolley lines stretched to communities such as Santa Monica, Pasadena, Long Beach, and Redondo Beach. They traveled to Whittier, where Frank Nixon, father of the future President, Richard M. Nixon, worked as a trolley conductor.

Huntington had a business plan. He built tracks into outlying areas while land prices were cheap. He offered low fares on his trolleys, enticing travelers and encouraging people to consider settling outside the city. Then he sold the land reached by the trolleys at a markup. His network of rails attracted new homeowners, who saw that thanks to the trolleys, they could travel easily to jobs in town or to holiday attractions in the mountains or by the shore. In just the first decade of the 20th century, Los Angeles County grew from 170,000 to 504,000 residents. Rapid, sprawling growth made Los Angeles boom sideways instead of building a more concentrated, high-rise, urban core.

. . .

Between 1865 and 1895, America was "mortgaged to the railways, and no one knew it better than the generation itself," observed author Henry Adams in his memoirs. The railroads' dominance of American life stunned his brother, historian Charles Francis Adams, Jr., who searched in vain for a word that meant "government by moneyed corporation."

Railroads altered America's sense of time and helped to create a nation of clock-watchers. Trains

## TRAINS KEEP AMERICA ON TIME

AN 1883 MAP ESTABLISHED
ZONES OF STANDARD RAILWAY TIME
THAT CONTINUE TO THIS DAY.

"WHAT TIME IS IT?" WAS A TRICKY QUESTION IN THE MID-1800s. NOON OCCURRED WHEN THE SUN REACHED ITS ZENITH, NO MATTER WHERE YOU WERE. BECAUSE OF EARTH'S ROTATION, NOON CAME 13 MINUTES LATER TO WASHINGTON, D.C., THAN TO NEW YORK CITY. AMERICA'S 300 TIME ZONES CONFOUNDED FAST TRAVELERS, WHOSE WATCHES INDICATED ARRIVALS BEFORE OR AFTER LOCAL TIME. THIS MAP HELPED MAKE TIME UNIFORM.

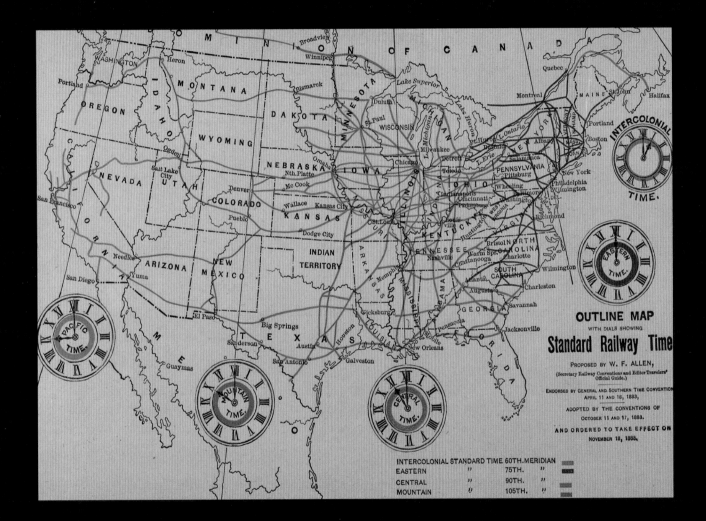

FROM 300 ZONES, FOUR MAIN ZONES—INDICATED BY THE CLOCKS ABOVE—WERE ESTABLISHED. RAILROADS BEGAN CONFERRING IN 1872 TO FIND SUCH A SOLUTION. IN 1883, *RAILWAY GUIDE* EDITOR WILLIAM F. ALLEN MAPPED A PLAN FOR THE GENERAL TIME CONVENTION, AN ORGANIZATION OF RAILROADS: HE PROPOSED TIME ZONES CENTERED ON THE 75TH, 90TH, 105TH, AND 120TH MERIDIANS. THE RAILROADS APPROVED THE SWITCH AND SCHEDULED IT TO TAKE PLACE ON NOVEMBER 18, 1883.

THE NEW TIME ZONES—EASTERN, CENTRAL, MOUNTAIN, AND PACIFIC—WERE SOON ADOPTED BY TIMEKEEPERS AT THE U.S. NAVAL OBSERVATORY. SOME PREACHERS BALKED AT ABANDONING "GOD'S TIME." NEARLY EVERYONE ELSE STARTED USING THE FOUR-ZONE SYSTEM. CONGRESS, HOWEVER, WAITED UNTIL 1918 TO ADOPT "RAILWAY TIME."

operated on a daily schedule, trips between towns or within a city completed in minutes or hours, compared with those on steamships that took days or weeks. Train passengers came to expect swift travel at regular arrivals. To be a few hours or even a few minutes late might mean missed connections, throwing the traveler off schedule significantly. "One well-regulated institution regulates a whole country," noted Henry David Thoreau. "Have not men im-proved somewhat in punctuality since the railroad was invented? Do they not talk and think faster?"

Before the railroads came, each town measured time locally: High noon was the moment of the sun's zenith. Noon in Chicago was 11:38 in St. Louis, a fact that could be verified by speed-of-light messages sent by telegraph. About 300 local time zones stretched from Atlantic to Pacific, with 38 in Wisconsin alone. Most railroads took small steps toward consolidation by establishing about one hundred zones of "railroad time." That many time zones still created confusion, as well as potential danger, when two trains operating on different clocks occupied the same track. Thus, on November 18, 1883, the railroad companies, like Joshua of the Old Testament, made the sun stand still. Residents of Chicago moved the hands of their clocks back nine minutes and thirty-three seconds to the new railroad standard for the Central Time Zone. Elsewhere, Americans reset their timepieces to one of four broad longitudinal zones across the continent—everyone, that is, except the federal government, which did not officially endorse the railroad time zones until 1918.

· · ·

Railroads stoked the engine of the national economy in three ways. First, they were giant consumers of natural resources. They demanded coal, glass, felt, leather, rubber, machine parts, and wood. The railroad industry was also the nation's largest market for iron, requiring 850,000 tons of iron rails in 1873 alone.

Second, since the railroads improved transportation within the United States, they helped stimulate foreign trade and investment. Britain had been buying American wheat, cotton, and beef even before the Civil War, but the expanded rail system opened up new lands to production and investment, broadening foreign interest in American goods. English and Scottish investors purchased many ranches in the Great Plains. In the 1880s, beef exports to Britain boomed. Railroad traffic also allowed Americans to receive foreign goods more easily. In the late 19th century companies brought sugar, cinnamon, bananas, and other foods and merchandise from overseas, distributing them to even the smallest towns.

Finally, railroads increased the speed and reliability of transport, invigorating internal markets. Compared with muddy roads and slow canals, rails made things move. Farmers and manufacturers enjoyed lower transportation costs at the same time that their possibilities for shipping long distance expanded. These improvements stimulated both production and sales. Town after town duplicated the kind of economic transformation that happened to Santa Cruz and Watsonville, when local railroad spurs linked them with the major lines, the rest of California and, from there, the nation. Along with food and manufactured goods, news and printed matter traveled hundreds of miles along the new tracks. Railroads laid the first foundations of what, a century later, mass media theorist Marshall McLuhan would call "the global village." Fast mail service established in 1884 put the morning's *Chicago Tribune* in the hands of readers in Council Bluffs, Iowa, nearly two states away. Circulations soared. Readers began to think about issues regionally and nationally. They also pored over advertisements for products manufactured in distant cities.

Once distance mattered less, each region of the country could specialize instead of having to be self-sufficient, which created economies of scale. Train cars full of hardy wheat grown on the Northern Plains arrived in Minneapolis, where workers at milling plants turned the wheat into snowy white flour. Massachusetts farmers no longer struggled to grow vegetables in their marginal rocky soil, but they worked their bogs, uniquely suited for growing cranberries. The German population of St. Louis brewed their national beverage, beer. In the early 1800s, when water transport reigned supreme, the bustling Ohio River town of Cincinnati processed livestock from three different states and earned the nickname "Porkopolis." But thanks to the railroads (and a Union blockade on Mississippi River traffic during the Civil War), by the 1860s Chicago surpassed Cincinnati in pork output. Soon Chicago would be, in poet Carl Sandburg's words, "Hog Butcher for the World, Tool Maker, Stacker of Wheat."

Consumers as well as producers benefited from the broader trade possibilities offered by the railroad lines. Before 1850, many Americans feared fresh fruits and vegetables, believing that they spread cholera and other diseases. Those who allowed themselves ate only locally grown produce. Produce was strictly seasonal: Fresh fruit in winter was a dream. New dietary knowledge laid to rest misconceptions about the healthfulness of fresh produce. People became more eager to buy fresh fruits and vegetables, and railroads started shipping them around the country. Los Angeles citrus grower William Wolfskill made the first long-distance shipment of oranges, to East St. Louis, in 1877. Soon wholesale marketing plans developed, and market owners across the nation set out fresh fruit for display, using the same wooden boxes in which it had been packed for transport. To attract attention, growers ornamented the crates, labeling them with rainbow-hued lithographs that promoted both the fruit inside and the sunny land that produced it.

New foods began to appear in American kitchens, thanks to new transport possibilities. Outside of a few Atlantic ports, few Americans had seen a banana until the late 19th century. Bananas spoiled easily, and marketers had considered them too risky to ship. By 1910, bananas were commonplace items, available nationwide, all year round, at a price so low they came to be considered pauper's food. The revolution in transportation now made the journey from jungle to breakfast table possible, and profitable, thanks to steam engines in ships and trains and refrigeration.

The corporate structure of banana companies helped make the difference, too. The firm that eventually became Chiquita began in 1885 as the Boston

Fruit Company. It sold Jamaican bananas in Boston. In 1899, the company joined forces with a Brooklyn native, Minor C. Keith, who had built railroads in Costa Rica and planted bananas along the tracks. The heat, tropical diseases, and harsh working conditions made it hard for Keith to attract and keep labor. He recruited Italian immigrants and convicted murderers and thieves from New Orleans, many of whom died in the jungles. For all his railroad tracks and plantations, Keith was called "the uncrowned king of Central America." His United Fruit Company transported bananas from Caribbean locales in trains and refrigerated steamships. Ninety-five ships filled out the United Fruit banana fleet in 1915, making it one of the largest enterprises in the United States.

Competition in the banana trade developed when four Sicilians in New Orleans—Salvador D'Antoni and brothers Joseph, Luca, and Felix Vaccaro—chartered a steamship in 1900 and began importing bananas. By 1906 they had built a railroad in Honduras and were sending a steady stream of banana vessels to docks at New Orleans, making that city the world's largest fruit importer. Their bananas were unloaded into freight cars chilled by ice in summer and heated by kerosene or alcohol in winter. From Fulton, Kentucky, a major railway crossroads, the bananas were shipped west, north, and east. Fruit purveyors displayed the Honduran bananas in stalls such as those at Baltimore's Lexington Market and Washington's Centre Market. Their techniques of vertical integration made the Vaccaro-D'Antoni venture successful. The company later came to be called Standard Fruit and, eventually, Dole.

*A Washington newspaper characterized the 600 stalls of Centre Market as "a social center [and] place of endless entertainment." Markets sold railroad-delivered and locally produced food. Shoppers, right, often bought directly from farmers' wagons. Vendors' business cards, above, advertised their wares.*

The Centre Market in Washington, D.C., two blocks long, operated until 1931 on the site of what is now the National Archives. City residents strolled through stalls, purchasing fruits, vegetables, meat, and dairy products. For a long time, beef bought at such a market was freshly butchered on the spot, but the transportation revolution changed that practice. Railroads could deliver butchered meat, in greater abundance and variety and at a lower price, to local markets—thanks to the stockyards of Chicago.

Iron tracks radiated out from the city on Lake Michigan like strands of a giant cobweb. Tracks owned by western companies went east only as far as Chicago. Tracks owned by eastern companies went just to Chicago, too. This confluence made the city a crucial distribution point. Livestock arrived and butchered meat departed, primarily eastbound.

In the mid-1800s, American consumers accepted pork that had been chilled or salted, but they preferred their beef freshly killed. At first, cattle were shipped into Chicago, then rerouted back out for butchering. As late as 1871, only 4 percent of cattle shipped to Chicago were butchered there. But shipping live animals had drawbacks. The animals had to be fed and watered in transit. Many lost weight, suffered injuries, or died. Shippers charged by weight, and the entire animal included pounds of entrails, bone, and gristle that were excised and discarded.

Shipping dressed beef would solve those problems, but that solution required the invention and engineering of railroad cars that kept butchered meat cold. Attempts at refrigerator cars had begun in the 1840s. A Chicago meat packer, George Hammond, built the first

successful refrigerator cars, nicknamed "reefers," in the late 1860s. Railroads charged meat packers for pulling their reefers and refused to consider investing in their own. Meanwhile, the meat packers kept improving on design. In the 1870s, Gustavus F. Swift, founder of Swift & Company, designed containers for ice and brine at both ends of a railroad car. Vented air from the ice boxes kept the hanging meat at a constant cool temperature.

The Armour Packing Company built its own reefers in Kansas City, and in 1900 boasted the nation's largest private fleet, totaling 12,000. By then, the meat packers had persuaded the Grand Trunk Line to reduce rates for refrigerator cars. Competing railroads followed suit. Western beef, cheaper to fatten, sold for a reasonable price, especially after shipping rates fell. The savings convinced more consumers in the East to buy Chicago-dressed beef. Swift introduced new cuts of beef, like chuck and round. "Cut it up and scatter the pieces," Swift told his agents, because "the more you cut, the more you sell." Local shops found it unprofitable to compete, and they stopped butchering on their own.

By 1890, cattle from the Northern Plains were herded up and hauled by train to the Chicago stockyards, where operations geared up to receive 12 million animals a year. The Northern Pacific Railroad had staged promotions to lure cattle ranchers north and west. The success of those campaigns meant that many meat animals came from Montana and the Dakotas. To handle the massive butchering job, Chicago stockyards perfected a disassembly line, learned from Cincinnati's pork packers. Instead of

*Cornelius Vanderbilt's Merchants Despatch Transportation Company was one of the first to run "reefer" cars, above, which transformed the beef and pork industry. Following pages: Western farmers raised beef, left, for eastern markets. Packing-house inspectors in 1916, right, mark hanging pork to show it has met Department of Agriculture standards.*

assigning one worker to dress one hog, stockyard managers split the labor into many smaller tasks. Each worker performed the same motions, over and over. In Upton Sinclair's 1906 novel, *The Jungle,* Jurgis Rudkus had butchered hogs in his native Lithuania for years, but he stared openmouthed at the massive, bloody ballet of the Chicago stockyards. "One [man] scraped the outside of a leg; another scraped the inside of the same leg.... Another made a slit down the body; a second opened the body wider.... It was like a wonderful poem to him."

Increased mechanization sped up the slaughter even more. Overhead trolleys carried slabs of beef slowly down the line. Specialized butchers cut and trimmed the meat as it moved from station to station. The Chicago stockyard line inspired Henry Ford. Instead of taking something apart as it moved along a belt, Ford speculated, workers could do just the opposite. Each person could perform one task, together building an object that grew more complex as it rolled along. Thus the modern assembly line and the cheap, reliable Model T were born of beef.

• • •

When the trains that carried goods into Chicago made return trips, they could carry other goods out. Railroad companies offered reduced rates to Chicago manufacturers, wanting to encourage shipments going out of the city. Producers of machinery and hardware, including Cyrus McCormick's reaper factory, got a boost from such discounts.

Another beneficiary of cheap transportation out of Chicago was Aaron Montgomery Ward. Ward had spent two years as a traveling salesman in the

Mississippi Valley. That job opened his eyes to rural America, where people were clamoring for quality products to buy, many feeling cheated by economic forces beyond their control. In 1872, Ward and his brother-in-law came up with a plan to use railroad networks to bring city merchandise to the farm. They bought goods in volume for low prices and shipped items cheaply and directly to customers. Ward's first one-page offering, in 1872, listed more than 160 items. Seven yards of denim sold for a dollar, a gold ring for two. By the turn of the century, Ward published his own catalog and listed 70,000 items, from tiddledywinks to goat harnesses. Cheap transportation and the lack of a middleman kept prices low. Ward promised satisfaction "Or Your Money Back."

Farmers and ranchers shouted the loudest to attract the railroads into their regions, envisioning access to more and bigger markets. The railroads turned out to be a mixed blessing. Farmers were small and independent producers; agricultural brokers and railroads were big, faceless operations. If a grain buyer offered a low price or a railroad charged a high shipping rate, all a farmer could do was accept the terms—or take his produce off the market. Price wars raged, aiding some towns and throwing others into economic turmoil. Populist William Jennings Bryan, three times a presidential candidate, and his wife, Mary, returned home to Nebraska after a world tour. They had purchased some bronze lions and other heavy freight in Japan. It cost more to ship the items from Kansas City to Lincoln than from Yokohama to Kansas City. "It is not surprising that the West urged railroad regulation," Mary Bryan wrote.

National economic forces caught farmers in a further bind. Corn and wheat production roughly tripled between 1866 and 1889, while the American population grew only 69 percent. Many railroad companies were deeply in debt and some even failed, leading to financial panics and deflation, a broad lowering of prices. Many farmers paid fixed mortgage rates, although the price of corn and wheat kept falling. In the mid-1890s, it was cheaper to burn corn for heat in Nebraska than to sell it and buy coal.

Farmers tried to pool their power. Joined by government officials, a banker, and a minister, Oliver Hudson Kelly founded the National Grange of the Patrons of Husbandry in 1867. Within seven years, the Grange had 22,000 chapters. In 1875, national membership neared 900,000. Farm-based political power reached its zenith in 1896 when William Jennings Bryan narrowly lost the Presidency to William McKinley. "You shall not press down upon the brow of labor this crown of thorns, you shall not crucify mankind upon a cross of gold," Bryan declaimed to the nation's masters of power and wealth, urging railroad regulation, among other controls. Despite the highest turnout of eligible voters in history, Bryan lost by 600,000 votes. He ran, and lost again, in 1900 and 1908.

Economic associations formed by groups of farmers had some successes, such as the Southern California Fruit Exchange. In 1893, about one hundred orange growers banded together to bargain with railroads and buyers. They sold their fruit under the name Sunkist. By collectively marketing oranges, the Exchange won an average price of a dollar a box,

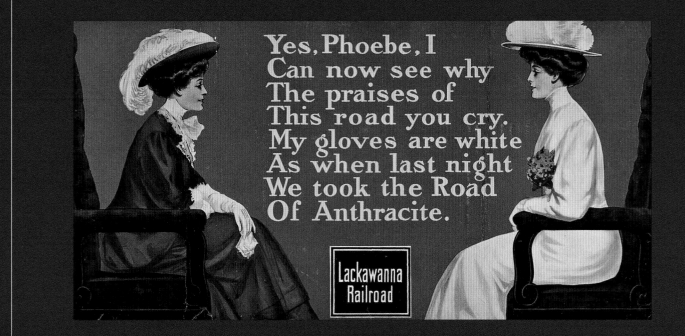

Yes, Phoebe, I
Can now see why
The praises of
This road you cry.
My gloves are white
As when last night
We took the Road
Of Anthracite.

Lackawanna
Railroad

## PHOEBE SNOW

### THE IMPECCABLE TRAIN TRAVELER

FROM 1900 TO 1917, THE FICTIONAL PHOEBE SNOW, ABOVE RIGHT, PROMOTED THE LACKAWANNA RAILROAD IN ADS SUGGESTING A CLEAN AND CLASSY RIDE. JINGLES ADVERTISED A NEARLY SOOT-FREE EXPERIENCE AND MADE PHOEBE FAMOUS.

A VAUDEVILLE JOKE of the early 20th century started with a question posed to a small boy: Who were the two most famous women in the world? His response: "My mamma's mamma and Phoebe Snow." Not bad company for Ms. Snow, a woman who retired at 17 – and never really existed in the first place.

Like the Gibson Girl, Phoebe Snow made the leap from advertising image to cultural icon. She appeared in 1900 to promote the Delaware, Lackawanna & Western Railroad, which ran from New Jersey to New York. The railroad burned anthracite coal, while competitors used softer bituminous coal, which left a sooty residue on passengers' clothes. Hence Phoebe Snow could dress confidently in white from head to toe and ride the Lackawanna. Her pristine white clothing adorned billboards, streetcar ads, newspapers, and magazines. Each image contained a verse set to the clack-clack rhythm of the rails. The most famous read:

*Says Phoebe Snow / About to go*
*Upon a trip / To Buffalo:*
*"My gown stays white*
*From morn till night*
*Upon the Road of Anthracite."*

Railroad advertisements often depicted white women riding in elegant cars. The images lured female passengers with promises of comfort and safety and intrigued men with hints of sexual adventure. Ads conveyed trains as respectable and clean and emphasized improved services since the Civil War.

Heavier trains and larger wheels refined the rides. Battery-powered lights and steam heat piped from the engines debuted in the late 1880s. The Pennsylvania Limited boasted in 1891 of a barber and valet for men and a maid for women. Passengers on a budget brought their own food or purchased it at the depot, but the well-to-do ate in dining cars that rivaled fancy restaurants. On June 29, 1907, for example, riders on the North-Western Limited could select caviar, littleneck clams, and roast duckling. While most railroad passengers struggled to get cozy in day coaches, the middle and upper classes enjoyed "high varnish" parlor and sleeping cars. Author Theodore Dreiser traveled to the 1893 Chicago World's Fair and thought "I was doing very well indeed" to be in a "gaudy" Pullman car decorated with rosewood panels, bevel-edged mirrors, carpets, and curtains. When 20 young schoolteachers boarded, Dreiser declared the train to be the ideal way to travel.

Such ideas apparently inspired advertising designer Earnest Elmo Calkins, the creative force behind the Phoebe Snow campaign. Lackawanna ads already showcased a woman in white. Calkins provided a name and jingles to make her memorable. His short verses left room for powerful visual images. Photographs of a model on a train to Buffalo guided the work of artist Harry Stacy Benton, whose drawings set Phoebe on her path to fame. The Lackawanna hired young women to dress in white and ride the line or appear at civic functions. In 1903, the railroad commissioned the film, *A Romance of the Rail,* featuring the Phoebe Snow character taking a Lackawanna train ride with her chaperone through the Blue Ridge Mountains. They fall in love and marry in the observation car.

Passenger traffic on Phoebe's railroad increased 80 percent in her first decade. She was still going strong in 1917, when the Lackawanna line retired her—and the anthracite—because coal was diverted to warships. In 1949, Phoebe Snow made a comeback as the name of the stylish streamliner service between Hoboken and Buffalo. This time she lasted 18 years, until 1967, when the Lackawanna removed Phoebe's train from service, mothballing for the final time the name that had once been so famous.

EARNEST ELMO CALKINS PENNED MORE THAN 60 POEMS, LIKE THE ONE BELOW, ON BEHALF OF PHOEBE SNOW. DESPITE HIS DEAFNESS, CAUSED BY CHILDHOOD MEASLES, HE HAD AN EAR FOR RHYME. CALKINS AND RALPH HOLDEN, A FORMER RAIL FREIGHT WORKER, FORMED A NEW YORK ADVERTISING FIRM AND SERVED CLIENTS INCLUDING THOMAS EDISON AND H.J. HEINZ, AS WELL AS THE LACKAWANNA RAILROAD.

Lackawanna Railroad

A coach or sleigh
Was once the way
Of reaching Home
On Christmas Day.
Now Phoebe's right
You'll expedite
The trip by Road
Of Anthracite.

more than triple the price that any one grower would have received.

At the same time, railroad labor was organizing. By the 1870s, some railroads had overreached their grasp. Many defaulted on their bonds. The depression that began in 1873 slashed railroad stock prices, and losses were passed on to employees. Typical wages dropped between 21 and 37 percent in the four years after 1873. The Baltimore & Ohio cut workers' pay roughly in half while demanding more labor. B&O brakemen, who had earned $70 a month in a job that risked injury and death, were told to make do with $30. In the summer of 1877, the B&O paid stock dividends but cut wages another 10 percent.

That announcement touched off strikes in Camden Junction, near Baltimore. Strikes quickly spread to Martinsburg (West Virginia), Pittsburgh, and other rail centers. As far away as San Francisco, citizens adopted resolutions in sympathy with the strikers. The first truly national strike briefly prompted the first general strike in American history, as workers in most important trades in St. Louis, Chicago, and Toledo stopped work in support of the railroad workers. Some strikes turned violent. Rail workers in Pittsburgh seized control of the city and burned 104 locomotives, 39 buildings, and 1,200 freight cars. Nine governors asked President Hayes to dispatch federal troops to restore order. Clashes with strikers cost more than a hundred lives before the railroads could set trains back in motion.

Most strikers returned to work for prestrike wages. President Hayes wrote in his diary in early August 1877 that they were "sober, intelligent and industrious" men who, having acted wrongly, had to be "put down by force." At the same time, though, Mark Twain wrote, "Pittsburgh and the riots neither surprised nor disturbed me; for where the government is a sham, one must expect such things."

Although the railroads claimed victory, their gain was limited. Samuel Gompers, President of the American Federation of Labor from 1886 to 1924, called the strike "the tocsin that sounded a ringing message of hope to us all." The suppression of labor grievances in 1877 kindled the growth of unions and led to further strikes, in 1885, 1886, and 1888. Eugene Debs organized the American Railway Union (ARU) in 1893, opening its doors to mechanics, day laborers, and any other "persons employed in railway service" and thus making it the broadest industrial union of that time.

Debs's union flexed its muscles in 1894 by supporting laborers who made sleeping cars for the Pullman's Palace Car Company. The company had laid off workers and cut wages to cope with a depression that began in 1893, but it did not reduce rents in the company town of Pullman, Illinois. Workers walked out. In a show of solidarity, the ARU refused to work on any train that pulled a Pullman car. The result was 1877 all over again: The violence ended only when federal troops broke the strike. The ARU disbanded, the Pullman strikers grumbled and returned to work, and labor unions suffered a setback that took decades to overcome.

One victory balanced those losses. The strike of 1894 prompted the formation of a presidential commission charged to resolve railroad conflicts.

Small-scale patent models from the late 1890s depict a variety of road-grading machines that could be pulled by horses. Graders shaped crude roads to smooth the ruts and elevate the center enough to channel rainfall to the sides. The machines reflected the public's growing interest in good roads. After a spring thaw or summer storm, every automobile passing over a road churned its surface anew.

# CONCRETE HIGHWAYS
### AND
## PUBLIC IMPROVEMENTS
#### MAGAZINE

Vol. XII       November, 1928       No. 11

An 1898 law established federal mediators, who settled 61 labor disputes between 1906 and 1913. Railroads felt the pressure from a number of sides, and slowly they came to accept the unions into the discussion.

Government attempts to regulate the railroads had begun with the Illinois Constitution of 1870, which balanced the needs of the railroads with those of the farmers. Illinois legislators regulated grain warehouses (often owned by railroads), forbade unfair shipping rates, among other rules, and established a commission to oversee enforcement. Other midwestern states also passed Granger laws, named for the Grange farmers who benefited from them.

The railroads resisted. At first, railroad money trumped farmer votes until the Supreme Court, in 1886, upheld the Illinois Granger laws, ruling in *Munn* v. *Illinois* that property rights can be restricted for the public good when the property, such as a railroad, is used in the public interest. The railroads argued successfully that only Congress could regulate commerce that crossed state lines, though.

Not to be outflanked, farmers demanded a federal office to supervise the regional and national railroads. In 1887, Congress created the Interstate Commerce Commission, the first government regulatory agency. The four-page law establishing the ICC provided little detail. Section 1 simply required "reasonable and just" transportation rates, for example. The laissez-faire spirit of the McKinley administration did not help. The Supreme Court reversed 15 of 16 ICC rulings in the 1890s.

McKinley's assassination in 1901 changed the political atmosphere. Financier J. P. Morgan, who had engineered the restructuring of the railroad industry during the depression of the 1890s, "cursed and staggered to his desk" when he learned of McKinley's death. Morgan feared that the new president, the progressive Teddy Roosevelt, would have more backbone than his predecessor. He was right. Roosevelt fought his own Republican Party in 1906 to win congressional approval of a bill giving solid regulatory and enforcement powers to the ICC.

. . .

As railroads began facing serious regulation, a challenge of a different sort altogether was arising—a challenge that seemed minor at first but that would ultimately prove momentous: the automobile.

None but the wealthy could afford the first automobiles. Expensive cars, Maxwells or Packards, were not for the masses. Fixing a blown tire could cost two weeks' working wages—and crude rubber tires blew out frequently on even cruder roads. By 1912, only 7 percent of the nation's road surfaces had been improved by grading, macadam, or brick. But from the late 1890s on, people were out there, driving their brand-new automobiles on them.

The Indianapolis 500, inaugurated in 1911, enjoyed immediate success, thanks in part to auto

*As automobiles developed in the early 1900s, reliable highways replaced muddy trails. Clockwise from upper left: The National Parks Highway takes shape in Lewis County, Washington, in 1924; mud puddles punctuate the road between Washington, D.C., and Richmond in 1919; by 1920, the Washington-Richmond road has a smooth gravel surface; and a 1928 magazine highlights the deluxe condition of Highway 10 near Asheville, North Carolina.*

headlamp manufacturer Carl G. Fisher. Fisher and three other investors financed the Indianapolis Motor Speedway as a testing ground for Indiana's auto industry. They replaced its rock-and-tar surface with bricks. A restless promoter and race car driver, Fisher toyed with that improvement in his imagination and conceived of a better road for all Americans.

In 1912, Fisher threw a dinner party for Indianapolis automakers and announced his vision of a "Coast-to-Coast Rock Highway." Materials would cost ten million dollars and labor and equipment would be donated along the way, he said. Dinner guest Frank A. Seiberling, founder of the Goodyear Tire and Rubber Company, promised $300,000 on the spot. Hoping to collect five-dollar donations from every American driver, Fisher gots lots of pledges. Some gave five dollars, others a hundred or a thousand, and captains of the auto industry even more.

A month later, Fisher had a million dollars in pledges and a lot of free publicity. "The biggest project ever undertaken in the automobile world," an Indiana newspaper called it. In 1913, backers formed the Lincoln Highway Association, thinking that the magic of the name would help sell the project. Henry B. Joy, President of Packard Motor Company, became the association's president.

In late summer, Joy announced the planned route: Starting at New York City's Times Square, the Lincoln Highway would meander 3,389 miles across the continent, through Pittsburgh, Fort Wayne, Omaha, Salt Lake City, Reno, and Sacramento, ending at Lincoln Park in San Francisco. Its enthusiastic supporters included President Woodrow Wilson, who sent in five dollars and received membership card number one. Civil War veterans and farmers warmed to the idea, as did the governor of Colorado, once the highway was rerouted through Denver.

Deciding that the project was too big and the donations too small to build the entire length of the highway, Joy embraced a plan to have states and communities along the way pay for construction. He proposed that the association build "seedling miles" of concrete in rural areas, giving farmers a sample of improved roads. De Kalb, Illinois, received the first such mile in 1914. The following year, more miles were poured in Nebraska, Illinois, and Indiana. The association also proposed that those who lived and worked along the route mark the Lincoln Highway with red, white, and blue stripes on poles, trees, or anything else vertical. Formal markers followed.

The Lincoln Highway did not reach coast to coast until the early 1930s. Even before then, though, it kindled Americans' desire to hit the open road. An estimated 5,000 to 10,000 drivers traveled some portion of the muddy Lincoln route to visit the 1915 Pan-Pacific Exposition in San Francisco. To promote their car and highway, Joy and two companions drove a Packard from Detroit to San Francisco. After 21 days on the road, the muddy mobile was displayed at the Exposition's Palace of Transportation. The following year, Wilson signed the Federal Aid Road Act, which provided the first federal tax dollars for improving the nation's roads. Where Tom Scott and the Texas & Pacific failed in 1877, the ordinary citizens of America succeeded in 1916. Uncle Sam was willing to build highways for the good of the country.

I HAVE STRUCK A CITY—A REAL CITY—
AND THEY CALL IT CHICAGO.

THE OTHER PLACES DO NOT COUNT. SAN FRANCISCO
WAS A PLEASURE-RESORT AS WELL AS A CITY, AND
SALT LAKE WAS A PHENOMENON. THIS PLACE IS THE
FIRST AMERICAN CITY I HAVE ENCOUNTERED. IT HOLDS
RATHER MORE THAN A MILLION PEOPLE WITH BODIES,
AND STANDS ON THE SAME SORT OF SOIL AS CALCUTTA.

HAVING SEEN IT, I URGENTLY DESIRE NEVER TO SEE
IT AGAIN. IT IS INHABITED BY SAVAGES. ITS WATER IS
THE WATER OF THE HUGLI, AND ITS AIR IS DIRT.

— *Rudyard Kipling,* American Notes, *1891*

# TRAVEL IN THE GILDED AGE

*Two men and a dog took America's first cross-country auto road trip in 1903. Opposite, clockwise from upper left: H. Nelson Jackson pushes his Winton during the historic trek; when there were roads, they were rough; a block and tackle pulls the Winton from a stream; and a cowboy leads the way through the sagebrush. Above, the Winton Motor Carriage Company touts its car—and Bud.*

Bud the bulldog wore goggles.

His master, Dr. H. Nelson Jackson, had them made to keep out the dust. Jackson's open-air Winton Touring Car, en route from San Francisco to New York in the summer of 1903, kicked up alkaline clouds that inflamed Bud's eyes. Goggles, plus an eyewash of boracic acid, kept Bud happy and healthy. For a snug fit, the goggle lenses had rubber sides, pierced by ventilation holes. A black ribbon looped below Bud's upright ears, and a hinge between the lenses curved across Bud's snout. The dog refused to start each day's drive until the goggles were on and adjusted.

Those goggles, along with Jackson's scarlet Winton, capture the flavor of travel in the Gilded Age. Railroads easily remained the most popular means of transportation and, along with steamships, set new standards of comfort for middle-class and well-to-do travelers. Automobiles and modern bicycles sprang forth within a single generation and beckoned the adventuresome to the open road.

Drivers and cyclists felt empowered and free. They chose their own routes and schedules, enjoyed closer contacts with nature, and flushed with pride over their new technical skills. Songs such as "The Auto Man" declared the driver to be "the greatest hit" of the new century, while the lyrics of "In My Merry Oldsmobile"—"You can go as far as you like with me"—suggested that something romantic, even sexual, animated the nascent automobile. Such clever toys had a price, however. In a decade when few Americans could afford to buy their own automobiles, not only could the wealthy Jackson afford custom-made goggles for his dog; he could also spend $3,000 for his Winton and another $5,000 to drive it on a cross-country journey. Meanwhile, the average industrial worker of 1903 earned less than $500 per year.

For his money, Jackson had the adventure of a lifetime, full of stories that he enjoyed telling and retelling. The Winton Motor Carriage Company of Cleveland, Ohio, recognized the trip's promotional value. The cover of the September 1903 edition of *The Auto Era,* the company's monthly magazine, featured a photograph of Bud modeling his goggles, with a caption that read, "I crossed the Continent in a Winton with Dr. H. Nelson Jackson."

Jackson, Bud, and Sewall Crocker, Jackson's chauffeur and mechanic, amazed the nation. They completed America's first transcontinental auto trip, only a decade after brothers Charles and J. Frank Duryea had built the first American car in Chicopee, Massachusetts. The trip in the Winton took 63 days at an average speed of about seven miles per hour.

Early automobiles were unlikely candidates for extended excursions. They had little power, broke down often, and had trouble navigating roads outside the cities—when there were roads outside the cities. Preparing for her own cross-country journey in 1915, New York resident Emily Post asked a California-born friend about the best road to the West Coast. "The Union Pacific," the woman answered. Pressed to identify a motor route, the friend finally said, "There isn't any." Until federal and state paving programs began in earnest after World War I, spring rains churned midwestern

*Special goggles protected Bud, a bull terrier, from stinging dust. A Wyoming reporter mentioned that Bud's "eyes are badly bloodshot from the exposure to alkali dust." The fabricated goggles guarded his eyes en route, but the writer also noted that, when possible, Bud "spends most of his time resting under the car."*

roads to soup, while rocks and sand choked the western trails. Railroad bridges often were the only spans across rivers. Post overcame the obstacles and reached California in four weeks. In her book, *By Motor to the Golden Gate,* she advised readers about routes, repairs, and a way to modify goggles with orange chiffon to prevent sunburn. A car with a high clearance would come in handy for vaulting boulders and fording streams, she advised—difficulties Jackson, Crocker, and Bud had faced 12 years earlier.

Two attempts to cross the continent before 1903 had ended in failure. The first, in 1899, saw John D. Davis and his wife, Louise, quit after a few hundred miles. Their Duryea "touring cart" suffered 25 breakdowns. The next attempt—by bicycle racer and automaker Alexander Winton, accompanied by his publicity agent—began in San Francisco but ground to a halt in the sands of Nevada. Winton shipped his car home to Cleveland by rail.

Jackson started his trip practically on the spur of the moment. Having quit his physician's practice in Vermont, he sat one May day in the University Club in San Francisco and joined a conversation about making a transcontinental auto journey. One man insisted it could not be done. Jackson disagreed. He consulted with his wife, then asked Crocker to help him make the trip. Crocker, a bicycle racer and gasoline engine mechanic, advised Jackson to buy a Winton for the journey. Jackson searched in vain for a new one, then finally settled on a four-week-old stock touring car, paying the owner $500 more than the new purchase price of $2,500.

Jackson christened his two-cylinder, 20-horsepower

*Charles and J. Frank Duryea, the first to make and sell gas-powered American automobiles, pilot an open-topped car, circa 1895. Frank, who had tested the car in Massachusetts in 1893, championed their mechanical steed. Horses by comparison were "willful" and "unreliable," he said, and befouled the pavement.*

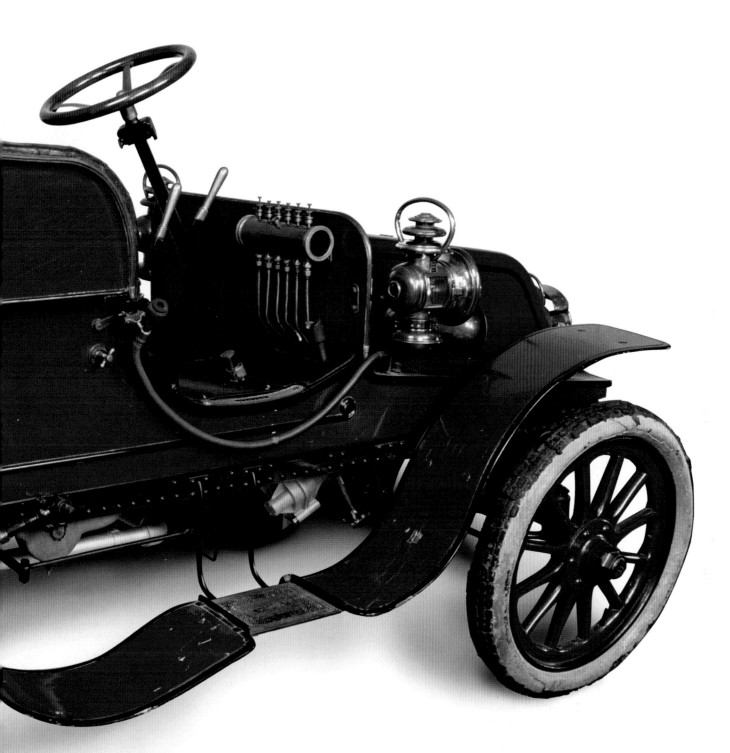

*H. Nelson Jackson's 1903 Winton, above, was named for his home state of Vermont. Hidden beneath its seats, the automobile's 20-horsepower, two-cylinder, water-cooled engine transferred power to the rear wheels via a chain. Jackson donated the car to the Smithsonian Institution in 1944.*

car "Vermont," honoring his home state. Cowboys on the western prairies later dubbed it the "Go Like Hell Machine." By modern standards, the Winton made diabolical demands on a driver. "Maintain a cool head at all times, and master the interesting details of operation before venturing near brick walls and telegraph poles," advised its instruction manual. The engine, mounted below the seats, had to be hand-cranked. A governor button on the floor regulated engine speed. Two levers near the steering column, on the right-hand side, worked two forward gears and one reverse. Once the car was moving, those inside had to monitor the "sight-drip oiler": a brass cylinder that distributed engine lubricant through six glass tubes. When the lines clogged, the driver had to stop the car, clean them, and refill them with oil.

Crocker and Jackson, a bookish-looking fellow with a neat mustache and wire-rimmed pince-nez, customized their car. They removed the "tonneau," or rear two seats, to make room for luggage. A gas tank beneath the hood held 10 gallons, but they added a 12-gallon container to improve distance between fill-ups, since only the occasional hardware outlet, general store, or blacksmith sold gasoline. Their gear included sleeping bags, rubber mackintoshes, a canvas water bag, guns, a block and tackle with 150 feet of rope, an ax, a spade, two jacks, and other tools to meet the demands of the road.

The two men—no dog yet—left San Francisco on May 23, 1903, bound for the dry country of southeastern Oregon. From there they aimed to go east across Idaho and Wyoming, through the Great Plains, along the southern edge of the Great Lakes, and on to New York City. They took a northern route to avoid the southwestern deserts, but the mountains of Oregon and Idaho proved formidable nonetheless. "Often the trail narrowed to ten feet, one-way thoroughfares established by nature," Jackson recalled some 30 years later. "Sometimes it was necessary to remove boulder blockades by hand. Slipping on shale and loose rocks, weaving around mountain ledges, we staked our careers against none too reliable brakes on steep descents. It is still possible to raise goose-flesh ... by recalling certain hair-pin turns where, jolting and skidding, we suddenly looked down unfenced sheer precipices."

Hardships came one after another. Crocker had to walk 29 miles when the gas tank ran dry in Oregon. Both men went without food for 36 hours until they found a shepherd who gave them corn and roast lamb. Mechanical failures included a broken axle, snapped bolts that sent a connecting rod through the crankcase, and numerous blowouts. The Winton was out of commission for a total of 18 days, awaiting various repairs. The two men shared driving duties. They rattled their bones on rocks and railroad ties, dodged mud holes, and occasionally navigated by compass in the Badlands.

The western terrain was often barely negotiable. Jackson "could not understand how people were allowed to use three miles of a public highway as an irrigation ditch," the *Laramie Boomerang* reported. Mud in Nebraska created "buffalo wallows" that halted the car 17 times in one day. Jackson and Crocker would free the Winton by digging ahead,

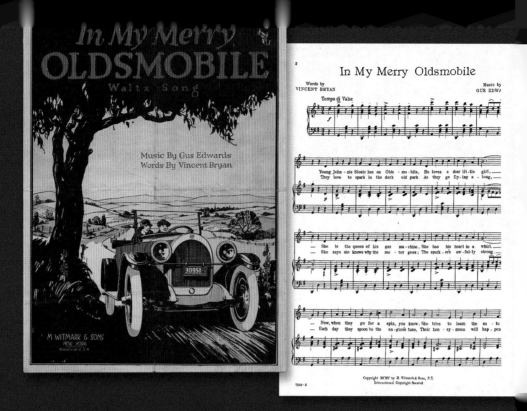

## A SONG FOR THE ROAD

### MUSIC MOVES AMERICANS

BEFORE THERE WAS A TRAIN, there was a train song:

> *O we're all full of life, fun and jollity,*
> *We're all crazy here in Baltimore.*
> *Here's a road to be made*
> *With the pick and spade,*
> *'Tis to reach to Ohio, for the benefit of trade.*

Not exactly "The Wabash Cannonball"– but "The Carrollton March," copyrighted on July 1, 1828, made up in historical significance what it lacked in catchy lyrics. Arthur Clifton wrote the song for the Baltimore & Ohio Railroad Company. The march commemorated the groundbreaking for America's first railroad in regular public service, on July 4, 1828. It also honored 90-year-old Charles Carroll of Carrollton, Maryland, who laid the railroad's first stone and called it his greatest act since signing the Declaration of Independence.

Modern transportation and sheets of po[...]
first widely published in the 1790s, grew up [...]
America. Railroads spread across the cont[...]
mid-1800s and linked the oceans in 1869. [...]
time, sheet music gained wide circulatio[...]
advances including steam-driven presses, s[...]
and lithography. Before recorded music and [...]
ished in the 1920s, printed sheets of lyrics [...]
combination of the two were a key compone[...]
tainment in homes, churches, and schoo[...]
music were printed by special publishing h[...]
as the Tin Pan Alley companies in Ma[...]
century's end, and by newspapers that inclu[...]
inserts in the Sunday editions. Songwriters [...]
loved to write about being on the move.

Hundreds of train songs described jou[...]
pleasant and disastrous. "Casey Jones," wr[...]
vaudevillians and published in 1909, pu[...]

describe the real-life wreck of an Illinois Central train nine years earlier. Other songs commemorated specific routes or railroads. "The Great Rock Island Route" (1882) claimed that "All great cities of importance can be found along its way," while "The Wabash Cannonball" (1890) bragged of a locomotive "mighty tall and handsome, and she's known quite well by all."

A song toasted the appearance of the "Velocipede" in 1869: "Give a turn and twist, With your hand and wrist," the lyrics advised. The 1910 song "Come Josephine, in My Flying Machine" featured a romantic duet sung aloft by pilot and passenger.

But nothing captured the songwriters' imaginations like automobiles. Americans sang about cars before most of them could afford one. Gus Edwards composed the quintessential auto song, "In My Merry Oldsmobile," in 1905, when Ransom Olds's car outsold all others. Vincent Bryan's lyrics made the waltz a hit:

*Come away with me, Lucille*
*In my merry Oldsmobile*
*Down the road of life we'll fly,*
*Automobubbling, you and I*

Many songs hinted strongly at the romantic possibilities of an auto trip. "Get Em in a Rumble Seat" (1927) offered the title's advice to the man who wanted his girl to "tumble." "He'd Have to Get Under – Get Out and Get Under" (1913) countered those claims with a more realistic account of romance in an automobile: Every time Johnny O'Connor snuggled with his sweetheart, his car broke down.

Colorful sheet music covers portrayed sleek women and sleek cars. That combination, which became a staple of automobile marketing, already was spelled out in a 1906 song. No boat or trolley would win her, hinted the woman in the song. "If you want me to ride with you, get an automobile."

POPULAR SONGS IN THE EARLY 20TH CENTURY, BELOW, INTERPRETED THE ROMANCE OF THE OPEN ROAD LITERALLY. "THE AUTO MAN" AND OTHER TUNES CONSTRUCTED MUSICAL STORIES IN WHICH YOUNG COUPLES TOOK ROMANTIC ADVANTAGE OF THE THRILLS OF SPEED AND THE TIME ALONE TOGETHER THAT AN AUTOMOBILE COULD PROVIDE THEM.

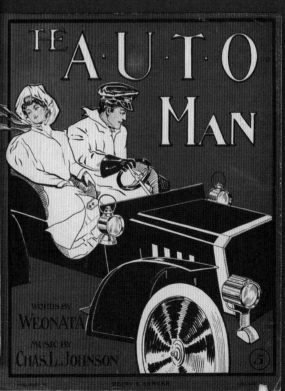

fixing their block and tackle solidly in the earth, and attaching the rope to the rear axle. Then they started the engine, put the car in gear, and let the wheels slip in the mud. The axle wound the rope like a windlass hauling up a ship's anchor chain, and the car pulled itself out of the hole.

Bud joined the trip in western Idaho, where Jackson bought the lovable bulldog. At first the dog bumped his face against the dashboard when the car jolted over rocks, but he soon anticipated the shocks. "He has become quite a chauffeur," Jackson told a newspaper reporter. "In fact, he watches the roads as closely as any one, and whenever there is going to be a jump, he carefully braces himself and is prepared for the bump when it comes."

Curious onlookers gathered as the Winton rolled by. "Quite a flurry of excitement was erected here Saturday evening by the arrival of an automobile," one rural paper said. "Very few of our citizens had ever seen this." An Idaho woman intentionally gave Jackson and Crocker false directions, sending them 60 miles out of their way just so her family could see a car. Crowds surrounded the Winton when it chugged into Omaha, just east of the midpoint of its journey, on July 12, 1903. The Winton and its passengers were "besieged" by newspaper reporters in Chicago. They arrived on New York City's Fifth Avenue at 4 a.m. on July 26. The trip's exact mileage remains unknown—Jackson and Crocker lost their "cyclometer" in Idaho—but estimates ranged from 4,500 to 6,000 miles.

After the trip, the cross-country hero, his trusty mechanic, and his faithful canine drove to Vermont. On the streets of Burlington, his home town, Dr. Jackson was fined five dollars for exceeding the speed limit of six miles per hour.

. . .

The Winton's cross-country journey awakened the nation to the sorry state of its roads. "When an automobile has to carry a wrecking outfit, with a tackle and derrick post to pull itself out of mudholes; when it has to go five miles out of its way to find a place where it can climb a railroad embankment and cross a river on the ties, and when it has to ford other rivers because there are no bridges at all, the scheme of a national transcontinental boulevard seems to have its advantages," Joseph Pulitzer's *New York World* editorialized.

Cars and roads improved, which meant that drivers could increase speed as well. They could make the trip across the continent in less time and with less worry. Long-distance motoring became more common across the nation, but automobiles and their drivers still attracted attention.

Alice Huyler Ramsey of Hackensack, New Jersey, created a sensation when she became the first woman to drive coast to coast in 1909. The sales manager of the Maxwell-Briscoe car dealership in Tarrytown, New York, proposed the journey as a way to promote his product. Ramsey said the seed of the idea "fell on fertile ground" when she heard it. Although only 22, she had been driving for a year. She drove a Maxwell Runabout purchased by her husband, who had never learned to drive himself. She had driven it 6,000 miles in the summer of 1908 and had made a flawless endurance run on

On the car:

SAXON

NEW YORK    APR 6. 191_
NEW ORLEANS
LOS ANGELES
SAN FRANCISCO
SEATTLE
MINNEAPOLIS
CHICAGO
DETROIT
NEW YORK

## SUFFRAGE AUTO CAMPAIGN.

### Two Women Will Tour to the Coast to Spread Propaganda.

An automobile suffrage circuit of the United States, the first of its kind, is to be made by Mrs. Alice Snitjer Burke and Miss Nell Richardson, who will leave New York on Thursday of this week, under the auspices of the National American Woman Suffrage Association. Their object is to carry the news of the plans of the National Suffrage Association for action in St. Louis and Chicago during the Democratic and Republican Conventions. The big "walkless" parade is to take place in the former city, where thousands of women in parade regalia will mass outside the convention hall. In Chicago there will be a parade, with 40,000 suffragists in line.

This is part of the news that Mrs. Burke and Miss Richardson will carry in Mrs. Burke's little yellow suffrage automobile, which she runs and cares for herself. This is the first round country automobile run of the suffragists. From New York the travelers will go South along the Atlantic seaboard, by way of New Orleans and Galveston and along the Texas, New Mexico, and Arizona border into California as far West as San Francisco. From there they will travel through Oregon and Washington to Seattle and East through South Dakota, Iowa, Illinois, and home to New York. The car will carry suffrage banners and literature and will be used as a rostrum for suffrage speeches at the dif-

Long Island. The Tarrytown Maxwell agent spotted her on that trip and announced that Ramsey was "the greatest natural woman driver I've yet seen."

In a donated Maxwell, Ramsey, her two sisters-in-law, and a friend drove across the continent, starting at Maxwell's Broadway showroom in Manhattan and reaching San Francisco in 59 days. It was before the advent of road maps, so Ramsey navigated by consulting laboriously detailed descriptive guides called Blue Books. Each book gave mileage between reference points and directions based on visual cues, such as, "At 11.6 miles, yellow house and barn on rt. Turn left." Following those instructions, Ramsey drove further than 11.6 miles. Asking about the yellow house, she learned from a local resident that it had recently been painted green. Blue Books only covered travel as far as the Missouri River. In wide-open Wyoming, Ramsey was reduced to following telephone lines. She guessed that the poles with the most lines led to the biggest towns.

Ramsey considered herself "born mechanical." Reporters called her "plucky." She patched flats, jacked the car out of mudholes, and repaired a short circuit in a spark plug. Her sisters-in-law unpacked cut-glass containers to carry water for the radiator.

"Good driving has nothing to do with sex,"

*Nell Richardson and Alice Burke, at the wheel, hit the road on a speaking tour to promote women's suffrage. They left New York in April 1916, traveled to the West Coast, and returned in October. Admirers festooned the Saxon auto with gifts, including a set of deer antlers and a big wooden key that said "Votes for Women."*

Ramsey once told an interviewer. "It's all above the collar." Yet Alice Ramsey was exceptional. Masculinity defined the auto, as surviving records from two states illustrate. In New Hampshire in 1906, women held 4.6 percent of the driver's licenses and owned roughly 1.8 percent of the cars; in Maryland three years later, they owned 9.1 percent of the cars.

Car advertisements of the period took for granted that men could master complex tasks. On the other hand, ads aimed at women sometimes focused on a car's styling or simplicity of operation, thus hinting at frivolous interests or inferior mechanical skills. Ramsey's well-publicized journey served notice that women could be as technically accomplished as men and should be considered as important a market by automakers.

Popular books celebrated women drivers. Lillian Garis, writing as Margaret Penrose, produced the *Motor Girls* series of novels from 1910 to 1917. The heroines drove off on their own adventures and served as role models for adolescent readers. One character told her male friends, "You boys are well enough where only muscle is concerned … but when it comes to a matter of brains, you're not in the same class with us." Young male readers enjoyed a similar series, authored by Garis's husband, as well as simplified automotive texts that introduced them to gas engines and primed them to become car owners.

In the years after Ramsey's success, cross-country trips became a way to call public attention to important issues. Nell Richardson, Alice Burke, and their cat completed a 10,700-mile circuit on behalf of the National American Woman Suffrage Association in 1916. They carried voting rights banners and literature in their yellow Saxon automobile and delivered what the *New York Times* called "propaganda" speeches in many cities. Their car returned covered with autographs, written by those who had heard them speak.

Three years later, a convoy of 81 Army vehicles traveled from Washington, D.C., to San Francisco in a combination field test and recruiting tour. The Army had bought many motorized vehicles for use in World War I, but the fighting stopped before they could be evaluated. The Transcontinental Motor Convoy analyzed the vehicles' performance in rough terrain. It also served as a patriotic postwar parade, certain to attract the attention of young men keen on new motor technology. "We were not sure [the trip] could be accomplished at all," wrote a young Lt. Col. Dwight D. Eisenhower, who accompanied the convoy. The vehicles made it, although they had more than 230 accidents. They slid off embankments and became entrapped in mud, but they pulled into San Francisco 62 days and 3,251 miles after leaving Washington. Eisenhower said the convoy started him thinking about the value of good roads. Nearly four decades later, he would sign into law America's interstate highway system.

Most ordinary drivers found joy in the open air, especially when they compared their lot with that of the railroad passenger. Novelist Theodore Dreiser, who wrote a book about his 1915 auto trip from New York to Indiana, said railroads had become "huge, clumsy, unwieldy affairs little suited to the temperamental needs and moods of the average human being." Railroad journeys were fixed: Passengers saw the same scenery over and over and trips followed rigid schedules. In contrast, the auto allowed limitless choices and left Dreiser "mentally poised in inquiry, which is always delightful."

. . .

Cars did not replace train travel, however. In many ways, the comforts and services of trains blossomed during this period of American history. An 1890 pamphlet of the Great Northern Railway Line touted the relaxation of a train trip, suggesting that "delightful journeyings and pleasant saunterings" were the only cure for chronic anxiety of the modern world. Trains could refresh the traveler who sought escape and help make getaway vacations possible not just for the rich, but also for the middle class. Easy, fast, relatively cheap travel put the beach, mountaintops, lakes, and countryside within reach of city dwellers.

Railroad companies published a flurry of pamphlets in the 1870s and 1880s, promoting vacation excursions and the national parks along their lines, starting with Yellowstone. First the Northern Pacific Railroad publicized this little known region, then discreetly lobbied for its protection as a national park. The railroad's "Wonderland Guide" touted the wonders of Yellowstone's geysers and canyons and suggested itineraries, effectively linking the company name with the park and western holidays. The Great Northern Railway promoted Montana's Glacier National Park, and the Atchison, Topeka & Santa Fe put its stamp on Arizona's Grand Canyon.

*Toys from the 1920s mirror the autos
and road-building equipment that were
reshaping America. A steam shovel,
concrete mixer, and road roller, above,
joined taxis, trucks, buses, and cars
as toy companies duplicated what children
might see on the road. Toy cars became
streamlined in the 1930s, as did their
full-size originals.*

The finest railroad cars seemed palatial. An 1875 sketch of the interior of a Pullman sleeper highlighted cushy chairs, drapery, and a pump organ with hymnals. Englishman James Macaulay traveled from Niagara to Chicago in a Pullman Hotel Car in 1887 and likened the experience to a cruise. "Two of us chartered a compartment like the cabin of a ship with a comfortable sofa above which a board was fixed at night, so as to form a second sleeping-berth.... Some of the drawing-room cars are as luxurious as those of royal or imperial carriages on European lines, with mirrors, lounges, chandeliers, piano and bookcases."

Many companies manufactured sleeping cars, but the Pullman Company, founded in 1867, dominated the field. Railroad workers known as Pullman porters ensured passengers' comfort. Each night, they converted the company's open-section seating cars into upper and lower sleeping berths. Pullman porters, all African Americans, were "very careful, obliging and attentive to their duties," according to an Australian passenger on a Pullman car in 1889.

Not all trips were so sublime, and the darker side of rail travel left its imprint on modern law. Injuries were common. People getting on or off a train in motion could suffer broken bones or worse. Some were mangled between or beneath the cars. The prevalence of accidents helped establish negligence as a distinct concept of liability law in the late 19th century, as citizens successfully brought legal charges against the railroad companies for injuries or deaths. Black passengers faced discrimination on the railroads, and the classification of riders by race and fare eventually laid the foundation for state-sponsored segregation.

A typical train featured a first-class ladies' car, open only to women and their companions. It was usually near the end of the train, for protection from head-on collisions and engine smoke. Also first-class, but deemed unfit for respectable women, was the masculine domain of the smoker car. Its furnishings were more rugged, befitting its inhabitants' propensities to drink, smoke, and spit. Many middle-class white passengers rode in mid-priced tourist or day coaches, while those at the bottom of the social hierarchy rode in baggage cars or in areas set aside for minorities.

Sharing space with members of another race implied a measure of equality that many whites were not ready to concede in late 19th-century America. Congress passed the Civil Rights Act of 1875, requiring equal accommodations for black Americans on all "public conveyances on land and water." Southern states were less than rigorous in enforcing the law, and federal officials often ignored it, which initially left the accommodations of black passengers in the hands of the railroads. Railroad companies framed rules to ensure the comfort of whites and the safety of blacks. Blacks

*Twenty-nine-year-old Lt. Col. Dwight Eisenhower, a War Department observer of the Army's 1919 motor convoy across America, stands tall west of Cheyenne, Wyoming, Major Sereno Brett at his left. The future president recorded the convoy's progress in photographs he took and annotated himself. His conclusion: Both roads and trucks needed improvement.*

Western Utah —

had to ride in "Jim Crow" cars—a phrase from an old plantation song that came to be associated with all forms of segregation. Angry and humiliated, black passengers sued but failed to end Jim Crow practices on the rails. In the 1880s and 1890s, appellate courts, federal courts, and other federal agencies upheld railroad segregation, as long as the accommodations represented "real and not delusive" parity.

African-American women faced particular difficulties. In white Southern culture circa 1900, the phrase "black lady" would have been taken as oxymoron. The railroad car had no place for a black woman, even if she bought a first-class ticket: Cultural mores discouraged racial mixing in the ladies' car. Black women, especially those traveling alone, shrank from riding in the all-male smoker, even though that was where agents usually shunted any black passenger with a first-class ticket. The situation caused black women to initiate more than their share of legal challenges.

Riding to Woodstock, Tennessee, on May 4, 1884, schoolteacher Ida B. Wells sat down in the first-class ladies' coach. The conductor told her she would have to move to the smoker. "I proposed to stay," Wells wrote in her autobiography. "He tried to drag me out of the seat, but the moment he caught hold of my arm I fastened my teeth on the back of his hand." As two other men helped the conductor drag Wells from the ladies' car, white passengers cheered. Refusing to enter the smoker, she left the train. She sued the railroad and was awarded $500. The railroad appealed. Tennessee's highest court

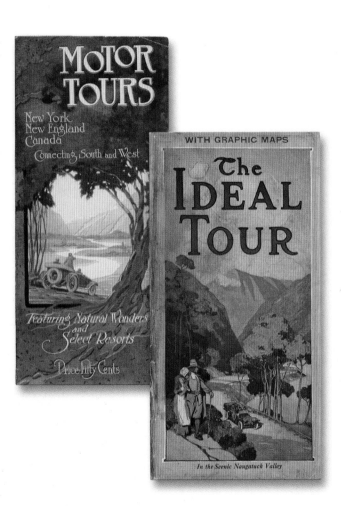

*Tourist brochures went head to head as destinations competed for vacationing families. The motoring pamphlets above hail the "Natural Wonders and Scenic Resorts" of the Northeast and Canada, left, and Connecticut's "Scenic Naugatuck Valley," vying for a reputation as America's favorite playground.*

## MAPPING THE RAILROADS

BY 1875, RAIL LINES HATCHMARKED THE NATION IN A COMPLEX PATTERN OF CONNECTIONS, REFLECTING LIFE AND MOVEMENT IN THAT ERA.

RAILROAD MAPS CHARTED THE SPREAD OF CITIES, INDUSTRY, AND AGRICULTURE. AFTER THE 1873 FINANCIAL PANIC, RAILROADS REORGANIZED AND QUICKLY EXPANDED. THIS "CENTENNIAL AMERICAN REPUBLIC AND RAILROAD MAP OF THE UNITED STATES AND OF THE DOMINION OF CANADA" SHOWCASES NEW TRACKS.

IN A BURST OF PATRIOTIC PRIDE, PUBLISHER GAYLORD WATSON'S HAND-COLORED 1875 MAP PROVIDES NOT ONLY THE NAMES OF RAILROADS CONNECTING THE NEWLY SPROUTING CITIES AND TOWNS, BUT ALSO A SKETCH OF GEORGE WASHINGTON, A LIST OF STATE POPULATIONS, THE TEXT OF THE DECLARATION OF INDEPENDENCE, A ROSTER OF GOVERNORS, AND A VIEW OF THE MAIN BUILDING OF THE CENTENNIAL EXHIBITION IN PHILADELPHIA.

ON THE MAP, A SHADED BOX LISTS MILEAGES FROM NEW YORK CITY NOT ONLY TO BIG CITIES SUCH AS NEW ORLEANS AND ST. LOUIS BUT ALSO TO SMALLER, YET VITAL, TRANSPORTATION CENTERS SUCH AS ATCHISON, KANSAS, AND DAVENPORT, IOWA. A DOMINANT COMMERCIAL HUB, CHICAGO SPINS ITS OWN WEB OF TRACKS THROUGHOUT THE UPPER MIDWEST.

overturned the ruling, holding that the smoking car served as a first-class coach for all black passengers. Wells refused to stay silent. She first told her story in a church paper. Discovering that she had talent as a journalist, she became editor of the *Memphis Free Speech and Headlight* and used the paper to crusade further for civil rights.

The United States Supreme Court had ruled that civil rights cases should be decided by the states. In the face of federal disinterest, the South gradually codified Jim Crow. Blacks in Louisiana raised a significant legal challenge in 1892 when Homer Plessy, racially mixed but considered black in the eyes of the law, entered a whites-only East Louisiana Railroad car. Railroad officials attempted to remove him, but Plessy refused to leave. He was arrested and convicted of violating Louisiana's Separate Car Act. He and a sympathetic Northern lawyer carried the appeal all the way to the Supreme Court. They said that the Louisiana law violated the 14th Amendment, which forbids states to "abridge the privileges or immunities of citizens of the United States" and "deny to any person ... the equal protection of the laws." Splitting hairs, the judges voted seven to one and endorsed segregation: Their 1896 ruling said the amendment guaranteed political and civil rights but not social ones. *Plessy* v. *Ferguson*

*A conductor and porter assist Santa Fe Railway passengers at La Grande Station Los Angeles in 1915. The station, a setting for the Judy Garland film,* Meet Me in St. Louis, *boasted Moorish architecture and a fine Harvey House restaurant, befitting a transportation industry that promoted a high-class image.*

established the rationale for "separate but equal" for not only trains but also buses, schoolrooms, public facilities, water fountains, and other social settings.

"Separate but equal" did not mean true equality. Train accommodations for African Americans in the South were often inferior. For example, prominent black ministers and their families, returning home from a religious gathering in Georgia in 1915, paid for first-class tickets but were forced to board a rickety wooden coach. Coal dust and dried sputum covered the floor, and the car lacked enough seats for all. One filthy toilet served both men and women. A white conductor spit on the floor and blew smoke in the faces of the female passengers.

Given the humiliation and threats involved in train travel, black Americans turned to the automobile. Cars gave black drivers a fleeting thrill of liberty. Alfred Smith, an African-American teacher in Washington, D.C., said he felt like a Viking behind the wheel. "It's mighty good to be the skipper for a change," he remarked. "It's good for the spirit to just give the old railroad Jim Crow a laugh."

· · ·

A sense of independence and freedom—that was important for American travelers. They had thrilled to those feelings when they first wheeled away on bicycles. Crude wooden bicycles had existed since 1817 in Germany. Riders shuffled along the ground to propel them. Pierre Michaux of Paris refined the design in the 1860s by adding pedals and cranks on the front wheel. His "Velocipede" became the first mass-produced personal transportation device. In 1870, Englishman James Starley created the

"Safety" bikes, such as a man's 1899 Cleveland model, opposite top, and a woman's 1889 Overman Victoria, below, had chain drives and equal-size wheels. A safer ride, promoted above top, helped the new bikes eclipse their giant-wheeled ancestors, above. Following pages: Wilbur and Orville Wright adapted bicycle technology to create aircraft like this glider flown at Kitty Hawk, North Carolina, 1911.

"Ordinary" bicycle, pairing a huge front wheel with a tiny rear one. Even without gears or a chain drive, the larger front wheel made this design go farther with each pedal revolution. Ordinaries proved difficult to ride, though. Accidents often pitched the rider headfirst over the front wheel. The solution was the "Safety" bike, with wheels of similar size and a chain drive.

Albert Pope, a Boston manufacturer of shoemakers' tools, grasped the significance of the bicycle at Philadelphia's 1876 Centennial Exposition: These new one-person automotion machines freed travelers from railroad routes and schedules. Pope bought the patent rights to European bicycle designs and opened a factory in Hartford, Connecticut. His Columbia model was a bestseller, and his factory became the city's largest employer. Mark Twain, a Hartford resident, bought a Columbia Expert bicycle in 1886 and signed up for 12 hours of lessons. "We got up a handsome speed," the 50-year-old Twain wrote after one of his first rides, "and presently traversed a brick, and I went over the top of the tiller and landed, head down, on the instructor's back, and saw the machine fluttering in the air between me and the sun. It was well it came down on us, for that broke the fall, and it was not injured." Later Twain wrote, "Get a bicycle. You will not regret it, if you live."

Riders in the 1880s used bicycles for urban travel and then, on weekends, to take in the country air. New Yorkers pedaled them to make deliveries in the crowded city. Theodore Roosevelt, the city's police commissioner in the 1890s, advocated bicycles for

his officers. By the mid-1890s, 300 American companies were making bicycles, and one million bikes had been sold.

Biking held special appeal for women, who could ride independently, shed their chaperones, and gain what women's rights advocate Susan B. Anthony called "a feeling of freedom and self-reliance." A woman on a bike knew she was safe from harm until she got off, Anthony said, adding that cycling did "more to emancipate woman than anything else in the world." For sedentary women, biking could produce muscle tone and a "natural bloom," as *Harper's Bazaar* described it. Frances Willard, the president of the Women's Christian Temperance Union, took up cycling in 1893. Her doctor had advised her, at the age of 53, to exercise outdoors. Willard had high hopes that the bicycle could keep men out of taverns and lead women beyond hearth and home.

Women's cycling achievements were doubly impressive, given their restrictive clothes. Willard wore ankle-length skirts when she rode her bicycle. Other women wore tight corsets, designed less for athletic abilities and more to achieve the severe hourglass figure considered attractive at the time. Bikes and women adapted to each other. The first women's model, the "Psycho Ladies' Bicycle," appeared in 1889. Its frame lacked a horizontal bar, so women in skirts could more easily mount and pedal. A screen manufactured by Theron Cherry of West Virginia hid a female rider's ankles from view and kept her skirts from billowing out and up. Gradually, the need for sensible riding clothes

helped change the American woman's wardrobe. Bloomers, as full as a skirt but divided into two legs, enjoyed new popularity during the cycling craze. Sears catalogs of the 1890s sold women's cycling suits with skirts that stopped mid-calf.

. . .

Bicycles aided the development of the car and the airplane, advancing the technologies of gears, brakes, and tires. The accomplishments of the Wright brothers owed much to the bicycle. Orville bought one of Pope's Columbias and raced it competitively. A short while later, in 1892, the brothers began selling and repairing bicycles in Dayton, Ohio. They turned the technical expertise they gained to designing gliders and airplanes.

One problem with previous inventors' efforts to develop heavier-than-air flight was mastering motion in three dimensions. The Wrights, schooled in the instability of the bicycle, understood that a pilot had to control every axis of movement. They envisioned a craft in which the pilot could intentionally lean or roll, much as a bicycle rider leans into a turn. They built gliders and tested wing modifications in a wind tunnel. They varied the angles, thicknesses, and length-to-width ratios of wings, then put full-size gliders to the test at Kitty Hawk, North Carolina, where the open country, soft sand dunes, and prevailing winds seemed perfect for their purpose. The Wrights made more than one thousand gliding flights in the fall of 1902. The following year, they built a small engine and mounted it on a biplane's lower wing. They added propellers, driving them with a chain-and-sprocket system

*A December 22, 1929, menu and music program, above, offered choices to passengers on the S.S.* Leviathan, *a luxury liner in North Atlantic service. Following pages: The* Leviathan *sails up the Hudson River, circa 1925, left. In its earlier World War I configuration, the same ocean vessel carried U.S. troops across the Atlantic to battle, then home again, right.*

similar to a bicycle's. When the sprockets came loose, the Wrights secured them with Arnstein's Hard Cement, a cycling glue that held bicycle tires to their rims.

On December 14, 1903, the first attempt at powered flight ended with a crash. The damage required two days to repair. Then the Wrights waited for the wind to pick up again. On the morning of December 17, a steady, frigid breeze blew out of the north at Kitty Hawk. The brothers shaved and put on white shirts with celluloid collars and ties. Orville climbed into the pilot's position and, at about 10:35 a.m., sent the plane chugging down a rail into a breeze of 27 miles per hour. The plane sailed for 12 seconds, surged 120 feet forward under its own power, then settled back to earth. The brothers alternated as pilot and made three more flights that day. During one, with Wilbur at the controls, the plane traveled 852 feet. After all its flights, the plane was sitting unattended when a gust caught it. An observer, John T. Daniels, grabbed a strut. The plane carried him along briefly, then veered toward earth and crumpled into a pile of wood, wire, and canvas. Unhurt, Daniels later boasted that he had survived the world's first plane crash.

By 1914, domestic airplanes carried passengers on a regular schedule. The St. Petersburg–Tampa Airboat Line charged passengers five dollars to fly between the two Florida cities. The service lasted only four months, though, and further commercial flights were slow to expand.

World War I demonstrated the military value of airplanes, cars, and trucks and simultaneously

stimulated their improvement. The Hispano-Suiza engine, featuring overhead cam shafts, powered thousands of Allied biplanes. Designed by Swiss engineer Marc Birkigt for a Spanish company, the engine was manufactured by Britain's Wolseley Motors, America's Wright-Martin Company, and five French companies. Refinements gradually doubled its initial 150-horsepower capability.

On the ground, motor vehicles and guns churned out by Allied factories helped turn the tide of war in Europe. Convoys of trucks transported men and supplies to battlefields on the Western Front. Fleets of taxicabs ferried soldiers to halt a German advance on Paris in 1914. Henry Ford's company built not only Model T automobiles, which served on the western front, but also swift, steel-hulled submarine chasers for the U.S. Navy, although they had not yet been deployed when the war ended in 1918. Transportation technology returned to civilian applications at war's end. Birkigt, for example, adapted his airplane engine design for use in the Hispano-Suiza H6 automobile, introduced at the 1919 Paris Motor Show.

After the war, Americans were slow to get past a fear of flying. Fledgling airlines foundered. In 1925, the federal government began contracting with private air companies to deliver mail. Those

*Twenties-era accommodations aboard the* Leviathan *promised an opulent oceangoing experience. First-class passengers enjoyed, clockwise from upper left, the luxurious Winter Garden; the stately Ritz-Carlton Restaurant, paneled in oak and mahogany; the gentleman's smoking lounge; and cheerful sleeping quarters. While the ship could carry 3,000 passengers, voyages averaged 1,300.*

aircraft began carrying passengers, too—only 6,000 in 1926, but 400,000 four years later. Air travel within the United States evolved during the next decade, but not until 1936 did Pan American Airways provide the first passenger air flight across the Pacific. In 1939, passenger planes started crossing the Atlantic.

. . .

For crossing any great body of water, though, ocean liners were still the preferred mode of travel into the middle of the 20th century. On ocean liners, as on railroads, passengers enjoyed comforts according to their classification and ability to pay. Immigrants packed the lower decks in steerage, the no-frills accommodation reserved for those who paid the cheapest fare. Thirty million had voyaged in steerage to the United States by the time immigration restrictions took effect in the 1920s. Travel in steerage was cheap, about $50 per person in 1910, but purchasers generally got what they paid for. "Everything dirty ... every impression oppressive," a congressional report said. Once immigration rates declined, in the 1930s, conditions improved substantially, and travelers on the lower decks enjoyed more space and greater comforts.

First-class accommodations glittered with opulence during the golden age of ocean travel, between the world wars. Ships belonging to more than 20 commercial fleets of luxury liners, representing many nations, took only five days to plow across the Atlantic in the 1930s. Of all these ships, none rivaled the United States Lines' *Leviathan*, the ultimate in glamour travel.

In the century's first decade, Germany's Hamburg-American Line had proudly operated the ship, at 950 feet long the world's largest ocean liner. Christened the *Vaterland,* it set out on its maiden voyage on May 14, 1914. It could carry more than 4,000 passengers, as well as 28,000 liters of German beer and 17,500 bottles of wine.

The vessel completed only seven Atlantic crossings under the German flag. At the start of World War I, the *Vaterland* was tied up at a pier in New Jersey, across the Hudson River from New York, its most recent pleasure destination. There it stayed until the U.S. government seized it in 1917. President Woodrow Wilson renamed it *Leviathan* for the biblical monster of the deep and put it into service for the American military. By war's end, it had ferried tens of thousands of American troops to Europe.

The ship then languished at berth in Newport News, Virginia, until 1922, when the United States Lines refurbished it as a commercial pleasure vessel. *Leviathan* made its first crossing to Europe as an American-owned passenger liner in July 1923.

Gone was the giant bronze bust of Kaiser Wilhelm II and the portrait of Ludwig of Bavaria. Instead, a portrait of President Warren G. Harding hung prominently. Naval architect William Francis Gibbs replaced the coal-fired engines with oil burners, put telephones in every room, redecorated the walls with English oak and mahogany, and designed clock faces with dolphins, seashells, and a nautical Santa Claus. *Leviathan's* owners also provided the finishing touch—a true luxury from America's current popular culture: prerelease screenings of Hollywood's moving pictures for the enjoyment of passengers.

On a single voyage, her passenger list included Hollywood stars Gloria Swanson, Douglas Fairbanks, and Mary Pickford; professional golfer Walter Hagen; and violinist Jascha Heifetz. The Ritz Carlton Company operated the ship's restaurant. Menu items one day in 1934 included pâté de fois gras on toast, venison in sauce Cumberland, smoked ox tongue, and St. Honoré tartlets. Guests could work out in the gym or swim in the 65-foot Roman bath, dance in the Empire-style ballroom, relax in a cozy library, or converse in a Louis XIV–style social hall.

Despite its splendor, the *Leviathan* proved unable to make a profit. The ocean liner business suffered after World War I, when the immigration levels dropped by two-thirds compared with those in the years before the war. Prohibition meant no alcohol was served on American-flagged ships. Pleasure-seeking customers booked passage with foreign competitors instead. The ship racked up huge fuel bills as well. After expensive overhauls and repairs, the *Leviathan* finally sailed to Scotland in 1938. The monster of the deep was butchered like a fish and cut up for scrap. With it went the last glitter of travel in the Gilded Age.

NEXT TO BEING STRICTLY HONEST,
THERE IS NO MORE TRYING STATE
IN THIS HUMDRUM REPUBLIC
THAN BEING SIMULTANEOUSLY A NEGRO
AND A TRAVELER.

— *George S. Schuyler in* **The American Mercury,** *1930*

# AMERICA
# GOES URBAN

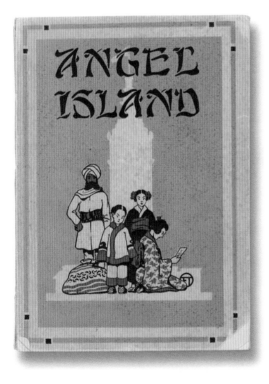

*From the 1890s, newcomers entered
America through immigration stations
such as the one on Ellis Island, in New
York. Opposite, clockwise from top left:
A German ship arrives in Baltimore,
Maryland, 1905; passengers disembark at
Ellis Island; a medical inspector checks
young immigrants, 1911; and children play
at Ellis Island. A 1917 book, above, tells
the story of immigrants at Angel Island.*

In 1890, eight-year-old Rose Schneiderman and her family left their home in Russian-controlled Poland. There were two steps in the family's move: First they left their village of Saven for the city of Khelm; then they sailed to America. Father Samuel went first, then the family followed on the steamship *Bothnia,* leaving Hamburg, Germany, for New York. There they joined droves of other new immigrants, living cheek to jowl in the city's bustling Lower East Side.

Samuel died when Rose was ten. The family split up temporarily, Rose going into an orphanage. When she rejoined her family, she was their main source of support. She went to work in a department store at the age of 13. At 16, Rose started working in a cap factory, making linings. The pay was better than in the store—six dollars a week instead of less than three. She worked long hours alongside thousands of other young immigrant women in New York's garment industry. The conditions were terrible. Rose had to furnish her own machine and buy her own thread.

As Rose Schneiderman worked in the factory, she saw that only men could get to the top of the trade. She helped organize a local chapter of the United Cloth Hat and Cap Maker's Union. A short woman with fiery red hair, Rose devoted the rest of her life to improving working conditions for women.

Through her labor efforts, Schneiderman befriended Eleanor Roosevelt, wife of the governor of New York, Franklin Delano Roosevelt. In 1933, Roosevelt was elected President of the United States. Rose Schneiderman moved to Washington, D.C., and began working directly with Roosevelt, whose New Deal administration would ultimately establish social reforms designed to improve the lots of working-class people and immigrants like her.

In some ways, Rose Schneiderman's story is unique. Few immigrants ended up working with the President. But in other ways, it is typical. Millions of immigrants came to the United States at the turn of the 20th century. Most of their journeys ended, like Rose's, in urban and industrialized areas. In the process, most of those journeys made an impact on the cities, the culture, and the economy of the nation.

More than 45 million people left their homelands and moved somewhere else between 1881 and 1924. Over half of them came to the United States. Historian John Bodnar calls them "the children of capitalism," since capitalistic agriculture and the spread of industrialization created the conditions that enticed—or forced—people to move. Immigrants came to America from Ireland, Mexico, Italy, China, and Quebec. They moved away from poverty, lack of opportunity, and pressures on the land—conditions at home that made migration elsewhere seem the best option.

Transportation innovations made the act of migration easier, at least. By 1900, steam-powered ships regularly crossed both the Atlantic and the Pacific Oceans to the United States. Millions of immigrants traveled that way, most in steerage class. When an investigator for the U.S. Immigration Commission traveled incognito on a ship from Germany to the United States, she described life below decks as smelly, chaotic, and cramped. "When the steerage is full, each passenger's space is limited to his berth, which then serves as bed, clothes and towel rack,

cupboard, and baggage space," she reported. "There are no accommodations to encourage the steerage passenger to be clean and orderly."

When Rachel Calof, an immigrant of the 1890s, first saw the steerage area in which she would be traveling, she knew that "it was evident that many people would be living in too small a space." She remembered constant noise. "We were on the same deck as the ship's machinery and the din of the engine noises was to assault our ears day and night."

Steerage was one cheap and reliable way of getting to the United States of America. New railroad lines helped people move as well. The first railroad connecting Canada and the United States opened in the 1850s, and by the 1880s, railroads crossed the Mexican border into the U.S. at four places, one in Arizona and three in Texas. The east-west transcontinental link may have been the most famous railroad of its day, but the north-south rails were also key to the growing transportation system, connecting Mexico and Canada to the United States and making it easier for people to cross the border into New Hampshire or Michigan, Texas or California.

· · ·

In the late 19th and early 20th centuries, most of the millions who arrived by boat landed on the East Coast, at New York City. Steerage passengers first stopped at Ellis Island, a small island in New York Harbor, just off the southernmost tip of Manhattan. The State of New York had begun inspecting immigrants in 1855. In 1892, a Federal Immigration Station opened on Ellis Island. There immigrants had to stop and answer questions about where they

*Advertisements, like this one in Swedish, encouraged people to make the journey to the United States by promising land and a new life. The railroad company that ran this ad owned land it hoped to sell to new settlers. Most immigrants, however, moved into the nation's cities.*

were from, where they were going, and whether they were in good health or not. By the time Ellis Island opened, federal law had created a laundry list of reasons that an immigrant couldn't enter the country. Prostitutes, convicts, lunatics, idiots, and "persons likely to become a public charge," people with contagious diseases, and most infamously, Chinese laborers, were barred from admission. At Ellis Island, officials inspected and processed as many as 5,000 to 10,000 immigrants daily during the first decade of the 20th century.

Rachel Calof underwent an Ellis Island inspection in 1894. "No previous experience aroused for all such anxiety as the test of Ellis Island," she declared. "With word or a gesture from an official, one standing a few feet from the gate opening to the golden land could be refused entry after having traveled so far." Those refused entry would be made to turn around and reboard the boat they came on. Into the 1920s, steamship companies were required to carry excluded emigrants home for free, so the firms conducted their own inspections before even beginning the transoceanic journey. For that reason, as many as 99 percent of incoming immigrants, including Rachel, made it through the Ellis Island inspections and on to Manhattan in less than a day.

West Coast immigrants also disembarked from steerage onto an island: Angel Island, in the San Francisco Bay. Established as an immigrant inspection point in 1910, Angel had a very different mandate from that of Ellis Island. Chinese people were detained there while their rights of entry were investigated, under the terms of the Chinese Exclusion

Act. According to the 1882 law, Chinese laborers could not come to the United States, although those already in the country could go home and then return. Merchants, students, and others could enter the country. These determinations were made while the hopeful travelers waited on Angel Island.

Many records burned during the 1906 San Francisco Fire, clearing the way for Chinese immigrants to claim rights of entry: Without a record to prove him wrong, an immigrant could claim that he was the son of a merchant already in the country, or had been born in the United States, or had been home for a visit but now reentered lawfully. Angel Island officials assumed that Chinese people arriving there were in cahoots with one another, trying to dupe the authorities. People who arrived by boat together were separated, and immigration officers interrogated people ruthlessly, asking them about the minutiae of their lives in China to ascertain whether they were trying to enter the country illegally. Hundreds of thousands of Chinese people, most of them male, were interrogated. About one in six was deported.

Detainees carved poetry into the walls as they waited to be interrogated. One unknown poet asked,

*For what reason must I sit in Jail?*
*It is only because my country is weak and*
  *my family poor.*
*My parents wait at the door but there is no news.*
*My wife and child wrap themselves in quilt,*
  *sighing with loneliness.*
*Even if my petition is approved and I can enter*
  *the country,*

*When can I return to the Mountains of Tan*
  *with a full load?*
*From ancient times, those who venture out*
  *usually become worthless.*
*How many people ever return from battles?*

Most people spent weeks on the island, some spent months, and a few spent nearly two years, waiting to see what their fates would be.

People also traveled into the United States over land borders. Although Mary Dancause was born in Manchester, New Hampshire, and was therefore a U.S. citizen, her parents had immigrated from French Canada and she spent most of her childhood back in Quebec, living with an aunt. She returned to New Hampshire when she was 12 and helped with household chores while her mother worked in the city's massive textile mills. Mary herself later worked in the mills and married into them, too: Her husband fixed the looms. They were among the large number of French Canadians who worked at Manchester's Amoskeag mills, drawn across the border by the promise of work and transported across the border by the railroad. By 1910, more than a third of Manchester's population was French-Canadian.

In those years, the Mexican border was equally permeable. Gonzalo Plancarte first came to the United States from Guanajuato, Mexico, in 1900. Like many other Mexican immigrants of the day, he worked on the railroads. After working two years in El Norte, Plancarte took his earnings home to Mexico City, where he got married and worked as a streetcar conductor. In 1909, he and his wife moved back to the United States, this time to Los Angeles. The transportation industry continued to provide good work for Plancarte, who joined the Southern Pacific Railroad Company, handling first freight and then baggage.

The same forces attracting Europeans, Asians, Canadians, and Mexicans into the United States pulled Americans themselves out of the country and into the cities. As farms became more commercialized, producing goods to be shipped far and wide rather than goods for the local consumers, there was less opportunity in the rural lifestyle. During the first half of the 20th century, millions of African Americans left the rural South to seek a better life, escaping racism and violence. Most moved first to small cities in the South, then to bigger cities in the North. Folklorist and novelist Zora Neale Hurston was born in Florida and lived in Memphis, Baltimore, and Washington before she moved to New York in the 1920s. There she became one of the literary lights of the Harlem Renaissance.

Millions of white Southerners migrated north as well—people like Hazel Smith and her husband, who moved from Kentucky to Cincinnati in 1925. Smith went north when she was 20. Although married, she left Kentucky without her husband, who stayed to work the land they had rented.

*Following pages: Ice vendors drove wagons like this one, shown in front of Birney Public School in Washington, D.C., in 1899. They joined a throng of entrepreneurs who delivered goods from horse-drawn carts and wagons throughout America's cities. These vehicles added to the mix of traffic on the nation's urban streets.*

Originally, Smith planned to make some money and go back home with "extra money to live on," but things didn't work out that way. Hazel got a job at a can factory, and her husband "got rid of all our furniture, turned this crop over in his uncle's name for him to pay off the bills we owed. And he come to Cincinnati. And he come on Wednesday and then on Monday he done had a job at Cincinnati Rubber Company. And he worked there as long as he worked—was able to work." The economic opportunities in the nation's cities exerted a powerful pull on the Smiths and millions of other rural Americans.

.  .  .

America had begun as an agrarian nation, with cities as centers of commerce and trade. By the end of the 19th century, cities had become even more important to the nation's identity, and in the succeeding few decades, the urban experience became the American experience. By 1920, for the first time in U.S. history, more people lived in urban than in rural areas.

The change didn't go unnoticed. Late 19th-century urban life in New York, Boston, and Chicago seemed to symbolize American progress and its discontents. Moses King's 1893 *Handbook of New York City* claimed, "To-day the City of New York is not only the metropolis of the United States, but in population, in wealth, in influence, in enterprise, in all that best distinguishes modern civilization, it is the rival of the great capitals of the Old World." To others, though, city life symbolized the worst of the paths that America was following. Jacob Riis's exposé, *How the Other Half Lives,* first published in 1890, took readers on a journey that "turned the corner from

prosperity to poverty" and revealed New Yorkers living in squalor, crowded into unsanitary tenements. Indeed, by the 1890s Manhattan was one of the most crowded places in the world. Every acre of the Tenth Ward—better known as the Lower East Side—housed more than 500 people.

Americans saw in their cities both hope and despair. Cities were the touchstones of a changing world, where the forces of immigration and industrialization and the most vivid contrasts in wealth and poverty could be seen on the streets every day. The cities changed as people flocked to them. A visitor in 1850 would find the same city almost unrecognizable in 1900.

In the 1850s, cities were compact walking districts, their size limited to boundaries that people could easily negotiate. Most people walked between home and work. In the city center, businesses and residences stood side by side. Proximity was at a premium, so the richest lived in the central core while the poor were more likely to live on the city's perimeter, among the buildings of industry and enterprise. In 1850 New York, for example, although the city had begun to spread north on Manhattan Island, most of the population was settled in the lower southern tip of the island. One 1890s observer remarked that in upper Manhattan, "many of the

little wooden houses still stand at hopeless odds with the new thoroughfares, to testify to the lines of country roads which have disappeared beneath a gridironing of city streets."

By 1900, cities were spreading and dividing into distinct zones of activity, changing the relationships between neighborhoods and creating new daily rhythms. Between 1880 and World War I, states one historian of this period in the nation's capital, downtown Washington became the core business area. "From a mixed neighborhood, downtown was transformed into a specialized area where people came to shop, work, go to the theater or other places of entertainment, and also to enjoy the crowds and bustling activity." This phenomenon was not limited to the District of Columbia: Around the nation, cities underwent a similar sea change. Americans even invented a word to describe this new zone. "Downtown" meant the compact, central area and the locus of business, entertainment, and commerce in a metropolitan area.

America's 20th-century cities differed dramatically from their ancestors in shape and direction of growth. Physically, they expanded both vertically and horizontally. Steel-frame construction allowed skyscrapers to reach new heights, with elevators transporting people inside them. Offices, commercial buildings, and apartments began to rise up toward the heavens and eclipse the church steeples that had previously dominated the skyline. Cities also spread horizontally, annexing surrounding land and the towns in it. Manhattan, Brooklyn, the Bronx, Queens, and Staten Island joined together as the

*As cars became a fact of urban life, they changed the ways people used the streets. In 1925, this observation station towered over busy Fifth Avenue in New York City. Towers were one of the many new systems, along with traffic lights and police, developed to regulate the flow of traffic in the nation's cities.*

boroughs of New York City in 1898. New York's population more than doubled between 1890 and 1920. Chicago and Los Angeles absorbed surrounding communities as well.

People reacted to the new scale of the nation's cities in a variety of ways. In Sinclair Lewis's 1917 novel, *The Job,* Una Golden, a "thoroughly commonplace, small-town girl" leaves her Pennsylvania home to move to the big city. Golden "expected to thrill at her first sight of the New York sky-line, crossing on the ferry in mid-afternoon, but it was so much like all the post-card views of it, so stolidly devoid of any surprises, that she merely remarked, 'Oh yes, there it is, that's where I'll be.'"

Una's first impressions were of a city that assaulted the senses: "New York immediately became a blur of cabs, cobblestones, bales of cotton, long vistas of very dirty streets, high buildings, surface cars, elevateds, shop windows that seemed dark and foreign, and everywhere such a rush of people as made her feel insecure." Real-life residents felt the same blur of confusion. Rachel Calof remembered that when she arrived in New York, "I was simply bewildered by the sights and sounds which assailed my senses. Everything was so strange; the immensity of the city, the manner of the people, the houses, the sounds and smells, all confused and astonished me. It was too much to absorb so quickly."

. . .

Transportation systems were supposed to help people navigate the city, but sometimes they just contributed to its confusing immenseness. Transportation systems shaped the daily pathways

of millions of city dwellers in New York and Chicago, hundreds of thousands in Los Angeles, Washington, Omaha, Montgomery, and Cleveland. Not surprisingly, as residents of the nation's biggest city, New Yorkers experimented with many forms of transit throughout the 19th and early 20th centuries.

Starting in 1827, Abraham Brower ran a horse-drawn omnibus—a multi-seated vehicle without tracks—down New York's Broadway. It was so successful that by the 1860s, thousands of omnibus drivers plied their trade on the New York streets. In 1832, the New York & Harlem Railroad Company opened up its service, which ran north along Fourth Avenue between 23rd Street and the Harlem River. Cities like New Orleans, Boston, Philadelphia, Baltimore, Cincinnati, Pittsburgh, and Chicago all followed suit. Horse-drawn railway systems reached their peak across the country in the 1880s, when 18,000 streetcars traveled 3,000 miles of track, with more than 100,000 horses and mules pulling them.

Horses pulled coaches along city tracks well into the 20th century, but starting in the 1870s, mechanized forms of transit began to move people around in the city. Cities tried a host of different kinds of systems—cable cars, elevated trains, subways, and electric streetcars.

The first of San Francisco's famous cable cars began running in 1873. By 1894, 86 miles of cable car line wound through the streets of Chicago. "A morning ride on a cable-car is as pleasant and invigorating as can be imagined," wrote one Chicago enthusiast, "and when the warm winds of summer have given place to snow and cold, there are still

## THE HARLEM RENAISSANCE
### A MEETING OF ARTISTIC MINDS

"IF WE WERE TO OFFER a symbol of what Harlem has come to mean in the short span of twenty years it would be another statue of liberty on the landward side of New York," wrote African-American intellectual Alain Locke in 1925. His article, "Harlem: Mecca of the New Negro," described the phenomenal flowering of creativity among African-American men and women in the 1920s. Painting, philosophy, music, dance, sociology, poetry, folklore, and literature coalesced into a modernist movement arising from the New York neighborhood north of 96th Street. Many rich and disparate voices joined the national culture – at jazz and blues clubs, at literary gatherings, and on the pages of magazines like *Opportunity, The Crisis,* and *Fire!!*

Even before the mid-1920s, Harlem had been a center of African-American culture. People flocked there from the South and from abroad, attracted by the job opportunities and heady atmosphere of America's largest city.

New York's black population had roots going back into antebellum times, and by the 1920s, the brownstones and apartment buildings of Harlem housed two out of three of the hundreds of thousands of black New Yorkers. Many Harlemites – like city dwellers around the country – were migrants. Charles S. Johnson, executive director of research for the National Urban League and founder of the literary magazine, *Opportunity,* called Harlem "one part native, one part West Indian and about three parts Southern."

An amazing concentration of talented musicians, authors, poets, and artists lived in Harlem in the 1920s. It was an era of tense race relations. Lynchings were common, and the country's cities had experienced race riots during and after World War I. Those times and their tensions come through in much of the work produced during the Harlem Renaissance.

Jamaica-born poet Claude McKay arrived in the

United States in 1912. He earned a living by working for the Pennsylvania Railroad but came to be known for his poetry. "If we must die, let it not be like hogs / Hunted and penned in an inglorious spot," he wrote in "If We Must Die," 1919. "Like men we'll face the murderous, cowardly pack / Pressed to the wall, dying, but fighting back!" Other poets and writers – Langston Hughes, Zora Neale Hurston, and Nella Larson – moved to Harlem in the 1920s. Artists, too, like Aaron Douglass and, later in the decade, William H. Johnson, were drawn to the thriving African-American urban scene.

Music—lively, energetic, and diverse – filled the Harlem air into the wee hours of the morning. Bessie Smith, the earthy blues singer from Chattanooga, joined the vaudeville circuit in the 1910s. She recorded her debut single, "Downhearted Blues," in a New York studio in 1923. The song was an instant success.

Jazz, the all-American music, grew up in Harlem. Georgia native Fletcher Henderson led his successful Rainbow Orchestra as they performed at the Savoy Ballroom. Playing songs like the "Sugar Foot Stomp," Henderson and his orchestra helped shape the sounds of jazz and the steps of swing.

The exciting synergy began to draw established performers to Harlem. Edward Kennedy "Duke" Ellington, one of America's finest jazz composers, moved to Harlem in the early 1920s from his native Washington, D.C. From 1927 through 1931, he and his band, the Washingtonians, electrified audiences at the whites-only Cotton Club with his piano innovations and songs like "Mood Indigo" and "Creole Rhapsody."

During the Depression of the 1930s, many of the Harlem Renaissance artists scattered. But this flowering of cultural activity in African-American urban communities – not just in New York, but also in Chicago, Washington, Detroit, and elsewhere – had a profound and lasting influence on the shape of American culture.

THE SHEET MUSIC FOR "SUGAR FOOT STOMP" BY JOE "KING" OLIVER, BELOW LEFT, SHOWED OLIVER'S 1922-24 CHICAGO BAND, INCLUDING, AT CENTER, A YOUNG TRUMPETER NAMED LOUIS ARMSTRONG. DUKE ELLINGTON, BELOW RIGHT, POSED IN 1933 FOR A STUDIO PHOTO BEFORE HIS FIRST EUROPEAN TOUR.

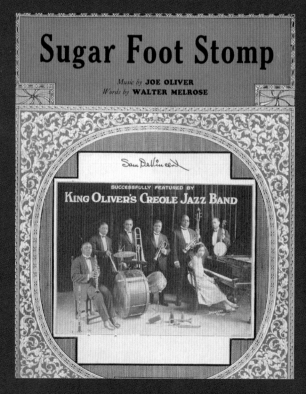

a large number who religiously occupy their favored seats on the grip-car and, well wrapped, take a health-giving constitutional on their way to business every morning."

New York and Chicago both built elevated railroad systems. Steam trains ran along New York's tracks at first, much to the chagrin of local businessmen. Those whose shops were located along the lines complained bitterly about the noise, dirt, cinders, and ashes that the steam trains produced. Opponents to New York's "El" declared that the raised tracks produced "a perpetual city of night" at street level.

New York and Boston both built subway systems. Boston's was the first. A petition circulated in 1894, stating that subway construction would "seriously interfere with travel and traffic, proving ruinous to hundreds of merchants and in the end failing to relieve congestion or promote rapid transit." In fact, the system was a great success, used by more than 50 million passengers in its first year of operation.

Work started on New York's subway system on March 24, 1900. In the end, it was 150 miles long and took 40 years to build. Despite the success of both cities' subways, able to carry people efficiently and without disrupting street traffic, only Philadelphia followed suit in the years soon to come.

In the 1890s, electricity helped transform the American city as electric streetcars, or trolleys, replaced horsedrawn systems. Cities around the nation electrified their existing tracks, changing steam and horse-drawn railroads into electrically powered streetcar systems and providing public transit to people who lived much farther away from the center of the city. Cheaper than subways, easier to construct than elevated trains, faster than the horse, and quieter and less dirty than steam locomotives, trolleys provided five billion rides a year by 1902.

A lot of city people used public transportation, and a lot of them complained about it, too. "Modern martyrdom may be succinctly described as riding in a New York omnibus," griped the *New York Herald*. The editorial called the omnibus "a perfect Bedlam on wheels" because it was so crowded. It went on to complain about horse-drawn street railways, saying that "People are packed into them like sardines in a box, with perspiration for oil. The seats being more than filled, the passengers are placed in rows down the middle, where they hang on by the straps, like smoked hams in a corner grocery."

In the 1880s, when Lawson Fuller was justifying his attempts to get a franchise for a cable line in New York, he recalled his first rides in public conveyances: "I had to hold on to a strap and stand up all the way down town, and I have been holding on to a strap ever since. The city is constantly and rapidly growing, and the facilities for travel are wholly inadequate." Fuller had similar complaints about New York's new elevated railways, too: "People are huddled together like sheep in a cattle train, and often are obliged to stand during the entire trip."

When Chicago ditched its last cable car in 1906, the *Chicago Tribune* bade the system "an unregretful farewell," noting for posterity how the "final cable train rattled and bumped around the loop." By 1913, the *Los Angeles Examiner* called conditions on its city's electric streetcars "little short of disgraceful."

Washington, D.C., began converting to electric streetcars in 1888. This one, owned by the Capital Traction Company, ran along Seventh Street from the Potomac River wharves to Boundary Street (now Florida Avenue). Since Washington banned overhead wires, streetcars drew power from an underground electrical conduit inside city limits and an aboveground wire outside the city.

In 1912, "The Trolley Car Swing" described the daily life of electric streetcar commuters, noting with good humor how trolleys threw customers of all classes and sexes together:

*And when the car goes round a curve*
*You begin to swerve,*
*Grab for a strap, fall in some woman's lap,*
*Clang, clang, watch your step.*
*That's the trolley car swing!*

No matter how much people complained, transportation systems structured the lives of all who lived in and visited them. Electric streetcars had an especially profound effect, changing urban residential patterns in striking ways. Streetcar systems spread settlement. They paved the way for new development, opening up new ribbons of land that had before been distant from the urban core and difficult to access. As historian Sam Bass Warner pointed out in his classic work, *Streetcar Suburbs*, metropolitan Boston had a radius of less than three miles in 1850. By 1900, it had expanded more than threefold. Thousands of people built houses in the newly accessible suburbs. In fact, many developers built streetcar lines in order to create real estate markets, as Henry Huntington did in Los Angeles.

• • •

The city of Washington, D.C., had a unique history, designed from the beginning as the seat of government. Like other American cities during the late 19th and early 20th centuries, though, it experienced urban growth.

Ten square miles were designated as the nation's capital on December 1, 1800. Although laid out in a grandiose plan, the early city was unprepossessing. Around 1810, one Portuguese diplomat is said to have called it the "City of Magnificent Distances," since it took so long to get from one place to another. In the 1840s, English novelist Charles Dickens renamed it the "City of Magnificent Intentions," because the vision for the city was so different from the reality.

Coming into Washington by train in 1869, one visitor noted, "The first glimpses of the federal city are not pleasant. The train passes through a succession of old fields, over which are widely scattered a few dirty, dingy frame houses." The Washington Monument stuck up in the air, half finished. It "has the aspect of a factory chimney with the top broken off," wrote Mark Twain in 1874 of the unfinished monument. In the 1870s, Washington's head of the Board of Public Works, Alexander "Boss" Shepherd, overspent his budget to plant some trees, build some sewers, and pave some streets. The city's wide avenues began to take on a more urbane feel.

Transportation systems helped connect the growing city. By the summer of 1867, Albert Richardson felt able to declare that "Washington is no longer the city of magnificent distances. Horse-railroads have abolished all that." Richardson's declaration may have been a bit premature, but soon street railways, cable cars, and electric streetcar lines reached out from the central core of the city. In 1870, only about 20 miles of streetcars served the city. By 1900, there were nearly 190 miles of track.

• • •

## WASHINGTON, D.C., REAL ESTATE, 1890s

RAILROADS GUIDE GROWTH INTO SUBURBS
IN PRINCE GEORGES AND
MONTGOMERY COUNTIES, MARYLAND.

IN THE PRE-AUTOMOBILE AGE, RESIDENTS WHO LIVED ANY DISTANCE FROM DOWNTOWN LIVED NEAR RAILROAD AND TROLLEY LINES, LIKE THE B&O'S METROPOLITAN BRANCH LINE, BELOW, OR THE ROCK CREEK ELECTRIC RAILROAD, BOTH IN WASHINGTON, D.C. AFTER PEOPLE BEGAN BUYING CARS IN GREATER NUMBERS, SUBURBAN DEVELOPMENTS POPPED UP BETWEEN THE RAILROAD-DRIVEN SETTLEMENTS AND FILLED IN THE MAP WITH COMMUNITIES.

FROM THE NORTHWEST IN THE ABOVE MAP, THE BALTIMORE & OHIO RAILROAD'S METROPOLITAN BRANCH RAN THROUGH RURAL MARYLAND, FROM ROCKVILLE TO THE D.C. LINE. INSIDE THE DISTRICT, THE BRANCH SERVED TAKOMA PARK AND OTHER SUBURBAN STATIONS. IT ENDED AT THE B&O TERMINAL NEAR THE CAPITOL, JUST BELOW THE MAP'S BOUNDARY AT LOWER RIGHT THE EXPANSE OF OPEN LAND EAST OF TAKOMA PARK SHOWS THE IMPORTANCE OF TRANSPORTATION: WITHOUT PROXIMITY TO A RAIL LINE, A SUBURB WAS NOT EASY TO ACCESS FROM THE CITY. HENCE THIS REGION REMAINED FARMLAND IN THE 1890s.

THE STREETS OF LEDROIT PARK, JUST ABOVE FLORIDA AVENUE, AT THE MAP'S LOWER RIGHT, WERE BUILT AT AN ANGLE TO THE DISTRICT'S GRID. THE REASON: TO SET APART THE SECTION AS EXCLUSIVE. MUCH OF THE LAND WITHIN THE DISTRICT REMAINED IN THE HANDS OF INDIVIDUALS LIKE PIERCE SHOEMAKER, WHOSE FAMILY LAND BECAME ROCK CREEK PARK, CALLED NATIONAL PARK ABOVE. BY THE TIME THIS MAP WAS MADE, THE CHEVY CHASE LAND COMPANY HAD LINKED THE AREA BY TROLLEY.

Electricity transformed the streetscapes and skylines of American cities. Electric lights redefined the city at night. On November 22, 1886, an electric light began to illuminate the torch held by New York's Statue of Liberty. Across the nation, restaurants, hotels, and businesses in many a city lit themselves up to advertise their modernity and attract customers. New York City's Broadway Avenue became known as the Great White Way because of all its lights. In 1907, when New York's Singer Building—at 612 feet the city's tallest—lit up, its brilliant, towering nighttime presence was topped by a flag that advertised the sewing machine company. All these uses of electricity distinguished the urban world from the countryside around it. Many rural Americans, on the other hand, had to wait until the 1930s to connect to an electric grid.

Cities glowed with new electrical lighting, but just as significantly, they hummed with the power of electric mobility. Streetcars stretched the city far beyond its traditional walking confines. In Washington, as transportation systems expanded, people built more homes. In 1881, editors at *Harpers New Monthly Magazine* called Washington cosmopolitan but still "a city without commerce and without suburbs—drive a mile or two in any direction and you find yourself in the midst of woods set but

*Urban congestion was a fact of life at the turn of the century. Even before the automobile took center stage in the Chicago Loop, left, trolleys, delivery wagons, hacks, and pedestrians crowded the city streets. Because their lines ran down the center of the street, trolley cars let out passengers into the middle of traffic, making city street corners even more perilous places.*

sparsely with houses or cabins." The comment was hyperbole, for a host of developments sprang up along the street railway, trolley, and railroad lines, as Washington, like many cities at the time, expanded outward. New neighborhoods like Takoma Park and Cleveland Park attracted residents looking for quiet living with city convenience.

One such neighborhood was LeDroit Park, within the original ten-mile square but north of the downtown district when it was built during the 1870s. Developers Amzi Barber and Andrew Langdon, who named their project after Langdon's father, set out to build an exclusive neighborhood. Close to a horsecar line, curved streets took off at angles from Boundary, now Florida, Avenue. Streets were named for trees, like Spruce and Maple. Developers requested that instead of Washington's traditional rowhouses, local architect James H. McGill design both detached and semidetached houses along the the streets. LeDroit Park was presented as an alternative to city life, even though just a block away from a streetcar line—and an option for white customers only.

LeDroit Park quickly grew into a neighborhood, no longer a rural enclave on the city's edge—and, soon, no longer a whites-only neighborhood. It lay next door to Howardtown, the African-American neighborhood surrounding Howard University, one of the nation's premier African-American higher education institutions. Throughout the 1880s, LeDroit Park developers tried to maintain racial exclusivity by literally fencing the neighborhood in. Protesting African Americans tore the fence down in 1888, and a "fence war" raged for three more years.

By the end of the century, LeDroit Park was home to a number of prominent African-American Washingtonians, including educator and activist Mary Church Terrell and Robert Terrell, the first black municipal judge. In 1897, poet Paul Laurence Dunbar lived in a boarding house at 1934 Fourth Street NW, which he glowingly described in letters to his mother. "Come at once," Dunbar invited her. "My house is very beautiful and my parlor suite is swell." When Dunbar married New Orleans–born poet Alice Moore, the newlyweds moved into another LeDroit Park house at 321 Spruce Street.

African Americans didn't find it easy to move into a new home at the end of the 19th century. "Washington is like most cities in our country," said Mary Church Terrell. "Colored people have to overcome difficulties when they try to buy homes. How huge they are I did not know until I tackled them myself. It was easy to find houses where self-respecting people of any color would not care to live. But finding the kind we wanted which either the owners themselves or their agents would sell us was a horse of quite another color." It took a white intermediary to help the Terrells buy a house in LeDroit Park. The owner would not sell to them directly.

By the time the Terrells moved to LeDroit Park, the Washington suburbs spread even farther from the city's core. Chevy Chase, Maryland, on the edge of the ten-mile square, was platted on 1,700 acres of land owned by Senator Francis G. Newlands and the Chevy Chase Land Company. They planned the development carefully, platted streets and lots, provided water and sewage systems, and built four

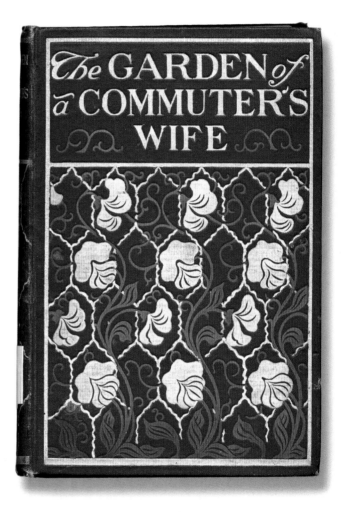

*Single-family suburban houses sprouted up on the fringes of the nation's cities as white families began to move to addresses like Chevy Chase, top right, and Takoma Park, bottom, outside Washington, D.C. Books like* The Garden of a Commuter's Wife, *above, helped women make the most of their new suburban isolation.*

model houses. The enterprising Newlands also built a streetcar line up Connecticut Avenue to Maryland, creating the critical commuting connection to the city center. By 1893, a streetcar, the Rock Creek Railway, ran past the new Washington Zoo, along Rock Creek Park, and out to Chevy Chase Lake.

In Chevy Chase, people were required to build their houses back from the winding streets. They were not allowed to build rowhouses. That way, the suburb was guaranteed to look and feel different from the city that fueled its economy. Suburban life served inborn human needs, as turn-of-the-century sociologist Charles Horton Cooley saw it.

"Humanity demands that men have sunlight, fresh air, grass and trees," Cooley wrote. "It demands these things for the man himself and still more earnestly for his wife and children. On the other hand, industrial conditions require concentration. It is the office of urban transportation to reconcile these conflicting requirements; in so far as it is efficient it enables men to work in aggregates and yet to live in decent isolation."

Many saw suburbs as an antidote to the ills of city life, where people from different classes and races mixed—"promiscuously," according to some—and where gambling, drinking, and prostitution were common on the landscape. Surburbs often prohibited alcohol, declaring their neighborhood dry and keeping saloons at a distance. In Chevy Chase, commercial business was banned from the subdivision altogether.

Many suburbs were racially exclusive, by design and by fact. The high cost of suburban housing kept

poor people and racial minorities out—but so did the law. Some city councils passed segregation ordinances. In 1917, the Supreme Court declared those laws unconstitutional, but early 20th-century suburbia remained a hotbed of racial restriction. Many deeds included legal covenants, disallowing a suburbanite from selling that property to a Jewish, black, or Asian home buyer—and these racially discriminatory covenants had the full force of the law behind them until 1948.

Streetcar suburbs set the physical pattern for early suburbia, with winding streets and building restrictions. They helped set the social pattern for the 20th century, too. In 1917, 45,000 miles of streetcar tracks checkerboarded population centers across the nation, and Americans took billions of streetcar rides. Soon the cars themselves had vanished, and relatively quickly, but their cultural influence on the shape of American suburbs remained.

. . .

In the 1920s and 1930s two other forms of transportation—the bus and the automobile—began to challenge the streetcar's dominance. It did not take long before American cities were struggling to accommodate both types of vehicles, especially the automobile.

In Los Angeles, for example, by 1924, nearly half the people entering the city's central business district arrived by car. Over a third of Washington's 600,000 residents owned and drove cars by the mid-1930s. Between 1916 and 1930, streetcar ridership in St. Louis fell by 30,000, while the number of people coming into the central business district more than

*As suburbs grew, lawns became a status symbol, and more and more Americans needed tools like this lawn-mower, left, from the 1920s. Suburban developers put up detached cottages and bungalows. Toy manufacturers followed suit, making dollhouses, above, that reflected the new housing ideal.*

tripled, to over 103,000 a day. With the exception of New York, cities saw a dramatic increase in automobile commuting. It was a nationwide phenomenon. The personal automobile became the daily transportation method of choice for most Americans who could afford it—and more and more could.

Congestion was already a fact of life in America's big cities. Thomas Edison thought cars would solve the problem. If New York's horses "could be transformed into motorcars overnight," he believed, it would solve traffic problems and "make Manhattan Island resemble 'the Deserted Village.'"

Such optimism was misplaced. Traffic snarled downtown areas. Parking issues arose. Many cities widened their streets to accommodate more traffic. On April 10, 1920, after much debate and opposition, Los Angeles's City Council banned parking downtown between 11 a.m. and 6:15 p.m. The move caused a storm of protest and a flood of editorializing by the Los Angeles press. A writer complained in the *Los Angeles Examiner* that "The people of Los Angeles want traffic and business expedited and not killed. The anti-parking ordinance is being condemned by merchants on the ground that it is ruining trade. If it is, the ordinance should be promptly amended." And so it was. Just 19 days later, the parking ban was lifted between 11 a.m. and 4 p.m. and

*The Great Depression of the 1930s caused suffering for many Americans. They hopefully elected Franklin Delano Roosevelt as President in 1932. Opposite, clockwise from top left: The "White Angel Breadline" was photographed by Dorothea Lange in San Francisco, 1933; a 1934 cartoon depicts Roosevelt as "Dr. New Deal"; women serve at a breadline in 1930; and a 1932 rally touts Roosevelt.*

replaced by a 45-minute parking limit. Parking bans were tried in other cities, but wherever they were initiated, they were soon abandoned.

The street was a chaotic place at the end of the 19th century. Streetcars ran down the middle of thoroughfares, picking up and depositing passengers. Pedestrians crossed streets wherever they wanted. It wasn't until 1913 that pedestrian crossing lines were painted at the corner of Fifth Avenue and 42nd Street in New York. Automobile traffic required a more codified system, in part because the speed of cars made them more dangerous than horsedrawn vehicles. City planners had to develop new traffic controls: One-way streets, traffic lights, stop signs, and parking meters—not to mention parking tickets—all appeared as more people drove their automobiles into the cities. In 1914, Cleveland began putting up traffic lights, and Newark banned left turns at one major intersection, trying to impose order on the city's traffic.

As automobiles created problems downtown, they also inspired satellite commercial nodes, outside the cities. By the end of the 19th century, the high cost of land drove residences out of downtown. The major players in the garment industry moved from New York's Fifth Avenue, the heart of the business district, west to Seventh Avenue in the 1920s. Wilshire Boulevard, located outside downtown Los Angeles, became a popular shopping district. Some businesses, particularly factories, moved out of the city altogether. In 1910, the Ford Motor Company opened a new factory in the Detroit suburb of Highland Park, after years of building cars in factories located in the city proper. Most people still worked, shopped, and found entertainment downtown, but throughout the 1920s and even into the 1930s, businesses continued to relocate.

Automobiles made it easier for people to work and shop away from the center of town. They also made it easier for people to move into areas more distant from city transit lines. Only eight thousand people owned cars in 1910. Eight million did by 1920, and while many of these millions were farmers, others were urban dwellers.

As more Americans took to the wheel, the shape of suburbia changed, filling in the undeveloped land between the radial transit lines. Neighborhoods such as Wesley Heights, within the ten-mile square of Washington, D.C., were designed with the automobile in mind. Now residents drove to work and home again, parking their cars each night in that new symbol of suburban convenience: the domestic garage. In the 1920s, the outlying areas grew twice as fast as the cities; in the 1930s, they grew three times as fast.

Urban areas saw hard times in the 1930s. After the Crash of 1929, the Great Depression affected everyone. America's downtowns, with their high rents and land values, struggled to survive. Urban landowners knocked down tall buildings and turned them into parking lots to try to forestall foreclosure on their property. Many still believed that downtown was the heart of a metropolitan area, its vitality the key to the region's fortunes.

Once the Depression was over, there was faith that American cities would rebound. City officials supported downtown neighborhoods, because they provided more than their share of property taxes. The notion of downtown remained powerful—but by the beginning of World War II, and certainly after, downtown was no longer the one and only place that residents went to work, shop, play, and congregate.

When Americans went to war in 1941, some of the forces that had been changing the shape of cities went temporarily dormant. Wartime restrictions and economic exigencies meant that Americans drove their cars less and rode buses and streetcars more. The country's resources went toward defeating the Nazis and the Japanese. Automobile factories converted to airplane manufacturing plants. Rubber and gasoline were rationed. New housing construction was curbed.

But when the war was over, in 1945, certain questions would return to center stage: What role would the nation's cities play in the economy? Where would people live, and how would they travel to work? The suburban dream hovered, coming closer within reach for millions of American families.

WHEN I STOPPED TO THINK, I COULD
NOT REMEMBER THAT I HAD SEEN MORE THAN
HALF-A-DOZEN HORSES ALL DAY LONG.
HOWEVER, I HAD SEEN A FIRE ENGINE, A SPRINKLING
WAGON, AN AMBULANCE, A FUNERAL PROCESSION,
A PASSENGER BUS, DELIVERY WAGONS, HEAVY TRUCKS,
AND PLEASURE CARS. ALL AUTOMOBILES!

AND TO THINK THAT IN 1900 THERE WERE ONLY
ONE HUNDRED AUTOMOBILES
IN THE WHOLE UNITED STATES!

— *Daniel J. Beeby and Dorothea Beeby,*
   **How the World Grows Smaller,** *a history schoolbook, 1924*

# ON THE RISE:
# A SOCIETY OF MASS CONSUMERS

*Mass production, developed by automaker Henry Ford, demanded simplified, repeated tasks. Opposite, clockwise from upper left: Flywheel magnetos come together at a Ford plant in 1913; factory workers test a Model T engine and chassis; tire makers stretch tire covers in 1910; and Model Ts roll down an assembly line. Drivers licensed in 1925, above left, and 1935, used the final product.*

It is centuries in the future, and they've cut the tops off Christian crosses, leaving only Ts.

A world state has replaced God in the year A.F. (After Ford) 632. Instead of traditional religious holidays, the people of Earth celebrate Ford's Day. They reverently trace the sign of the Model T. "Oh, Ford!" they curse. But when things get better they purr, "Ford's in his flivver. All's well with the world."

This is the Brave New World that British novelist Aldous Huxley envisioned in his 1932 novel of mass production taken to nightmarish extreme. Playing off Henry Ford's proclamation that "Machinery is the new Messiah," Huxley envisioned a world that worshiped industry, uniformity, and science. Other contemporary critics echoed Huxley's concerns. Charlie Chaplin's 1936 film, *Modern Times,* portrayed the Little Tramp as a human cog in an infernal production line. French filmmaker René Clair compared factories to prisons in his 1931 film, *A Nous la Liberté (Give Us Freedom).* The film's protagonist, a prison escapee, ends up running a phonograph assembly plant and finds wild success by applying the brutal methods of cell block regimentation.

Huxley chose a pivotal date for the start of his futuristic calendar: the year the Model T appeared on the market. The Model T Ford automobile, and all that flowed from it, added new strands and unraveled old in the social, psychological, and economic fabric of America. A French theologian and historian, Father R. L. Bruckberger, said Ford's assembly line, coupled with the high wages he paid, affected the 20th century more than the Bolshevik Revolution.

Henry Ford said he would build a car "for the great multitude"—and he did, selling 15 million Model Ts. This Model T roadster rolled off the assembly line in 1926, the last full year of production. Ford Motor introduced the swankier Model A in 1927 to compete with rival General Motors in variety and annual model changes.

Ford made the automobile affordable for many adult Americans, creating unprecedented mobility and freedom. Car culture sewed together city and country; consolidated schools; scattered homes in new suburbs, chain stores and gas stations along new highways; expanded recreational opportunities; and ultimately sucked some of the life out of metropolitan downtowns. Automobiles became the foundation of a new economy. But Ford's revolution did not end with cars. He gladly publicized his methods, spreading his techniques so others could produce goods cheaply and uniformly. Radios, vacuum cleaners, and other home appliances soon appeared in huge numbers, each one exactly like the next. Mass production, a term Ford popularized, helped create a culture of mass consumption. It made Americans not only want more things, but also want them again and again, in new models and new colors. Consumers eagerly abandoned yesterday's goods for tomorrow's.

Mass production changed the labor force. On the one hand, the five-dollar-a-day salary paid by Ford to his laborers more than doubled previous wages. It gave them the income to participate in the brave new economy and to buy the cars they made. On the other hand, mechanized factory work numbed the mind and spirit. Employee turnover at the Ford Motor Company hit 380 percent in 1913. Absenteeism also kept his factory understaffed. Only by offering such unusually high wages could Ford Motor attract—and keep—workers.

Ford dismissed concerns about turning men into robots. In his memoirs, he said that he could never stoop to doing the same repetitive tasks every day, "but to other minds, perhaps I might say to the majority of minds, repetitive operations hold no terrors.... The average worker, I am sorry to say, wants a job in which he does not have to put forth much physical exertion—above all, he wants a job in which he does not have to think." Some of Ford's workers begged to differ. "The chain system you have is a slave driver!" the wife of a Ford employee wrote him in 1914. "My God!, Mr. Ford. My husband has come home and thrown himself down & won't eat his supper—so done out! Can't it be remedied?"

Contrary to myth, Ford did not invent the automobile. Nor did he build the first popular model. He had well-established competitors at the beginning of the 20th century, including steam and electric car makers. Many automotive pioneers had attempted to adapt the familiar coal-fired boiler technology of steam locomotives to automobiles. The Stanley Steamer, manufactured in 1897 by twin brothers Francis and Freelan Stanley in Newton, Massachusetts, featured a boiler heated by kerosene or gasoline that powered a carriage-sized vehicle.

Unfortunately, the steam car—the most common type of automobile until 1901—was hard to drive. Until the flash boiler was introduced in 1901, it took 20 minutes to fire up a steam car engine. It could explode, and many did. Boiler explosions frightened several cities into banning the steam car.

Electricity seemed more promising. After all, trolleys ran efficiently and cleanly along city streets. Electric cars, such as the early models produced by Albert Pope, were clean and quiet. Their main problem was that their heavy batteries had to be recharged every 40 or 50 miles.

While such cars might fit the needs of city dwellers, they were impractical in the country. Muddy roads often overwhelmed their low power, and electric lines necessary for recharging had yet to be strung throughout much of rural America. Compared with electric or external combustion engines, gasoline-powered autos had fewer drawbacks. The internal combustion engine compressed a tiny bit of fuel and air in a cylinder and exploded it with a spark, moving a piston and transferring the resulting power to an axle. Gasoline engines could run for a long time, thanks to the relatively efficient conversion of a tank full of gasoline into the energy of motion. The spread of paved roads and gasoline filling stations, along with Charles Kettering's 1912 invention of the electric starter and other improvements, cemented the victory of the gasoline-powered automobile over its rival technologies. Steamers and electric cars vanished in the 1920s.

An early mobile steam engine set Henry Ford on the path of his career. Born in 1863, Ford began thinking about how machines could replace horses while he was growing up on a farm near Dearborn, Michigan. He was 12 when he first saw a steam engine, "the biggest event" of his youth, he said. The engine and boiler, mounted on wheels and coupled with a water tank and coal cart, powered threshing machines and sawmills. The driver happily showed off the engine and explained how it worked. That day, Ford later recalled, planted in him the desire to create "a machine that would travel the roads."

Ford hand-made the two cylinders of his first gasoline vehicle from a steam engine exhaust pipe. A leather belt sent power to the rear wheels of his 1896 "quadricycle," which featured four bicycle wheels and a buggy frame. In 1899, he joined a group of investors and formed the Detroit Automobile Company, which they later renamed the Henry Ford Company. He and his backers soon clashed over production plans, though. Ford lost that fight and was forced out in 1902.

A rival car maker, Henry Leland, took over and reorganized the company that Ford left behind. Leland, a master mechanic and engineer, produced high-priced, high-performance cars. He renamed his firm the Cadillac Motor Car Company, after Antoine de la Mothe Cadillac, the French Army officer who founded Detroit in 1701. After a few years of production, he transported three Cadillacs to London in 1908, organizing a unique demonstration of his skill in machining parts to precise specifications. A crowd watched as Leland had the cars reduced to piles of nuts, bolts, and other bits of metal. The pieces were mixed up, so it would be impossible to know which cars they had come from. Then Leland reassembled them into Cadillacs that ran perfectly.

Another of Ford's rivals in gasoline engine technology, Ransom E. Olds, opened a factory in Detroit in 1899. Olds laid out a progressive assembly system capable of manufacturing multiple copies. Economies of scale helped keep the price of the car affordable—the classic Curved Dash Oldsmobile sold for $650. Engineering gave it a smooth ride. The public celebrated the "merry Oldsmobile" in the

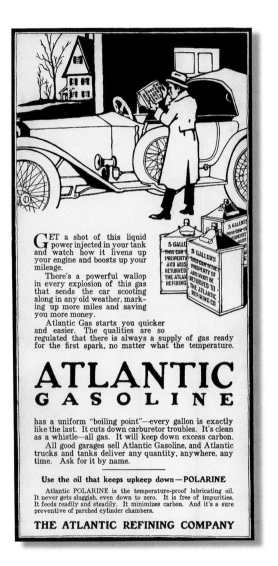

*Early motorists bought gasoline from
hardware and grocery stores. In about 1915,
the Atlantic Refining Company advertised
its gas, above, for sale at garages but could
deliver "any quantity, anywhere, any
time." Following pages: Motorists enjoy the
convenience of a 1923 filling station in
the New York area. By the 1920s, motorists
commonly filled up at roadside stations.*

popular song and bought 5,000 in 1904, more than
twice the entire production run of Detroit's Cadillac
plant in that same year. Olds's chief financial backer
decided to take the company in a new direction and
build expensive cars. Olds quit, and then he decided
to form the REO (for Ransom E. Olds) Motor Car
Company, which enjoyed modest success.

The tendency to build luxury cars created a new
market opportunity for Henry Ford. After leaving his
initial firm, he joined a new group of investors and
formed the Ford Motor Company in 1903. His new
firm began to produce a variety of medium-priced
models and, with them, achieved a noteworthy sales
record. Americans purchased more than 1,700 Ford
automobiles in the company's first 15 months. That
success gave stockholders more than a 100 percent
return. Henry Ford bought out some of his backers
and became the majority stockholder.

By the time he gained control of the company, in
1907, Henry Ford had witnessed automobile
economics at work. The company's cars sold for
$1,000 to $2,000 in 1905-06. Sales plummeted that
year. Few Americans could afford to buy the Ford
vehicles. The average weekly wage was less than $13
in 1900, so a car cost more than a year's income.
Ford decided to cut prices. Sales shot up, even
though the nation was suffering an economic slump.
Ford put two and two together. More than ever, he
was convinced that the American consumer wanted
a light, powerful, low-priced car. He scrapped the
production of multiple models and turned all of his
energy toward producing vast numbers of a single,
elegantly simple model. He staked his future on

turning out cars as alike as "pins or matches," with no variations between them for his workers to worry about as they assembled the parts.

"I will build a motor car for the great multitude," Ford announced. "It will be large enough for the family but small enough for the individual to run and care for. It will be constructed of the best materials, by the best men to be hired, after the simplest designs that modern engineering can devise. But it will be so low in price that no man making a good salary will be unable to own one—and enjoy with his family the blessing of hours of pleasure in God's great open spaces."

The Model T, introduced in 1908, proudly lacked extravagance. It was plain, even homely. It had a single-cast engine block capable of 20 horsepower, a somewhat awkward transmission, and three speeds, including reverse. The vanadium-alloyed steel chassis was light but tough. Its colors were black ... and black. And it was cheap: Half of the Model T replacement parts that were sold at repair shops cost less than 50 cents each. Its plain and pragmatic design won the applause of many. One sect of the fundamentalist Dunkard religion banned other cars as "haughty and sinful" but saw no prideful iniquity in members who drove the Model T. Honest, hardworking Americans embraced the car.

Ford's manufacturing facility was organized so that mechanics with a variety of skills worked together to assemble one Model T. Then that crew moved on to make the next car. Factory experts hired by Ford gradually changed the process. Trying to improve on the cruder 19th-century techniques already in place

for the mass production of guns and sewing machines, they designed truly identical parts and arranged equipment in sequence to speed assembly. Mechanics specialized in certain tasks, which increased efficiency. Parts scooted along gravity slides to the locations where they were needed. Work flowed more logically. Ford opened a giant factory at Highland Park, built to take full advantage of his new production techniques. His massive investment in single-use tools—such as an automatic drill that cut 45 holes simultaneously in a cylinder block—saved time and motion. Assembly time decreased and total production increased. In 1912, Ford made 82,000 Model Ts, and the pace kept quickening.

Workers burned up assembly time by walking back and forth among stations. A timesaving breakthrough occurred on April 1, 1913, when technicians rigged a waist-high frame of pipes. Workers stood in positions on either side of it. A magneto (a standard engine part that converted mechanical power to electricity for the car's ignition) came down the frame to the first worker. That man added a part, then slid the magneto down the frame to the next worker, who added another part, slid the magneto further, and waited for the next one to come down the line.

Under the old system, in which each worker built an entire magneto on his own, a line of 29 workers would have completed one magneto each every 20 minutes. On the moving assembly line, working as a team, they improved productivity. Now they were completing an average of one magneto per person every 13 minutes and 10 seconds. After making a few improvements to the line—using a conveyor belt, regulating its speed, and raising the height of the line to a more comfortable level for the workers, for example—an assembly crew could turn out one magneto per person every 5 minutes.

The moving line succeeded so well that the company applied it to other subassemblies and, in January 1914, to the final assembly of the Model T itself. Ford's revolutionary system essentially transformed the Highland Park plant into one giant machine with a single purpose. By late 1914, the plant workers could complete a car in 93 minutes, a job that used to take them hours. As assembly costs fell, Ford cut prices. The car that cost $950 in 1909 sold for less and less as the years passed, dipping down to $290 in December 1924. Meanwhile, production rose. Ford manufactured 585,000 Model Ts in 1916 and 2,000,000 seven years later.

By no means could all Americans afford the luxury of an automobile. In 1918, companies in the United States manufactured a million new cars, but they also cranked out half a million brand-new horse-drawn wagons as well.

Of those Americans who did purchase an automobile in 1921, more than half chose the Model T. A car so simple and so practical inspired a generation of owners who tinkered and made their own repairs. Twine, wire, gum, and clothespins could fix the car, they claimed. True, the Model T sometimes misfired and ran hot, and jokesters said the Ford shook more hell out of people than Bible-thumper Billy Sunday. But on an icy morning, a homegrown mechanic might coax the engine into life by pouring boiling water over the carburetor or lighting a small fire under the oil pan.

Model Ts became characters in the American culture. They inspired volumes of quips and epithets. "Flivver" meant "failure" in the contemporary slang, while "Tin Lizzie" applied the common nickname of African-American maids to the black steel car. "We can joke all we want to about the Ford car, and the Ford owner, being a good fellow, laughs along with us," asserted the editor of a 1915 Ford joke book. "At the same time, though, he pats his pocketbook, lets in his clutch, and rides serenely away, proud of his possession and confident of his good judgment."

Henry Ford did not seem to mind Model T jokes, at least not during his company's heyday. He told his favorite one to President Woodrow Wilson: Carrying out the instructions in a will, a grave-digger made a hole big enough to bury both the dead man and the car he loved. In his will, the man had written that since his Model T had gotten him out of every other hole in life, he was confident it would pull him out of this last one.

. . .

What Henry Ford did not know was that his Model T was digging its own grave. Ford staked his company's success on continued demand for a single product. His rivals at General Motors had a different idea.

The General Motors Company was founded in 1908. Whereas Ford's genius lay in production, Alfred P. Sloan, Jr., mastered modern business methods. Sloan and Pierre du Pont, two early presidents of

Gasoline pumps evolved along with automobiles and traffic. A portable device produced around 1910, right, took the gas to the auto. Motorists pulled up to the 1916 S.F. Bowser pump, below, and the 1932 Wayne Oil Tank pump, far left. Displays such as the enamel sign for Mobiloil, circa 1930, drew attention to specific brands.

General Motors, pushed the company to success by marketing cars not for the masses, as Ford did, but for a wide spectrum of customers. They decentralized their operations, in contrast to Ford's top-down autocracy, enabling swift adjustments as consumer demand changed. They declined to copy Ford's dead-end investment in single-use tools, instead investing in basic tools that could serve different purposes and contribute to a flexible mass production plan.

General Motors produced cars in five price categories, offering consumers choices they could not get from Ford. The basic Chevrolet, with the lowest price and highest sales, rivaled the Model T. However, Chevy owners might aspire to work their way up what Sloan called the "price pyramid," one day buying the luxury Cadillac, a product line GM had acquired from Leland's independent company. Sloan considered trade-ins sizable down payments, and in that way helped loyal GM customers climb up that pyramid. To make financing easier, in 1919 the company created the General Motors Acceptance Corporation, which offered credit and installment payment plans.

The most visible innovation by General Motors was the introduction of annual model changes in its vehicles' designs. The concept of annual models began with the Chevrolet in 1924, one year after Sloan became president of General Motors, and then spread to other divisions. The modifications drew attention to technical improvements and became a way for the proud buyer to announce to the world that he owned the latest (and therefore the greatest) General Motors car. The Chevy models did

*"Cheapest Supply House on Earth," proclaimed the cover of the 1899 Sears, Roebuck catalog. Railroad networks, road improvements, and rural mail delivery beginning in 1896 let farm families buy nearly anything with ease through mail-order houses. In 1898, Sears declared a price war on Montgomery Ward and surpassed it in total sales two years later.*

noticeably improve, thanks to the flexibility of design inherent in the GM management style. Americans bought into the notion of living ever better with ever newer cars.

Amid all these changes, the Model T suffered. Ford's market share plummeted to 30 percent in 1926 and fell even further in early 1927. That year, as Americans bought a million Chevrolets, Ford halted Model T production. Company managers rethought, retooled, and six months later reemerged with a new, more handsome automobile: the Model A. It appeared just in time. The Depression cut new car sales by 75 percent in the early 1930s and killed off most of the small automakers. Ford Motor adopted the custom of annual model changes, along with some of the business practices of its rivals, and survived. By the 1930s, three big automakers dominated the United States market: Chrysler, General Motors, and Ford. Smaller competitors, such as Studebaker and Nash, struggled to survive.

. . .

By the time of the Depression, cars had irrevocably changed the way ordinary Americans did business. In the previous century, when trains had ruled the countryside, mail-order catalogs had ruled the everyday trade. Railway express, rural free delivery, and parcel post allowed farmers to receive items from Montgomery Ward and its rival, Sears.

Founded by Richard Sears, who began by selling watches in the 1880s, the newer mail-order company had surpassed Ward's in total sales at the turn of the century. The Sears catalog eventually supplied everything from Ouija boards to maternity bras,

from coffee grinders to cedar-shingled houses. The 1900 Sears catalog had more than a thousand pages.

Once a farmer could buy a car, though, and drive it over hard roads to shop in the city, he and his family no longer had to rely on mail order. They could compare prices and quality among stores in town and choose the best bargains. Catering to this newly mobile population, chain stores mushroomed in the 1920s. Sears opened a retail store in Chicago, its home base, in 1925, then branch stores opened soon in Philadelphia, Dallas, and Seattle. The retail stores specialized in selling auto-related items, such as Sears-brand Allstate tires.

Not to be outdone, Ward opened an Exhibit Store in Plymouth, Indiana, in 1926. At first, the store followed a plan that had succeeded at local fairs and in a small shop in Marysville, Kansas. Customers examined sample goods in person, but then had to order theirs through the catalog. When the Plymouth store's customers insisted on buying the display stock, Montgomery Ward took the hint and opened regular retail stores in other towns. They, too, concentrated on tires, batteries, and other accessories for the growing number of cars being driven in, around, and across the nation.

In 1932, Americans owned 24 million cars. Numerous businesses and industries sprang up or evolved further, to support all the automobiles on the road and the needs of those who were driving them. Firestone, Goodyear, and other rubber companies manufactured tires. Oil companies hit gushers in Texas, Oklahoma, and California, and the petroleum industry hired a million workers in the 1930s.

Those workers strung more than 90,000 miles of pipeline, through which flowed the raw material for all the petroleum products that trains, trucks, and ships delivered to America's many drivers.

Once, retailers had sold oil and gas alongside dry goods, hardware, and bicycles. Now petroleum products were being sold by service stations, which specialized in answering auto owners' specific needs. The Bowser Self-Measuring Gasoline Storage Pump of 1905 and its descendants simplified filling auto gas tanks. Colorful, houselike buildings appeared across the country, and signs for Texaco, Gulf, and other gasoline brands sprouted right alongside them. Some, such as the Canfield Oil station in Lakewood, Ohio, offered easy pull-through access on busy street corners. Others opened up on the roads running out of towns. By the mid-1930s, America had 200,000 gas stations. The 48-mile stretch of U.S. 1 between New Haven, Connecticut, and the New York State line averaged one filling station every 895 feet and one restaurant for every two stations.

The price of gas fell from 29 cents a gallon in 1920 to 27 cents a gallon in 1927, despite taxes added to the price to finance road construction. Stations relied on gimmicks and special offers to attract customers. "No one knows what a real SERVICE station is until he crosses the Mississippi River," one 1930s traveler wrote. "Your tank is filled, your oil checked, your tires tested, your radiator filled, and your windshield polished without a word of instruction on your part." Customers might receive free glassware, china, or savings stamps that could be redeemed for gas or gifts. Gulf stations were the first to issue free

maps, in the 1920s. Rand McNally sold its first national atlases in 1924, but it also printed and sold maps emblazoned with gas company logos. A customer would "Put Your Sign Post in His Pocket," promised Rand McNally, when he walked away with a map bearing your gasoline's brand name.

The maps were easy to follow. States assigned simple numbers to their highways, and federal highways joined the system in 1925, consolidating a multitude of local route names into a single set of numbers. For the sake of consistency, federal highways received odd numbers if they ran north-south, even numbers if they ran east-west. Shield-shaped signs were posted with those numbers along every route. Driving privileges, too, became bureaucratized. New York led the parade of states requiring car registration. State license plates were universal by 1918. Drivers' licenses spread more slowly, required by only 35 states as late as 1935.

. . .

As automobiles became common, some of the romance faded out of driving. Instead of reveling in the adventure of the open road, Americans adopted behind-the-wheel routines. The focus shifted from the trip to the destination.

Early long-distance auto travelers like Dr. Jackson camped beside their cars or stayed in traditional hotels. Entrepreneurs who saw the growing glut of automobilists built cabins right alongside highways, near resorts and tourist homes. A "cabin camp" that opened in Douglas, Arizona, in 1913 may have been the first. By the mid-1920s, others had spread up and down the West Coast, and the trend crept eastward.

## THE HOT PILLOW TRADE

### J. EDGAR HOOVER ATTACKS

TOURISTS STAY AT TEPEE-SHAPED CABINS, ABOVE LEFT, NORTH OF LAWRENCE, KANSAS, IN 1936. THE CABINS INCLUDED HOT AND COLD RUNNING WATER. ISOLATED BUNGALOWS SOMETIMES ATTRACTED HARDENED CRIMINALS, AS IN THE COMIC STRIP, ABOVE RIGHT.

IN 1935, SOUTHERN METHODIST University's sociology department dispatched its students to investigate motels and tourist camps near Dallas, Texas. Decades later, the students' findings still boggle the mind.

One camp operator rented a single cabin 16 times in one day. Another camp, consisting of four units, attracted 109 Dallas couples in ten days. Of those, 102 put false names on the register. What these renters were doing was obvious, even to the young scholars of a private religious college. One typical camp "is no resting place for the weary, but is an abode of love, a bower of bliss, in which amorous couples devote themselves to the worship of Venus," said the SMU study, published in 1936. A camp owner admitted that quick sex assignations, called "the hot pillow trade" in contemporary slang, constituted 90 percent of his business.

The motel and its country cousins – the tourist camp, cabin camp, motor court, and the like – had come to dominate travel accommodations in the 1930s. *Business Week* asserted in 1940 that the traditional hotel's share of travel lodging fell from 75 percent to 32 percent over the previous decade. Motels had grabbed most of the trade. While cheap, convenient highway lodgings attracted weary vacationers and business travelers, they also drew less savory characters.

The Roaring Twenties had ushered in a change in American values. Bathtub gin drinkers thumbed their noses at Prohibition; women sought greater freedom; family and church lost ground to the new gods of consumerism and personal liberty. In this context, the automobile and the motel opened new frontiers for romance—and crime. At least six hitchhiking murderers took young girls with them and hid from the law in auto camps, reported Federal Bureau of Investigation Director J. Edgar Hoover in a 1940 article in *The American Magazine*.

America "has a new home of disease, bribery, corruption, crookedness, rape, white slavery, thievery, and murder," wrote Hoover. He warned that many of the nation's 35,000 tourist camps constituted a threat to their communities' peace and welfare. Unfortunately, local police could not crack down on businesses outside city limits, and many county sheriffs seemed unwilling or unable to act. The public should demand an end to "loose laws and loose enforcement," said Hoover, and get lodging recommendations from auto clubs, better business bureaus, and law enforcement agencies.

Grassroots responses to sleazy motels already had begun. The American Automobile Association's *Directory of Motor Courts and Camps,* first published in 1920, listed hundreds of reputable motels and cabin camps. Southeastern entrepreneurs formed the Tourist Court Owners Association in 1932. The following year, Californians created a business group called United Motor Courts, which campaigned against quick-sex rentals. That same year, the International Motor Court Association began producing a trade magazine, *Tourist Court Journal,* which soon became the authority on professional motel practices.

Reputable motels policed themselves. Flanagan's Camp, consisting of 27 cottages in Macon, Georgia, banned questionable couples and liquor. Ring's Rest, on U.S. 1 outside Washington, D.C., refused rooms to travelers from nearby towns. Many motels posted rules of behavior alongside the usual information about rates. "Absolutely no one except those originally registering for the room will be allowed to occupy same. No boisterous or profane language or undue noise will be tolerated.... We take the number of all cars," the Lighthouse Lodge of Longview, Texas, announced. With tougher zoning regulations and stronger law enforcement practices in the mid-1930s, the hot pillow trade in Hoover's "Camps of Crime" began to cool down.

BEGINNING IN 1934, FRED E. RINGE, SR., AND HIS FAMILY RAN RING'S REST, BELOW, A CABIN CAMP AND FORMER SPEAKEASY ON U.S. HIGHWAY 1 IN MUIRKIRK, MARYLAND. CABINS WERE CLEAN AND FUNCTIONAL, FURNISHED WITH OIL HEATERS, TABLES AND CHAIRS, SINKS, PITCHERS AND BASINS, MATTRESSES ON IRON FRAMES, PILLOWS, AND BLANKETS.

Midway between auto tenting grounds and modern hotels, cabin camps simplified long-distance driving. Travelers did not have to carry their own bedding, towels, or soap. Many camps offered meals, eliminating chores that would have taken time away from the drive. Customers could travel by auto coast to coast with just a suitcase and save money: no investment in camping gear, no expensive hotels. Instead a traveler would stop for the night and relax in a clean little room with a double bed, a table, two chairs, a mirror, and possibly a washbasin and toilet.

Many cabin camp owners, like Fred E. Ringe, Sr., supplemented their income by putting in gasoline pumps and opening a small store. A widower and service agent for an adding machine company, Ringe bought an old speakeasy and its four cabins in 1934, turning them into a camp he called Ring's Rest.

He worked to make the cabins attractive and clean. His children made beds, pumped gas, and collected money. Ringe put up a red neon sign that read "CABINS" to attract tourists and business travelers driving along U.S. 1 south of Laurel, Maryland. Circus performers en route to winter quarters in Florida sometimes stopped, as did travelers on their way to see the cherry blossoms in Washington, D.C.

Customers would knock at the side door of the Ringe house, and a family member would show them to a cabin and collect payment in advance. At the time, cabin camps had been taking a bite of the standard hotel business. Hotel operators mounted a campaign to portray the cabins as vice dens. Even FBI Director J. Edgar Hoover alleged they were criminal hangouts. Ring's Rest, however, refused any business that might have resembled the "hot pillow" trade. Customers whose license plates looked local were told to move on.

·  ·  ·

A different type of traveler frequented Hamon's Court on Route 66. Seven cabins and a gasoline station, it was established in 1941 by Lucille and Carl Hamons, a mile southwest of Hydro, Oklahoma.

In the early years of their business, Lucille Hamons noticed that many customers seemed to be carrying "everything they owned." The people passing through were travelers who had pulled up stakes in Arkansas, Missouri, Kansas, or eastern Okla-homa, hoping to find work in California. "We used to always say the way you could tell the Arkies from the Okies was that the Okies would have two mattresses on their car and the Arkies would only have one," recalled Lucille Hamons.

Many who passed through bought water bags to cool and refill their radiators in the desert. Some families stopped for food and gas but had no money. Lucille Hamons ran the business by herself during the long spells while her husband hauled hay, and sometimes she would accept travelers' personal goods as payment. Occasionally she even bought their broken-down cars—at least that way they got enough money for bus fare to the West Coast. Lucille Hamons's generosity through nearly six decades of service earned her the nickname "Mother of the Mother Road."

The families helped by Lucille Hamons represent the massive movement of people out of America's midlands. It started in the 1920s and accelerated in the 1930s, when the Depression and the Dust Bowl coincided. Nearly four million people had left Oklahoma, Texas, Arkansas, and Missouri by 1950. More than a third of them settled in California.

At least 800,000 farmers and other agricultural workers abandoned the Midwest during the same two decades. Farmers made up a significant percentage, but not a majority, of this westward migration. There was a time when California had drawn them with the promise of rich fields to work, but during the Depression, farmers felt more driven than drawn. Their crops had failed during the prolonged drought, and they carried not much more than hope for a better life elsewhere.

In Oklahoma alone, 55 percent of the agricultural labor force hit the road. Gasoline engines eased their flight—the same engines that had evicted them from the land, as farm tractors replaced field hands and horses. Americans owned 850,000 tractors in 1930. Three decades later, the number had swelled to 2.4 million. President Franklin Roosevelt's Agricultural Adjustment Act of 1933 saw to it that farmers got paid to leave their land fallow, trying to prop up cotton prices through the laws of supply and demand. Landlords dismissed their tenant workers. "I let 'em all go," a Texas landlord told Farm Security Administration photographer Dorothea Lange in 1937. "I bought tractors on the money the government give me and got shet o' my renters.... They've got their choice—California or the WPA."

Many did choose the Works Progress Administration, another Roosevelt relief agency. At its peak

in 1938, the WPA employed 3.2 million Americans, who worked on the construction of airports, schools, hospitals, bridges, highways, and other public-minded projects. Federal relief agencies accounted for four billion dollars' worth of road construction in Roosevelt's first nine years in office. Many other unemployed Americans followed the path of the Joad family in John Steinbeck's 1939 novel, *The Grapes of Wrath*. They headed west, driving Route 66 to California.

The Haggard Family of McIntosh County, Oklahoma, followed Route 66 to Bakersfield, California, in July 1935. The family—father James, mother Flossie, and children Lillian and James Lowell—had grown cotton and raised dairy cows and pigs. Drought killed the crops, and a barn fire destroyed not only the next year's seed but also the family's farm equipment—along with the family's prized 1931 Ford Model A. James Haggard ran a service station in Checotah for a few months before the family decided to move. Flossie Haggard had a sister, Flora, in California, whose family loaned the Haggards $40 to make sure they had enough to pay their travel expenses. They loaded a secondhand 1926 Chevrolet and trailer with their family possessions, including a sewing machine. They packed up bacon, potatoes, fruit, and vegetables, hit the road, and arrived in the San Joaquin Valley four days later.

"It was like a long camping trip," recalls Lillian Haggard, 14 years old at the time. "We ate along the road side or sandwiches en route. Slept, camplike." She remembers enjoying the fresh colors of the mountains, trees, and sky. A photograph of the journey shows her dipping her feet in a mountain stream east of Albuquerque, New Mexico, indicating "a bath was on my mind."

In California, the Haggards worked for two months milking dairy cows by hand, then James got a job at the Santa Fe Railroad shops. The family moved into an empty refrigerator car on a lot, rent-free for nine months as long as they cut out windows and doors to make the car livable. "I've never heard of an Okie who'd work," the railroad car owner said. "I've never heard of one who wouldn't," James shot back. The Haggards worked hard, refurbished their train car, and found their life improving. Many migrants who moved to California gave up and went back home, but every time James raised that idea, Flossie scotched it. On April 6, 1937, she gave birth to another son, Merle, who would one day become famous for singing with pride of being an "Okie from Muskogee." Those were his family's roots. He was actually born in Kern General Hospital in Bakersfield, California.

Another family from eastern Oklahoma took a different path to success in the West. Arthur and Martha Dillard Williams lived with their six children in a two-room log cabin without electricity in the African-American town of Boley. The Williamses were cotton sharecroppers. When the livestock and crops failed, the family drove to California in 1936. As daughter Christina McClanahan recalls, her father traveled ahead to get a place to stay, then her mother's brother and his wife drove cross-country in a 1929 Chevy from California to fetch the rest of the family. The Williamses secured their suitcases to the running board, hooked up a small trailer to carry other belongings, and provisioned themselves with fried chicken and fruit. Then all nine—mother, aunt, uncle, and six kids—set off together on Route 66. ("Was there any other way to come?" McClanahan asks.) All six children squeezed into the back seat, some sitting forward and some leaning back. "We squabbled with each other," McClanahan says. "My mother was always telling us to be quiet and be still."

In California, the family found work picking and chopping cotton. Arthur Williams saved enough money from his work as a farmhand and from WPA and state relief to purchase a 1935 Chevrolet and two-and-a-half acres at Buttonwillow. The Williamses had two more children. They grew cotton and vegetables and eventually the family installed electricity in their home. The children entered racially integrated schools. She and her family members considered themselves fortunate, recalls Christina McClanahan. Like Flossie Haggard, she had a son who would become famous. Brent McClanahan played running back for the Minnesota Vikings during the 1970s.

. . .

Such triumphs ran counter to the popular image. Migrants objected to Steinbeck's portrayal of ignorance and poverty. Marked as outsiders in their new surroundings, they strove as hard as California natives to achieve the American dream. The news media spread the stereotypes. Many well-known photographs of down-on-their-luck farm families owe their existence to Paul Schuster Taylor, an economist who consulted for the California State Emergency Relief Administration. Taylor believed words could

## EXPERT TRAVEL HELP

THE AMERICAN AUTOMOBILE ASSOCIATION'S (AAA) TRIPTIKS SIMPLIFIED LONG-DISTANCE AUTO TRIPS WITH PERSONALIZED MAPS AND INSTRUCTIONS.

MOST OF THE FIRST AUTO TRAVEL "MAPS" WERE CLOSER TO GUIDE-BOOKS. THEY DESCRIBED SPECIFIC ROUTES OR ILLUSTRATED KEY INTERSECTIONS WITH PHOTOGRAPHS. WHILE TRYING TO READ SUCH A GUIDE, A DRIVER HAD TO NEGOTIATE BAD ROADS, WATCH THE ODOMETER, AND DECODE THE COLORS AND SYMBOLS THAT IDENTIFIED REGIONAL HIGHWAYS BEFORE NUMBERS WERE ASSIGNED TO THEM IN THE 1920s.

THE AMERICAN AUTOMOBILE ASSOCIATION (AAA), FOUNDED IN CHICAGO IN 1902 TO PROMOTE MOTORISTS' INTERESTS, MADE THINGS EASIER. IT PUBLISHED A BONA FIDE MAP OF NEW YORK STATE IN 1911. THEN AAA BEGAN PRODUCING LONG, NARROW "STRIP" MAPS, LIKE THE DETROIT-TO-TOLEDO MAP, ABOVE LEFT. ONE OF THE FIRST CHARTED THE ROUTE FROM NEW YORK CITY TO JACKSONVILLE, FLORIDA. THE AAA'S EXPERTS, CALLED "PATHFINDERS," HELPED DRIVERS VERIFY DISTANCES, ROAD CONDITIONS, AND CONSTRUCTION IMPEDIMENTS.

INDIVIDUALIZED MAPS, CALLED "TRIPTIKS," DEBUTED IN 1937. THE AAA CUSTOMIZED EACH ONE, SUCH AS THE 1947 VERSION ABOVE, PER MEMBERS' REQUESTS. TRIPTIKS COMBINED STRIP MAPS, WRITTEN DIRECTIONS, POINTS OF INTEREST, AND AAA OFFICE LOCATIONS. AS THE AAA ENDED ITS FIRST CENTURY, MEMBERS COULD MAKE THEIR OWN TRIPTIKS ON THE INTERNET.

not document the needs of migrant farm laborers. He got relief agency funds to hire a photographer, although on the books, the job was called "clerk-stenographer." In the process, he also got a wife.

Dorothea Lange, a studio portrait photographer, took documentary photographs first for Taylor and then for the federal Resettlement Administration (later the Farm Security Administration). She accompanied Taylor as he examined living conditions among the migrant harvesters. Lange and Taylor were married in December 1935, and continued visiting migrant families together. She snapped sensitive photographs and demonstrated a rare talent for capturing her subjects' words. "We got blowed out of Oklahoma," one said. "It seems like God has forsaken us back there in Arkansas," said another.

Lange's photograph, "Migrant Mother," became the quintessential image of the Depression. At a pea pickers' camp at Nipomo, California, in March 1936, Lange walked toward a woman in a lean-to tent. She looked desperate. Her children huddled around her as Lange began taking pictures. The woman said she was 32 years old, and she had just sold her car tires for money to buy food. "The pea crop at Nipomo had frozen and there was no work for anybody," Lange wrote. "But I did not approach the tents and shelters of other stranded pea-pickers. It was not necessary; I knew I had recorded the essence of my assignment."

When Lange sent her pictures to the Resettlement Administration in Washington, she included the photograph of this contemplative mother with her hand to her cheek and her daughters burying their faces in her shoulders. She also gave one of her photos to the *San Francisco News,* which printed it alongside an editorial about hundreds of hungry migrants at Nipomo. The United Press wire service spread the story and the famous image around the country. After that, the federal government provided 20,000 pounds of food for the migrants—but the relief came too late for the family in Lange's picture. They had moved on.

Four decades later, Florence Thompson—the migrant mother in Lange's photograph—told her own story to the *Modesto Bee* newspaper and to photographer Bill Ganzel of Nebraska Educational Television. An American Indian, she had left Oklahoma in the mid-1920s. Her husband, Cleo Owens, worked in a California sawmill but lost his job in the Depression. He picked fruit to earn money, took sick one day, and died of a fever, leaving Florence pregnant with their sixth child. She took work where she could find it. She picked peas, cotton, grapes, and potatoes. She also worked in a restaurant for 50 cents a day plus leftovers. Her daughter, Ruby Sprague, told Ganzel, "When we were growing up, if mother weighed one hundred pounds, she was fat." Her adult children later bought her a home in Modesto, but she preferred to live in a trailer. "I need to have wheels under me," she explained.

At the time Lange took her photograph, the family car, a Hudson, had broken down. They were stranded in the migrant camp, waiting to get it repaired. Many migrant families had a car, to follow the harvest. "To even the poorest of them an automobile is a vital necessity, and the cost of its operation cuts a large figure in the family budget," Taylor wrote in

*American Exodus,* a book published in 1939 that showcased Lange's photographs. "The car must be fed gasoline and oil to make the next harvest, or to get to and from the fields, and its wheels must be covered before the feet of the children."

. . .

By the 1930s, automobiles had replaced trains as the most common travel method in America. Among vacationers in 1935, 85 percent went by car. Train travel cost less, but Americans seemed willing to pay for the convenience and independence of traveling in their own vehicle. Railroad traffic fell during the 1920s and 1930s. Auto travel multiplied sixfold.

Two events boosted the railroads' fortunes, though. One was World War II. Factories stopped making cars and retooled to make tanks, planes, trucks, and jeeps. Submarines off the American coast disturbed normal shipping, and highway travel fell off as the government rationed gas and tires. Trains took up the slack. Railroad passenger traffic doubled between 1940 and 1944, to 910 million riders, and remained high until the economy returned to peacetime footing.

The other change in railroading came with the introduction of diesel engines. It was a change that had a longer-lasting impact, not only on trains but on automobiles. GM's Electro-Motive Division created a lightweight diesel engine, first used in a train in 1934. Improving on German engineer Rudolf Diesel's 19th-century designs, the GM model compressed air and a small amount of diesel fuel in a cylinder, but it needed no spark to ignite it.Instead, the heat from extreme compression exploded the mixture.

Diesels cost more than steam engines, but their advantages made up for the expense. They could go farther without stopping. Powerful diesel engines could pull heavier loads at half the fuel cost. Unlike steam engines, they ran efficiently at a wide range of speeds. While steam engines had been manufactured in small batches to match specific terrains, diesel locomotives were as interchangeable as the mass-produced GM parts that went into them. They could handle any climb, descent, or turn, and could be linked together to pull as a single unit. Orders for diesels soared. The last commercial steam engines were hammered together in 1949.

The spread of the diesel engine played havoc in the labor force. Diesels needed routine inspections every 4,000 miles, not every 150, as steam engines did. That reduced the need for maintenance and repair. The nature of repairs also changed. Mechanics joked that it took six minutes to find a problem with a steam engine and six hours to fix it, while diesel trains reversed the numbers. The new engines required mechanical know-how associated with car and truck engines, such as electrical skills, but not the special skills that had evolved in the 19th century to service steam engines. Boilermakers, for example, knew how to work with sheet metal and

*Like many migrants of the 1930s, Flossie and James Haggard, right, moved their family from Oklahoma to California. Daughter Lillian kept notes on the trip, which included a description of a welcome stream near Albuquerque, inset. In California, James found a railroad job. His son, Merle, was born in Bakersfield. Decades later, he became a country music star whose songs recalled his family's past.*

repair steam engine boilers. Diesel trains had no boilers, though, so boilermakers scrambled for welding and reconditioning jobs. Blacksmiths traditionally had crafted unique parts for steam engines. GM's interchangeable diesel parts cut their workload, too.

Diesel trains still needed conductors to oversee passengers and freight. They still needed engineers to operate the engine and control the speed. But steam engines had required firemen to feed coal into the firebox, matching the blaze to the demands of terrain and load. Diesels had no fireboxes. Unions fought to keep firemen on board the new trains. The Southern Railway answered a 1950s court order to hire firemen by employing primarily elderly black women. The railway aimed to shame the union and demonstrate that on a diesel train, anyone could do a fireman's job. A compromise maintained firemen on diesel trains, understanding that they were being hired for training to become engineers.

Many of the steam train jobs held by African Americans continued on diesels. Racial discrimination kept blacks employed in menial jobs as waiters, cooks, maids, and track laborers. Many filled the relatively prestigious job of Pullman porter—in fact, the Pullman Company for many years had the nation's largest African-American payroll.

*Americans knew her at first only as "Migrant Mother," the title of Dorothea Lange's 1936 photo of a widow and two of her children at an agricultural workers' camp in Nipomo, California. Decades after the photo had become an icon of the Depression, the mother was identified as Florence Thompson. She had left Oklahoma in the 1920s.*

Company employees ensured that customers equated Pullman cars, common until the 1950s, with elegant accommodations. Nationwide, thousands of porters made beds and turned down sheets, carried bags, brushed coats, adjusted the heat, and performed myriad tasks for the sake of passenger comfort. Pullman porters created the first black union, the Brotherhood of Sleeping Car Porters, in 1925. Members worked hard and were admired in their communities. The union's first President, A. Philip Randolph, and other members became leaders of the civil rights movement.

• • •

Across America, towns that had prospered during the era of the steam locomotive adjusted to changes as the diesel era began. Spencer, founded in 1896 in Rowan County, North Carolina, was one such railroad town. Financier J. P. Morgan created the Southern Railway Company in a reorganization the year after the panic of 1893. The town of Salisbury sat, strategically, halfway between Atlanta, Georgia, and Washington, D.C., so many trains came through, switched tracks, or stopped there for service. Nearby Spencer became the service center for all the Southern Railway trains. The back shop, where the trains were serviced, was the largest commercial building constructed in North Carolina between 1900 and 1920.

Hundreds worked in the huge complex of Spencer shops. The county's population rose from 7,000 to more than 44,000 in the second decade of the 20th century. The Spencer freight yard was Southern Railway's largest, handling 1,800 freight trains

*Pullman railroad travel guaranteed style and comfort in the early 20th century. Opposite, clockwise from upper left: A conductor greets a passenger in Iowa, 1925; a porter serves passengers in the lounge car; in the sleeping car, a porter makes up a berth; and the oldest Pullman porter greets customers. Above, staged photographs in a 1924 magazine for Pullman employees display etiquette in dealing with customers.*

a month in the 1930s. At the same time, 800 passenger trains pulled through the depot. When trains came in, transfer workers removed freight—Sears and Ward catalog goods, for example—and carried it from boxcars to the proper track and train for delivery. Packers loaded and unloaded the cars, while drivers operated hand trucks, forklifts, and tractors to move the freight from car to car.

Factory production and shipping shrank during the Depression. The Southern Railway posted its first loss in 1931. Smaller shops along the Southern lines closed, in the short run bringing more freight to Spencer. Steam trains continued to serve their country: Southern Railway's No. 1401, for example, helped pull President Roosevelt's funeral train from Georgia to Washington, D.C., in April 1945. By 1953, however, low-maintenance diesels had completely replaced steam locomotives on the Southern. The switch to diesels cut the need for repair and maintenance crews, and the labor force at the Spencer shops dropped from 2,500 to 500. Shops built for steam engines could not be adjusted to service diesels, and repair work, along with the freight transfer business, shifted to other yards.

· · ·

World War II once and for all demonstrated the power of mass production, as railroads buzzed with activity and the auto industry converted to wartime production. As he had with his Model T, Henry Ford specialized in volume production for the sake of the war. Under license to Willys-Overland Motors, the Ford Motor Company cranked out jeeps. The two companies, working from Willys blueprints, made about 600,000 of the war's amazing all-purpose vehicles. Government officials, wanting Henry Ford's expert advice, asked him to examine production methods of B-24 bombers in late 1940. Ford dispatched his son, Edsel, and a company official to the San Diego Consolidated Aircraft bomber factory, which was turning out about one plane a day.

Knowing he could do much better, Ford sold the federal government on a plan to build a new factory at Willow Run, Michigan, to drastically increase bomber production. In 1942, one year after America entered World War II, Ford's Willow Run plant was churning out 365 B-24s each month. At its peak, 42,000 people worked at Willow Run, producing a stunning 540 bombers a month.

General Motors converted to war industry with similar success. The home of flexible mass production stopped making Cadillacs in February 1942 and started producing M-5 tanks, each one containing twin Cadillac V-8 engines. GM engines also powered American fighter planes: the P-38, P-40, and early versions of the P-51 fighter. On the West Coast, Henry Kaiser applied assembly-line techniques to ship construction. His Portland shipyard turned out solid Liberty ships ready for action. A single ship took only ten days to build.

As car factories retooled for airplane production, the supply of new vehicles quickly dwindled. After selling nearly four million cars in 1941, the auto industry manufactured only one hundred new vehicles two years later. The car became a hot com-modity: The used car market exploded as war workers—especially those on the West Coast who had to drive to jobs in factories—hunted for transportation. By April 1943, a used car on the West Coast was selling for more than it had originally cost. Car registrations began to fall off, and by June 1943, the number of cars on the nation's roads had dropped by an estimated 2.5 million.

Those who did own a car had a hard time driving it anywhere. Federal speed limits were set at 40 miles an hour in May 1942, then dropped to 35 in September, as the war continued. On December 1, 1942, gasoline was rationed nationwide. Curbs on gasoline purchases had already been put into place in the East. Now the rest of the country had to abide by such restrictions. By driving more slowly, Americans would conserve rubber—an important sacrifice since, as a government report put it, America was "a HAVE NOT nation" when it came to rubber. The war in the Pacific had slashed supplies. Some owners just put their cars on blocks for the war's duration

Meanwhile, wave after wave of wartime machines rolled out of American factories, crushing the Axis powers by their sheer bulk. Mass production techniques, fine-tuned in America's automobile industry, contributed mightily to the Allied victory. Thus the century's pivotal technological development, which had so frightened Aldous Huxley, helped to destroy a far more real danger—the century's greatest threat to freedom.

THE FORD IS MY AUTO;
I SHALL NOT WANT ANOTHER.
IT MAKETH ME TO LIE DOWN BENEATH IT;
IT SOURETH MY SOUL.
IT LEADETH ME INTO THE PATHS OF RIDICULE
FOR ITS NAMESAKE.
YEA, THOUGH I RIDE THROUGH THE VALLEYS
I AM TOWED UP THE HILLS,
FOR I FEAR MUCH EVIL.
THY RODS AND THY ENGINES DISCOMFORT ME;
I ANOINT MY TIRES WITH PATCHES,
MY RADIATOR RUNNETH OVER;
I REPAIR BLOWOUTS IN THE PRESENCE
OF MINE ENEMIES.
SURELY, IF THIS THING FOLLOWETH ME
ALL THE DAYS OF MY LIFE,
I SHALL DWELL IN THE BUG-HOUSE FOREVER.

— *from* **Funny Stories about the Ford,** *1915*

# CHAPTER 7

# ROAD TRIP:
## FUN, PROFIT, AND THE AMERICAN DREAM

*A cross-country auto trip in the late 1940s combined friendship and fun. Four friends drove from Rochester, New York, to Hermosa Beach, California, stopping at state lines for photographs. Clockwise from upper left: Janet McDonnel, Ethel May Krockenberger, Caroline Millbank, and all three with Mary Jane Pecora. Souvenir pennants from the 1940s, 1950s, and 1960s, above, preserved tourists' memories.*

Drive where you want, when you want. Stop when you feel like it. See things, meet people, and write about them.

Those were the instructions that the Scripps-Howard Alliance gave to reporter Ernie Pyle in 1935. Pyle had pitched the idea of a continuing roving assignment to the national association of Scripps-Howard newspapers shortly after he finished a freighter journey from Los Angeles to Philadelphia.

Pyle's punchy accounts of that trip impressed the newspaper chain's editor-in-chief, G. B. Parker. He admired their "Mark Twain quality" and agreed to give the soft-spoken Indiana journalist a try as a syndicated columnist. "I've had a good stroke of luck," Pyle wrote a friend. "It's just the kind of job I've always wanted and hope I can make a go of it."

Make a go of it he did. Pyle produced his travel column until 1940, when World War II called him to duty as a civilian combat correspondent. Toward the end of his wandering, he announced that he had been to every state at least three times. He completed 35 crossings of the continent, stayed in 800 hotels, wore out a Ford and a Dodge convertible coupe, and went through five sets of tires. He mailed six columns a week to Scripps-Howard from places such as Death Valley, Zion National Park, and rural Alabama. The pieces earned him thousands, if not millions, of fans.

"I have no home," Pyle wrote during his American travels. "My home is where my extra luggage is, and where the car is stopped, and where I happen to be getting mail this time. My home is America."

Each morning, Pyle ate breakfast in a hotel restaurant or diner. His order never varied: crisp bacon, one medium-boiled egg, dry toast, and coffee or milk. The bill ranged from 30 cents to a whopping $1.25, an amount that flabbergasted him, at a resort in British Columbia.

As he left a hotel he had enjoyed, he marked its name in his copy of the Hotel Directory of the American Automobile Association (AAA), to remind himself to stay there again. Then he and "that Girl who rides with me"—his wife, Jerry—loaded their car with his Underwood typewriter, her newspapers and books, and their assorted luggage and headed out for destinations unknown. At the start of their travels in 1935, the Pyles fit everything into six suitcases and satchels. The number grew to ten. Emptying the car in 1938, Ernie Pyle found the archives of a well-seasoned traveler, including 50 road maps, a pile of old magazines, a Wyoming fossil, and big envelopes stuffed with mail.

Readers admired Pyle's job. He encouraged such envy, despite his secret difficulties. Behind his relaxed prose lurked shyness and a feeling of inadequacy as a writer. But Pyle's writing made his life on the road seem positively idyllic. "When I sit again at the wheel of our car after being away from it ... I feel like busting, it is so good," he wrote before taking the Overseas Highway to Key West. His columns made readers cast off their blues for a moment and vicariously soak up the joy of travel.

The best moment, he told his readers, was that sweet sip of liberty he tasted when his car pulled onto the highway. "The happiest I am at any time on a long trip is when we have been laid up several days in one place and then finally one morning we pack up, check out, fill up with gas, and light out into open country. Once in that car and under way, we don't have to talk to anybody, keep up with events ... answer letters, remember things, or grudgingly fit ourselves onto other people's worlds. We are alone, and free."

He chose his routes from gas station maps and seldom averaged more than 40 miles an hour. Ernie and Jerry might go only a few miles, or they might go farther. Once Pyle drove 570 miles in a day, from Arizona to Los Angeles, and then swore he would never go that far in one day again.

Aside from such rare extremes, when readers asked him if he ever got tired of the driving, Pyle replied with assurances to the contrary. Auto travel provides an escape from problems and routines, he said. He never had to buy coal for the furnace. He never had to crawl out of bed to do farm chores. If he and Jerry found a place they didn't like, they could shake off its dust and move on. And if the place was pleasant, they could leave before it lost its luster.

. . .

Novelist John Steinbeck also felt the "virus of restlessness," beckoning him to the "broad and straight and sweet path." Migration and the highway life were common themes in his novels, and he drew on his own observations of the road to breathe life into his fictional characters. To gather material for a series of nonfiction works, Steinbeck set out in the fall of 1960, driving a GM pickup truck equipped with a Wolverine camper, to see America anonymously. He

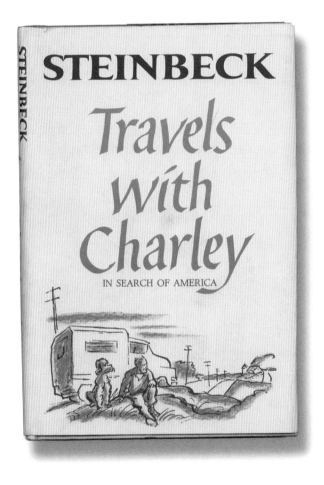

named the truck "Rocinante," in honor of Don Quixote's horse. Steinbeck chose to go north from his New York home to Vermont and New Hampshire, then south and west into the heartland. He tried to keep his gear to a minimum but, like Pyle, quickly accumulated freight. "I carried too much of everything—too much food, too many books, tools enough to assemble a submarine," he wrote. In terms of companionship, he packed light. A French poodle, Charles le Chien, traveled with him and lent his name to a book Steinbeck wrote about his experiences, *Travels With Charley*.

The trip had its good moments. Steinbeck bought fresh eggs, explosively juicy apples, and fresh cider in New England. He shared a bottle of brandy with a family of potato harvesters from Quebec while unwinding amid the autumn forests. He met truck drivers and waitresses and learned the rhythms that the road imposed on those who lived on it and near it. Rocinante and Charley broke the ice, as curious folk asked to check out Steinbeck's rig or made small talk about his dog.

But Steinbeck also knew the downside of extended travel. The road's regimen of driving, cooking, cleaning, and taking care of Charley imposed its own pressures. The ugliness of American cities, "like badger holes, ringed with trash," appalled him. Urban traffic made him anxious. Superhighways staggered his senses with roaring truck convoys and screaming road signs.

"These great roads are wonderful for moving goods but not for inspection of a countryside," he wrote. "You are bound to the wheel and your eyes to

## WEST TO A NEW LIFE

**LONG ON HOPE BUT SHORT ON CASH, MIGRANTS HEADED TO CALIFORNIA.**

STALLED ON U.S. 80 OUTSIDE LORDSBURG, NEW MEXICO, IN 1937, A FAMILY, BELOW, EN ROUTE TO A NEW LIFE IN CALIFORNIA, WAITS AND WONDERS. THROUGH THE 1930S, HUNDREDS OF THOUSANDS OF MIGRANTS FROM TEXAS, OKLAHOMA, ARKANSAS, MISSOURI, AND KANSAS JOINED THEM IN SEARCH OF WORK IN THE LAND OF SUNSHINE AND ORANGE TREES.

IN 1935, NOTES THE MAP KEY, ROADS BOTH PAVED AND UNPAVED LED FAMILIES WEST, MANY FROM THE DUST BOWL—A REGION OF DROUGHT LARGELY AFFECTING MIDWESTERN STATES. THERE TRACTORS HAD ALREADY REDUCED THE NEED FOR LABOR ON SMALL FARMS. THIS, COUPLED WITH THE DROUGHT AND THE COLLAPSE OF CROP PRICES, UPROOTED RURAL FAMILIES. ROUTE 66—HERE A STRONG RED LINE—FUNNELED MANY "ARKIES," "OKIES," AND "DUST BOWLERS" TO CALIFORNIA.

THOUGH VERDANT, CALIFORNIA'S LARGE FARMS PAID LOW WAGES FOR SEASONAL WORK. THE PICKING SEASON VARIED BY CROP AND CLIMATE. MIGRANTS DROVE FROM JOB TO JOB. MANY LACKED FOOD AND SHELTER, BUT THEY HELPED ONE ANOTHER. SOME RECEIVED GOVERNMENT RELIEF. "IF YOU'RE IN TROUBLE OR HURT OR NEED—GO TO POOR PEOPLE," MA JOAD SAYS IN *THE GRAPES OF WRATH*. "THEY'RE THE ONLY ONES THAT'LL HELP."

the car ahead and to the side-view mirror for the car or truck about to pass, and at the same time you must read all the signs for fear you may miss some instructions or orders.... When we get these thruways across the whole country, as we will and must, it will be possible to drive from New York to California without seeing a single thing."

. . .

Pyle's and Steinbeck's wanderings illustrate the development of auto travel between 1920 and 1960. The mass production of automobiles, coupled with the spread of paved roads, opened new opportunities for work, but increasingly Americans also looked to the car for fun and adventure. They could rough it in the autocamps that proliferated in the 1920s or unwind in the variety of lodgings that gradually replaced those camps. The road took on some of the trappings of home, offering food and shelter, domestic comforts, and opportunities for social interaction all along the way.

As Steinbeck demonstrated, vehicles sometimes became home, as more Americans became automotive gypsies, living semipermanently in tents, trailers, and motor homes, or in cars, trucks, and buses that had been customized to accommodate beds and other furnishings. The "auto gypsies" at the wheel and in the passenger seats might be retirees touring the country, itinerant businessmen and -women, or, like Steinbeck, captains of leisure and students of American life.

When he needed to relax and find inspiration, mystery novelist Erle Stanley Gardner took to the desert in a "house car," a boxy living space mounted on a car chassis. Cornflake inventor Will Keith Kellogg hit the road in an elegant, buslike house on wheels to learn new things, treat his insomnia, and rest.

Most travelers didn't own a house car or trailer. More and more, they drove their cars during vacation, often for days or weeks at a time, and found places to bed down along the road. The circles of traveling vacationers broadened after World War I, as more working-class white and middle-class black Americans began taking travel vacations, just as upper- and middle-class whites had been doing already. Progressive employers recognized the value of a respite in raising worker morale and productivity. Henry Ford's Detroit plant, for example, gave two weeks' paid vacation to 100,000 workers in 1930. While Pyle's travel routine could hardly be called a vacation, as he constantly faced deadlines, his example of just picking up and going wherever he desired—taking in the sights and enjoying the freedom of the road—served as a template for the American pleasure trip, as did Steinbeck's journeys with a furry black dog.

. . .

The drop in auto prices and availability of easy credit in the 1920s dramatically increased the proportion of working-class Americans who bought cars. Automobile ownership expanded the possibilities of where to go and what to do on vacation. City dwellers could visit the mountains or the seashore, get out to the country or into a different city, or relax at resorts that catered to budgets ranging from extravagant to frugal. With increasing car ownership, driving became a pleasurable part of a vacation.

R. H. Kuhlman, an employee of the National Cash Register Company in Dayton, Ohio, described "An Ideal Vacation" in 1920. It included a three-and-a-half-day drive to Washington, D.C., where he visited the national monuments and the zoo before making a side trip to Baltimore and Annapolis. "This is about the best two weeks' trip that I know of," he wrote. Another NCR worker and his family covered a thousand miles in an auto tour of Ohio and said they had a "dandy" time. So many NCR employees were taking to the road on vacations during the mid-1920s that the company's newsletter included advice about leisure travel.

Ushered in by the 1929 stock market crash, the Great Depression raised unemployment and kept wages low, but many Americans still owned cars and, particularly among the middle and upper classes, still took vacations. In 1936, slightly more than half the respondents to a *Fortune* magazine poll said they intended to go on some kind of vacation that year. Furthermore, the survey found, vacationers aimed "to get as far away as they have time to go, preferably to another part of the country."

Fun-seekers who wanted to enjoy the road as well as the destination could take the legendary Route 66 from Grant Park in Chicago, Illinois, all the way to Santa Monica Boulevard and Ocean Avenue on the California shore. The highway had star status. Postcards, maps, and promotional materials advertised Route 66 as "The Main Street of America." It crossed eight states, often driving right through the center of towns. Steinbeck called 66 the "mother road, the road of flight," as he described its role in the lives and dreams of midwestern migrants in *The Grapes of Wrath*. Route 66 held a grip on the imaginations of job-seekers, who called it the "highway of hope" and saw it as their path to a new start in the West.

But Route 66 was much more. Travelers followed 66 straight into the heartland of America. They drove on 66 into Abraham Lincoln's hometown of Springfield, Illinois; through the land of outlaws and Ozarks; past Missouri's hills and caves and into Kansas grasslands; past cowboys and cattle in Oklahoma and Texas; through spectacular deserts and canyons in New Mexico and Arizona; and, after midsummer 1955, to the most fantastic American destination of them all: Disneyland.

Route 66 was an adventure in American culture. It was Red's Giant Hamburg in Springfield, Missouri. "I would have put 'hamburger,' but I ran out of space," said Sheldon "Red" Chaney, talking about the sign near his roadside stand. Chaney, a former World War II GI, opened up his cafe in a converted gas station and sold "sooper burgers" for 37 years. He parked a Willys jeep in the yard and put a washing machine motor inside it. He attached thin rods to the motor, stuck a foil ball on each rod's end, and set the whole thing spinning to attract attention.

*The promise of groceries, gas, Native American crafts, and supplies for the long road ahead called to motorists at the Great Divide filling station in New Mexico, circa 1940. Route 66, America's main artery from Chicago to southern California, wandered through prairies and deserts where roadside businesses beckoned like oases.*

*"Rides are fair – but the weather is fairer,"
Pete Koltnow wrote his girlfriend in 1950,
in one of a series of postcards from Route
66, above. Koltnow had hitched the same
route in June 1948, when he photographed
Thom O'Connor, left, who had given
Koltnow a ride in his LaSalle convertible.*

Route 66 was the Big Texan Steak Ranch in Amarillo, where dinner consisted of a 72-ounce steak with all the trimmings, priced at ten dollars. Customers could get it for free—if they could eat every bite in an hour.

And Route 66 was El Rancho, a hotel in Gallup, New Mexico, whose guests included Spencer Tracy, Katharine Hepburn, and Humphrey Bogart. Route 66 was also the Wigwam Village, a motor court made of concrete tepees in Holbrook, Arizona. Route 66 was the stovetop heat of the California desert as it gave way to coastal oases, green trees, and cool breezes.

. . .

Route 66—a 2,400-mile-long, 18-foot-wide highway—was born of the dreams of a man from Oklahoma. Amid the mud and muck that plagued his home state's roads in the early years of the 20th century, Cyrus Avery yearned instead for swift, smooth pavement. Born in 1871, Avery had moved to the Midwest from his native Stevensville, Pennsylvania, graduated from college in Missouri, and then settled for good in Tulsa in 1907, the year that Oklahoma gained statehood. Settled relatively late by European Americans, Oklahoma lagged behind the nation in highway development. Avery wanted better roads for his hometown, his state, and his country.

In 1921, Cyrus Avery was elected president of the Associated Highways Associations of America, composed of 42 separate highway organizations. That same year, Avery personally invested in his dreams of bringing more traffic to Oklahoma roads by building 25 tourist cabins, a gas station, and a restaurant outside of Tulsa.

Avery worked himself further into the nation's network of highway agencies. He became Oklahoma's highway commissioner in 1923 and then a leader of the American Association of State Highway Officials in 1924. The association urged U.S. Secretary of Agriculture Howard M. Gore to establish a board of national and state highway officials who would work together and designate a "comprehensive system of through interstate routes" that would have "national significance." Gore designated Avery as a "consulting highway specialist" and assigned him to direct the mapping of the key national highways.

Avery drew a route from Chicago to the Pacific, passing through his beloved Tulsa. The officials assembling the highway system decided to use the now-familiar shield-shaped signs to mark national routes, to use numbers below one hundred for the major roads, and to reserve multiples of ten for the most important east-west highways. Avery wanted his Tulsa route to bear the number 60. When Kentucky and Virginia successfully fought for that number, highway officials from Illinois, Missouri, and Oklahoma met and, in 1926, settled on the number 66 for Avery's route west.

The entire pathway of Route 66 had been laid out by October 1925, although the exact placement of rural pavement came later. Eight hundred miles of the highway had already been paved when the route became official in 1926. The rest still consisted of dirt, gravel, brick, asphalt, and even wooden planks. Most of the hard surfacing began at the ends; the middle sections received the last of the pavement, in 1938.

Even though huge sections were still unpaved, the U.S. 66 Highway Association—formed by Avery and supported by the eight states through which the route traveled—advertised in the *Saturday Evening Post*. In 1932, their ad told readers that by driving Route 66, they would "stay on pavement longest going west." "The Great Diagonal Highway" was the best way to travel to the Los Angeles Olympic Games that summer, read the ad, and it offered more information on the marvelous road by mail. Seven hundred coupons, clipped from the magazine to request information, poured into the association office within a week of publication.

. . .

Though he had vied for a different number, Avery embraced 66. It was easy to remember, and it had a catchy sound when said aloud. According to legend, Phillips Petroleum named its gasoline "Phillips 66" when a company executive realized he was driving 66 miles per hour on Route 66 while heading to a meeting.

Songwriter Bobby Troup immortalized the highway in "Get Your Kicks on Route 66," written during a road trip with his wife, Cynthia, after World War II. As the two of them headed out of St. Louis for California in a green Buick convertible, Cynthia whispered the now-famous line. "God, what a marvelous idea for a song!" Troup said. He took out a map and picked out musical-sounding city names. The lyrics included a traveler's itinerary:

## CARS SHAPE THE CULTURE

### AN AMERICAN JOURNEY

FRANK LLOYD WRIGHT looked at the neighborhood gas station and saw the future. It was only 1931, but the visionary architect already expected that the car would restructure daily life. Wright regularly drove between Wisconsin and Arizona, so he was acquainted with the car culture. He forecast the decline of city cores. Central-ization sprang from the former inefficiency of individual transportation, he told *Popular Mechanics*. The advent of autos cut the umbilical cord to downtown; drivers embraced the decentralized sales of gasoline. Wright wondered: Why couldn't the same distribution system work for food, clothing, and other things?

In fact, such changes were underway. Restaurants were among the first to reinvent themselves for an auto-crazy nation. Movie theaters and shopping centers followed. Cars became dining rooms, entertainment centers, and fun houses—at the expense of the city.

Roadside soda fountains began making deliveries to parked autos after 1910. "You need not get out of your car," a travel writer wrote of the widespread food stands in Florida. "You draw to the kerb, sound your horn, and a white-jacketed, sailor-capped youngster brings you your lunch on a tray that he clamps to the door of your car." More than 100,000 Americans owned roadside stands in the early 1930s, selling everything from orange juice to tamales to potted flowers. Architecture evolved to catch motorists' eyes. Drivers who saw a two-story ice cream cone or a coffee pot as big as a house didn't need to ask what was featured on the menu.

Attractive employees, cheap food, and minimal adult supervision made drive-in restaurants popular with teenagers. They also thronged enclosed shopping malls. The first, Southdale, opened in 1956 near Minneapolis. Visitors drove by car to become pedestrians in an enclosed shopping mall, where they were likely to bump into friends.

Drive-in movies appealed not only to teens seeking independence, but also to parents seeking a cheap family night out. The drive-in theater debuted on June 6, 1933, in Pennsauken Township, New Jersey, just outside Camden. Designer Richard M. Hollingshead, Jr., said his idea "virtually transforms an ordinary motor car into a private theater box.... Here the whole family is welcome." Mom and Dad could watch a movie without dressing up or hiring a babysitter. Kids could wear pajamas and fall asleep in the back seat.

That first night, cars occupied nearly all of the 336 parking spots at the Automobile Movie Theater, coming to see Adolphe Menjou in the 1932 film, *Wife Beware*. The sunset hour dictated starting time, but Hollingshead discovered that if films ended too late, viewers had trouble getting up the next day. The sound was bad, the image distorted at odd viewing angles, and patrons either sweated with their windows up or suffered insect bites with them down. Hollingshead struggled to make a profit and sold the theater after a couple of years. In the 1940s, drive-in theaters began to catch on. America had 95 in 1942. A decade later, 690 drive-in theaters were constructed in a single year.

Not everyone at the drive-in watched the show. Only a few weeks after Hollingshead's theater opened, the *Motion Picture Herald* noted, "Perhaps it will occur readily enough to the reader what fun Young America could have in a coupe under the added stimulation of a sophisticated romance." The managerial instruction manual for one drive-in chain urged regular patrols to "prevent any sort of misconduct."

Drive-in theaters declined in later decades, thanks in part to smaller cars, which made hours of sitting and viewing uncomfortable. Television—that most decentralized entertainment medium—contributed to the demise of the drive-in theater as well. With it, people could view movies without ever leaving their living rooms.

CARS SPREAD OUT LIKE A FAN BEFORE THE SCREEN OF AN OPEN-AIR THEATER ON U.S. 1 NEAR ALEXANDRIA, VIRGINIA, IN 1941. DESCRIBING THE DRIVE-IN PHENOMENON, A NATIONAL GEOGRAPHIC WRITER SAID, "THE CARS' FRONT WHEELS ARE SLIGHTLY RAISED, SO THE NATURAL SIGHT-LINE OF PATRONS MEETS THE CENTER OF THE SCREEN."

*Now you go through Saint Looey; Joplin, Missouri;*
*And Oklahoma City is mighty pretty;*
*You'll see Amarillo; Gallup, New Mexico;*
*Flagstaff, Arizona; Don't forget Winona,*
*Kingman, Barstow, San Bernardino.*
*Won't you get hip to this timely tip:*
*When you make that California trip*
*Get your kicks on Route Sixty-Six!*

When Troup finished the song in Los Angeles, he pitched it to Nat "King" Cole. The public loved Cole's 1946 bluesy pop version. The song resonated with many who traveled, or who hoped to travel, Route 66. The income from record sales allowed the Troups to buy a house in California.

· · ·

Four young women who worked for the phone company in Rochester, New York, took a cross-country trip in 1947, making sure they got some kicks of their own on Route 66. Mary Jane Pecora and Caroline Millbank each owned a car, and both drove, carrying passengers Janet McDonnel and Ethel May Krockenberger. Ethel packed with great expectations, tucking her mink stole into her monogrammed luggage, lined with blue satin.

The trip had its small adventures, especially after they got onto 66. The front tires of Millbank's car blew out as they crossed some railroad tracks in Missouri. While waiting for repairs, the women visited Meramec Caverns in Stanton, a popular tourist haunt that billed itself as the "Greatest Show Under the Earth." The travelers joined a wedding celebration at a restaurant in Arizona. Morning skies

over Flagstaff took their breath away: bright blue contrasting with fresh, white snowfall. All arrived safely at the Millbank family house in Hermosa Beach, California, on Thanksgiving Day. They preserved their memories of the trip through photographs, including one of every sign that marked their crossing a state line.

Peter Koltnow, a civil engineering major at Antioch College in Ohio—who would go on to become president of the Highway Users Federation—hitchhiked on Route 66, once in 1948 and again two years later. The first trip took him, at age 19, from New York to Los Angeles. For the second trip, Koltnow thumbed his way to a Bureau of Reclamation job in Yuma, Arizona. In a series of June and July 1950 postcards to his girlfriend, Dot, who was to become his wife, he described adventures that included a frighteningly fast trip through the Ozarks—"but 900 miles in 21 hours is good." Drivers seemed saner when the roads got straighter in the flatlands, he wrote.

Koltnow found the roadside roulette of hitchhiking unpredictable. He waited for five hours in Victorville, California, before a driver picked him up. Usually, however, he could get a ride in less than half an hour, and the drivers were pleasant enough. "Nice people pick you up," he recalled. "The nicest people were in Oklahoma. Salt of the earth! [But] I had the hardest time getting a ride in Texas."

His scariest moment occurred after he got into a car on Route 66 west of Albuquerque. The car's driver decided to pass a Dodge while going uphill. As he slowly did so, a big truck appeared over the crest and bore down on them. Koltnow's driver jerked the wheel at the last moment, to avoid a head-on collision.

"In my mind's eye I can remember seeing the rust pits in the chrome of the truck," Koltnow said. Petrified, the pair carried on in silence for two hours, then the driver said, "That was close, wasn't it?" To Koltnow's surprise, the driver turned out to be a Catholic priest in everyday clothes.

. . .

Early highway travelers had limited choices about where to spend the night. After World War I, autocamping was the simplest way, but it made for quite a primitive adventure. Autocamping enthusiasts usually carried their own tents and blankets, their own food, and the means to prepare it. They parked in schoolyards, along the edges of roadways, in farmers' pastures, and in parks and forests.

During the 1920s, millions of Americans touted this "auto gypsy" lifestyle, simple and close to nature. Now more families could take vacations, avoiding the high cost of hotels. In reality, autocamping merely transferred domestic chores from the convenience of the home to the open air, with much of the labor falling on wives and mothers, who still were expected to cook and clean.

Autocamping attracted all kinds of vehicle owners from all rungs of the social ladder. Writer Elon Jessup, discussing the rise of autocamping in 1921, hailed it as "the most democratic sport in America," because "everybody plays the game." Millionaire Cornelius Vanderbilt, Jr., enjoyed autocamping that year, too, and said he "brushed shoulders with every type of humanity imaginable."

Another upper-crust motor traveler, Vermont writer Frederic Van de Water, chatted with a Maryland naval officer, an Ohio school principal, a Brooklyn photoengraver, and three Montana cowboys around a campfire in Yellowstone National Park. Visitors to Yellowstone and other parks often had no choice but to camp, since the number of hotel rooms proved inadequate for the rush of tourists. Of the 98,225 visitors to Yellowstone in 1922, more than half stayed overnight. Of those, 1,500 stayed in hotels, and nearly 50,000 fended for themselves.

Van de Water hailed those who chose autocamping: To him, they embodied America's melting pot ideal. He thought camping could reduce sectionalism and bring together people who otherwise might never meet. There was a grain of truth to such generalizations. American autocamping blended the rich, the poor, and every class in between, people from city and country, people from every region. With a few notable exceptions, campers left their social status behind and treated their autocamping neighbors as equals.

. . .

It may have appeared that new cross-country travel opportunities could help ease the class, race, and regional differences threatening the American

*A 1934 Trav-L-Coach trailer was named "Old Faithful" for its decades of service to Virginia and Rudolph Cate, upper right, and their parents, Eben and Vernie, who drove it to Maine every summer. "Auto gypsying" grew popular in the 1920s and '30s, as free spirits lived in trailers, house cars, and tents like that of the couple in Florida, lower right.*

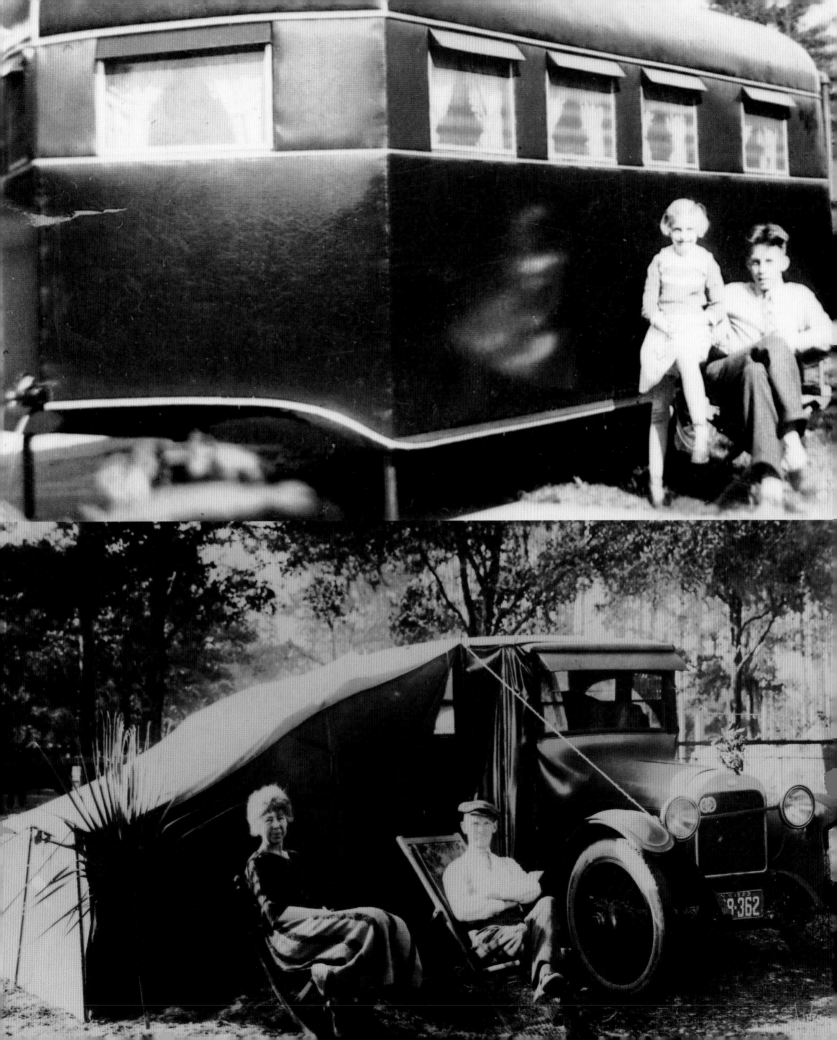

dream. In the 1960s, Steinbeck found a measure of highway egalitarianism in roadside camping. Through the mid-20th century, though, the freedom of the open road did not guarantee full rights for everyone. African Americans and other minorities were excluded from many public accommodations. Migrants and the destitute alienated many autocampers and were seldom fully welcomed among them. Owners of the most expensive house cars often took advantage of their self-contained lodgings, shut their doors, and sealed out their neighbors.

Alongside autocamping, literally, came the spread of roadside garbage. Tin cans, cheese rinds, and other autocamp trash marked the Lincoln Highway across Nevada as effectively as the red, white, and blue highway signs, one traveler observed. The *Saturday Evening Post* said highways were becoming "trails of trash and swill." To entice campers away from the roadside and reduce conflicts with private landowners, cities began opening free municipal campgrounds.

Waterloo, Wisconsin, established what may have been the first such camp in 1920. Typical camps in small towns offered lights, laundry tubs, and a few other amenities. Potable water was free, although health inspectors' surveys in the mid-1920s found a high percentage of camp water unfit for drinking. Cities hoped that campers would spend money in town, but penny-pinching autocampers rarely offset the expenses of running the camps. Most people camping in Boston, for example, spent less than a dollar a day, and most of that went for gas. Camps started charging visitor fees,

typically 50 cents. Fees and time limits on stays also served to screen out migrants.

Fees created competition among the municipal camps and opened the door to private enterprise. Once drivers paid for accommodations, they looked carefully at what they got for their money. Private operators lured them with gas stations, improved campsites, and cabins. Private homes started sprouting signs that read "Tourists Accommodated." About a thousand tourist homes operated in 1935 in Richmond, Virginia, alone.

But the cabin camps of the West overwhelmed the room-to-rent phenomenon of the East. *Architectural Digest* reported in 1933 that the building of cabin camps was a rare "booming" sector of the economy during the Great Depression. Cabin camps numbered about 5,000 in 1927 and more than tripled in the next eight years. Most charged one dollar per person per night. As more travelers stayed in cabins, the autocamps lost their appeal. Then the Depression altered the demographics. Vacationers still camped, but so did desperate job-seekers. By the mid-1930s, nearly all municipal camps had closed, and new laws prevented roadside camping.

In the 1930s, diehard auto gypsies had discovered the new alternative: the trailer. "We can travel deluxe on a couple of bucks in back of the family car," proclaimed the 1937 song "Our Little Home on the Highway (The Trailer Song)." That year the house-trailer industry hailed itself as the fastest-growing business in America. The Covered Wagon Company began producing travel trailers in Detroit in 1929, after founder Arthur Sherman got soaked in a tent trailer during a camping trip. Sherman exhibited a prototype at the Detroit Automobile Show in January 1930. In 1936, after a move to Mount Clemens, Michigan, his company was mass-producing a thousand units a month. By the end of the decade, the business had expanded to include 76 distributors selling tens of thousands of wheeled homes every year. More than 300 competing manufacturers, including Pierce-Arrow, crowded the field. Americans hit the road in 300,000 trailers in 1936.

One of those Americans was Eben Cate, a rural mail carrier from Lakeport, New Hampshire. Cate fell in love with a two-year-old, 18-foot-long Trav-L-Coach in a showroom and bought it in October 1936 for $650, intending to take his wife and two children on pleasure trips. The post office gave Cate two weeks' vacation a year. Every summer in the late 1930s and early 1940s, the Cate family climbed into their Chevrolet and pulled that trailer to York Beach, Maine, to spend those two weeks near the ocean. The insulated trailer had electric lights, beds, a kitchen, a gas stove, and monk's cloth curtains. The Cates added a toaster, old silverware from the house, and board games such as Monopoly and checkers. The trailer stayed in the family for nearly half a century, earning the nickname "Old Faithful."

. . .

At about the same time that the Cates hauled Old Faithful down the road, the family of J. N. "Ding" Darling, editorial cartoonist for the *Des Moines Register,* was taking trips in "Bouncing Betsy." Like many Americans lured by the freedom of the road, Darling reasoned that a trailer "could take us

anywhere we wanted to go on land without benefit of railroad tickets, hotels, or timetables. It must be something like having a private car and a pass on all the railroads." His wife objected to any attempts to make her porter, cook, steward, dishwasher, engineer, or conductor. Thus forewarned, the Darlings set out for a winter vacation in Florida.

Difficulties arose on the journey southward. Cargo shot out of cabinets and rolled on the floor until Darling and his wife figured out the best way to secure it. At first they had trouble finding free places to park for the night. Once in the South, though, they found camps where they could stay, and the Darlings joined the informal fraternity of trailer folk on Southern roads.

In Florida at last, Darling wrote, "It was GRAND. Nearly every center of population we passed through had an elaborate trailer camp where the trailer traveler could rent for a modest fee space for their caravan by the day, week or month. Electric current, water and sewer connections were available for each individual parking lot. Some old residenters had landscaped their front yards, canopied their entrance and suspended flower boxes from their trailer windows. But for the most part a trailer city looks like a huge herd of blue, pink and green elephants lying down, closely packed, and giving the suggestion that they might get up and stampede at any moment."

Trailers mimicked the interior of a home, but they could not fully duplicate it. The beds were seldom as good, and the living space was much smaller. If the trailer even had a bathroom, taking a shower might mean sprinkling from a hot-water bottle while

standing over a drain. Author Howard Vincent O'Brien said of his travels in 1936 that cramped trailer life was "distinctly on the nudist side" and likely to remove inhibitions in those traveling in groups.

. . .

Highway travelers could also take the bus. Intercity bus lines evolved out of private jitneys, which carried passengers without fixed routes or times. In 1914, Model T driver L. P. Draper picked up people at Los Angeles trolley stops and dropped them off at their request, several blocks down the road. He charged them a "jitney," slang for a nickel. The idea caught on, and by the following year, hundreds of jitney services operating throughout America were cutting into trolley business. By the mid-1920s, though, burdened by government regulations, jitneys had all but vanished.

At about the same time, a group of entrepreneurs in northern Minnesota formed the Mesaba Transportation Company. They needed ways to transport workers, and other passengers if they wished, among the mining towns of the Iron Mountains. Building on early success, the company poured its profits into buying larger vehicles and expanding the region it served. During the 1920s, mergers and restructurings built Mesaba into a huge interstate operation. The company decided it needed a new name to reflect its larger operations. It settled on the image of a sleek and swift racing dog, a greyhound, for its corporate name and logo.

Between 1929 and 1932, more than one thousand bus companies went under. Greyhound and its rivals survived by reducing operating costs and attracting new riders. To encourage bus trips to the Chicago World's Fair of 1933-34, they orchestrated a mass media campaign that included scenes from the motion picture, *It Happened One Night*.

Director Frank Capra had based the film on "Night Bus," a Samuel Hopkins Adams short story printed in *Cosmopolitan* magazine. The two main characters, a snobbish runaway heiress and a hardboiled newspaperman, meet and fall in love on a bus trip. Romantic and comedic sparks flew between Clark Gable and Claudette Colbert in the 1934 movie, which showed buses in a new light. Sexual suggestiveness in a cabin camp scene didn't hurt, either. The Greyhound–World's Fair promotional partnership netted more than half a million dollars in profit, earned in part by the hordes of fairgoers who paid a dime to ride the bus through the fairgrounds.

. . .

As cabin camp owners competed for business, they reached for the trappings of hotels, still retaining informality and roadside locations. Fanciful architecture sometimes boosted their curb appeal. Log cabins, wigwams, and colonial or Spanish exteriors beckoned the weary travelers. One entrepreneur coined a new word for the highway homes away from home, and it stuck.

Architect and developer Arthur S. Heineman

*A General Motors "First Streamliner" bus, left, exits a St. Louis Greyhound depot in 1932. Greyhound, which began as the Mesaba Transportation Company in the 1920s, survived the Depression while many rivals shut down. Low fares proved attractive, especially later, during World War II. An ad circa 1943, inset, hailed the All American Bus Lines as "America's Most Economical Trans-Continental Travel Service."*

This classic Indian motorcycle with a Princess sidecar was manufactured in 1923. Bicycle racer George Hendee and engineer Carl Hedstrom founded their company with the mission to build the first "motor-driven bicycle for everyday use." They produced Indian motorcycles from 1901 to 1953, styling various models for gentlemen riders, police officers, and thrill-seekers.

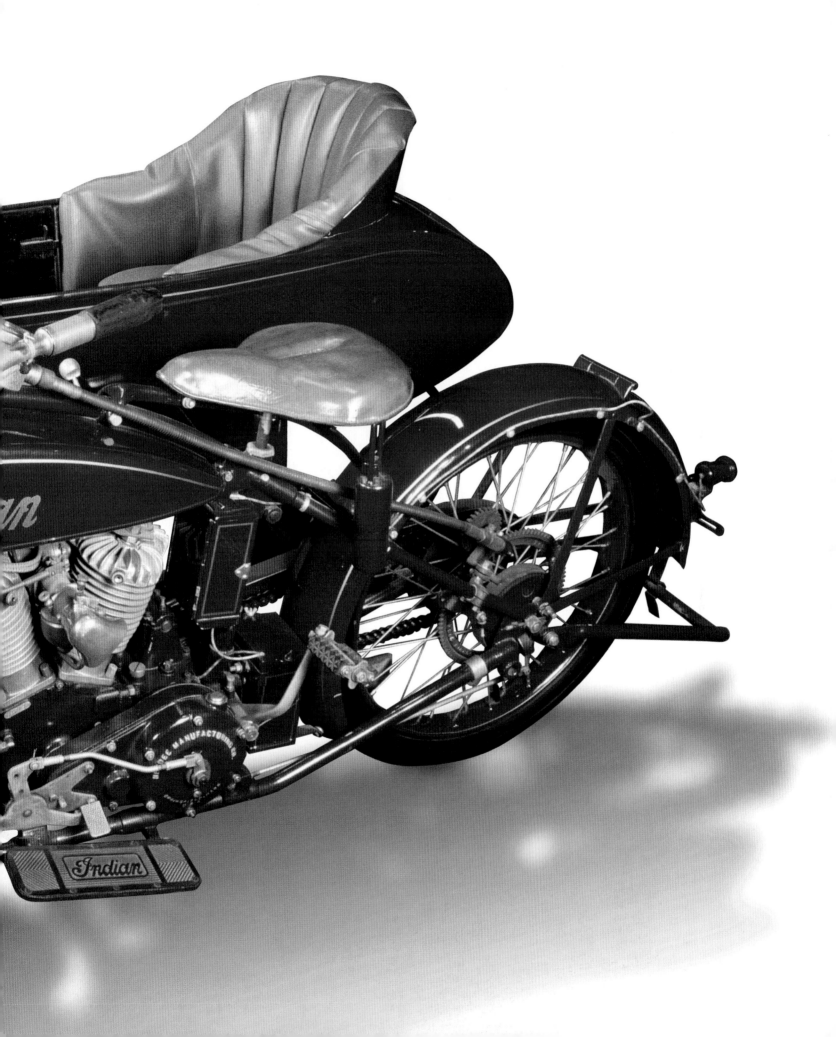

PENNANT HOTELS
at Rolla and
Columbia, Mo.

PENNANT TERMINALS
Des Peres, Mo., U. S. 66
Rolla, Mo., U. S. 66
Miami, Okla., U. S. 66
Springfield, Mo., U. S. 66
Tulsa, Okla., U. S. 66
Columbia, Mo., U. S. 40

A COMPLETE PENNANT TERMINAL

DRIVE IN

# ALAMO PLAZA HOTEL COURTS

Over 600 Rooms and Apartments In 10 Courts In 6 States

WACO, TYLER, AND BEAUMONT, TEXAS

SHREVEPORT, LA.              OKLA. CITY, OKLA., JACKSON, MISS.              LITTLE ROCK, ARK.
MEMPHIS, TENN.                       BATON ROUGE, LA.                       NEW ORLEANS, LA.

opened the Milestone Mo-tel in December 1925 on Highway 101 in San Luis Obispo, roughly halfway between Los Angeles and San Francisco. It had the look of a Spanish mission, with tile roofs and a three-tiered bell tower. Waitresses wore satin vests and big-brimmed hats. *Ristras,* or decorative bunches of red peppers, accented the theme. Heineman hoped to build a chain of Milestones from San Diego to Seattle, 200 miles apart from each other, but he only finished the prototype.

More successful was the word he coined for his enterprise—Mo-tel—created by combining "motor" and "hotel." The hyphen quickly evaporated, and the word "motel" soon applied to any lodging designed for travelers that lacked the large, formal spaces of traditional hotels, such as ballrooms, but was larger and more elaborate than a cabin camp.

Motels offered a toilet and shower in most rooms. They tended to stand by the edge of a highway instead of downtown, and they were usually composed of several small, single-story buildings instead of a high-rise structure. Distinctions blurred during the 1950s and 1960s, as motels evolved and became even larger and more fancy.

Motel owners formed two types of chains. The referral chain grouped independent owners into associations that recommended lodgings, a plan that arose out of practices already in place in the trade. Travel bureaus and auto clubs had given out seals of approval since 1909. Two decades later, independent cabin owners allied to put official-looking referral seals on their signs and advertisements, proclaiming standards of quality. They also printed brochures with lists of fellow association members.

The second, the franchised chain, constructed identical lodgings in many locations, assuming that motorists who liked one would like all motels built like it. Franchised chains, which grew to include Holiday Inns and Best Westerns, began humbly in Texas. Voters in McClennan County approved matching funds for state and federal highway dollars in 1928. More roads meant more motel locations and business opportunities.

Eight concrete roads were planned, radiating out from the county seat of Waco like the spokes of a wheel. Auto dealer Edgar Torrance and his friend, Judge Drummond W. Bartlett, decided to take advantage of the new connections by opening a building with 24 tourist apartments on the east side of town. They would be classier than cabins, the two entrepreneurs decided, built around a common yard and screened from road noise.

Torrance and Bartlett opened the first Alamo Plaza Tourist Court in 1929. It looked like a miniature of the Alamo. They kept building more, and this first successful franchise chain grew to 34 motels across the South and Southwest. By the early 1960s, a growing system of federally funded interstate highways—and competition from new motel

*Images decorated a promotional fan in the late 1920s, upper left, portraying the luxurious hotels and "Pennant Terminals" of the Pierce Petroleum Company. Although the company dreamed of opening hotels every 150 miles from New York to San Francisco, only five were built. A more successful chain, Alamo Plaza, lower left, began in Waco, Texas, in 1929, and grew to 34 hotels by 1960.*

chains—took their toll on Alamo Plazas. The number of motels nationwide peaked around 61,000, and other chains grew to dominate the field.

The appeal of an Alamo Plaza was that it mixed comfort, affordability, and a touch of class. "Catering to Those Who Care," crowed the newspaper advertisement for an Alamo Plaza Hotel Court that opened in 1941 in Baton Rouge. "Telephone in Every Room. Simmons Furniture Thru-out. Hot and Cold Water. Radio in Every Room." Room rates began at a dollar for a single. For that, the customer got a carpeted bedroom and a tiled bathroom. Black maids and porters, considered a sign of prestige, served the guests—although they or their relatives could not rent rooms there, or in any Alamo Plaza.

Racial segregation ruled in much of the country. Southern blacks moved north in large numbers during the second decade of the 20th century. Racial tensions developed into violence in 25 cities, peaking in 1919. The clash over public spaces fueled many race riots. In Chicago that summer, for example, a black youth stepped over an invisible line in the sand and entered a portion of beach reserved for whites only. Angry whites drowned the boy. Racial and ethnic tensions boiled over as immigrants and minorities sought the good life that America promised but found themselves denied equal rights and opportunities.

Henry Ford believed that the automobile solved racial problems, since it promised his fellow whites a way to escape the "antagonistic, competitive, mutually exclusive" ethnic mix building in America's cities. "We shall solve the City Problem by leaving the City," Ford said in a famous declaration.

He urged Americans to seek out communities where residents knew their neighbors and shared a "commonality of interest."

But for African Americans, the automobile did not represent such an easy answer. They could not drive away from their problems. Many found it hard to buy auto insurance in the 1920s and 1930s, because white-owned insurance companies considered black drivers to be bad risks. Even if black travelers could afford all of the costs of leisure travel, they could not be sure of their reception on the road.

"The white New Yorker ... may choose from a thousand different places the one to which he will go with his family," a writer stated in 1912 in *Crisis,* the magazine of the National Association for the Advancement of Colored People (NAACP). "He has but to choose and pay his board. But you, if you are colored, will knock in vain at the farmhouse door for board and lodging."

Motels and hotels could be just as inhospitable. Even the park superintendents at a National Park Service Conference at Yosemite in 1922 discouraged blacks from overnight visits because "the parks have no facilities for taking care of them." Dr. T. Price Hurst, a black motorist and Harvard-educated physician driving from Montreal in 1932, sued the Prince George Hotel in New York City for refusing him a room he had reserved. He won $400 damages, but it was not until the courts upheld the Civil Rights Act of 1964 that hotel and motel discrimination ended.

In the meantime, black travelers either risked humiliation when trying to get a room for the night, or they relied on guidebooks that pointed them to friendly restaurants, motels, and resorts. In 1936, travel agent Victor H. Green began selling *The Negro Motorist Green-Book* in New York City. He established nationwide distribution with the 1937 edition.

Green said he aimed to give black travelers information that would keep them from "difficulties" and "embarrassments." Organized alphabetically by state, the book listed tourist homes, hotels, trailer parks, restaurants, and even barber shops and beauty parlors that accepted black patrons. Green provided advice about highways as they opened and counseled drivers on how to improve their gas mileage and avoid accidents as well.

Several resorts catering to middle-class blacks prospered in segregated times. W. E. B. DuBois favored the cottages at Idlewild in northern Michigan, which opened for business in 1915. Guests flocked to boardinghouses in Newport, Rhode Island, run by fellow African Americans. Highland Beach, Maryland, offered beaches, tennis courts, and cottages for the wealthiest of black visitors. Jews opened their own resorts as well, particularly in the Catskill Mountains, located conveniently for the large Jewish communities in New York City.

Public transportation was just as segregated. Jim Crow rules relegated blacks to second-class train cars in the South from the late 19th century on. Dr. Charlotte Hawkins Brown, an African-American teacher, Massachusetts-educated, and the founder of the Palmer Memorial Institute in Sedalia, North Carolina, made it a habit of paying for a Pullman berth every time she traveled, knowing full well that

*Beginning in 1936, the annual* Negro Motorist Green-Book *listed restaurants, lodgings, and other businesses that welcomed African-American travelers. A happy purchaser told Victor H. Green, the guide's originator and publisher, that it would prove to "mean as much if not more to us as the AAA means to the white race."*

they were reserved for whites only. She slept in a Pullman car in 1920 while en route to speak at the white Woman's Missionary Convention in Memphis.

As the train traveled through Alabama, a dozen white men threatened her and marched her back to the Jim Crow car. Brown moved to the day coach for black passengers, walking past white women who were going to the same destination as she was—a convention whose goals included making "Negro women unashamed and unafraid." When Brown underwent a similar removal to the Jim Crow car in 1936, white women on the train protested, but the railroad company turned a deaf ear.

Southern train stations and bus depots had racially separate waiting rooms, dining rooms, drinking fountains, and bathrooms. In the Southern Railway station in Salisbury, North Carolina, whites enjoyed a much larger waiting room. Blueprints for the station underscored the inequality of the arrangements, naming the room for white women a "Ladies Parlor" and vestibule but labeling the black counterpart simply "Colored Women." At the railroad service shops in nearby Spencer, where workers transferred freight and repaired locomotives for Southern Railway, water fountains and locker rooms stayed segregated until the late 1950s. Black workers

*Activists fought segregation on many fronts in the 1940s and '50s. Clockwise from upper left: A 1944 Detroit parade calls for the death of Jim Crow rules; marchers protest school segregation in 1947; signs divide the races at a Memphis bus terminal in 1943; and Rosa Parks rides an integrated bus in Montgomery, Alabama, in 1956, after a yearlong boycott, sparked when she was arrested for refusing to give up her bus seat to a white man.*

were expected to use the back door to enter and exit a restaurant in town.

The Supreme Court's 1892 ruling in the railroad case of *Plessy* v. *Ferguson* had legalized the doctrine of "separate but equal" in all public venues. Fittingly, legal challenges to segregated public transportation helped bring an end to that doctrine. Congress had laid the foundation in 1887 with the Interstate Commerce Act, which banned discrimination on trains, but the ruling in *Plessy* v. *Ferguson* left that act with no teeth for settling segregation complaints. In 1935, a new federal law, the Motor Carrier Act, used nearly the same language as the Interstate Commerce Act and banned discrimination on interstate buses.

In America's changing social climate after World War II, new legal challenges to racial segregation invoked both laws. In 1953, the National Association for the Advancement of Colored People (NAACP) launched an attack on segregation in rail travel by filing suit with the Interstate Commerce Commission (ICC). It accused 12 Southern railroads of segregating black and white passengers, in violation of the law and the Constitution.

Sarah Keys, a member of the Women's Army Corps, brought a similar suit against the interstate bus industry after she refused to move to the blacks-only section of an interstate bus traveling through North Carolina. In the same month that the ICC heard Keys's complaint, May 1954, the Supreme Court dismantled the doctrine of separate but equal for public schools in its landmark *Brown* v. *Board of Education* decision. The ICC joined the civil rights bandwagon in November 1955, concluding that segregation on interstate trains and buses, as well as in the public waiting rooms of train stations and bus depots, violated federal law.

While the ruling said nothing about transit systems that did not cross state borders, activist organizations sprang up in southern states to challenge local segregation laws. On December 1, 1955, Rosa Parks, a 43-year-old black seamstress who had once worked as a secretary for the Montgomery chapter of the NAACP, refused to give up her seat to a white man on a crowded bus in Montgomery, Alabama. Police arrested her and took her to the city jail, where she was booked for violating the law against integration. Black citizens organized a bus boycott that began on Monday, December 5, and lasted for 381 days. To manage the protest, they formed the Montgomery Improvement Association (MIA) and elected as its president a little-known 26-year-old minister named Martin Luther King, Jr.

During the long boycott, the MIA helped organize car pools and encouraged walking as an alternative to driving. Walkers took inspiration from an elderly woman known as Mother Pollard. When a minister urged her to drop out of the boycott because of her advanced age, she refused, telling him, "My feets is tired, but my soul is rested."

Counsel for the MIA filed suit in 1956, challenging state and local bus segregation laws. The United States Supreme Court's November 1956 ruling on the case, known as *Browder* v. *Gayle,* dissolved the Jim Crow laws that had separated blacks and whites for 60 years. On the morning after the court decision, four men boarded a Montgomery bus and sat in the front seats, formerly reserved for whites only. They were Martin Luther King, Jr.; his friend, Ralph Abernathy; a white minister, Glenn Smiley; and a Pullman porter and community leader, E. D. Nixon. Their action signaled an end to the bus boycott that had divided the city and crippled the bus company.

It would take another decade of civil rights agitation before public accommodations across America were to become color-blind. Diehard white segregationists defied integration laws. Civil rights advocates responded with more boycotts and demonstrations, and the ICC and Justice Department enforced the law. By June 1963, the Justice Department reported that it knew of no segregation by any air, rail, or bus facility, not even in the Deep South. In the next few years, the ICC learned of sporadic violations by individual employees of transit companies, but even those died out.

Meanwhile, blacks and whites accustomed themselves to a racially mixed nation. Some had to take the process slowly. "When you've been under wraps for years, you don't suddenly get out of bed and try a 100-yard dash," a Virginia NAACP official said. Each city, region, and state had to find its own path, but integration on buses and trains eventually occurred nationwide.

As restrictions and barriers fell, the freedom of travel took on new meaning. No longer did it just symbolize the exhilaration of the open road, but also the expanded liberties of all who traveled on it.

SIXTY-SIX WAS STILL A NARROW TWO-LANE HIGHWAY
HARRY TRUMAN WAS THE MAN WHO RAN THE SHOW
THE BAD KOREAN WAR WAS JUST BEGINNING
AND I WAS JUST THREE YEARS TOO YOUNG TO GO
COUNTRY MUSIC HADN'T GONE TO NEW YORK CITY YET
AND A SERVICE MAN WAS PROUD OF WHAT HE'D DONE
HANK AND LEFTY CROWDED EV'RY JUKEBOX
THAT'S THE WAY IT WAS IN FIFTY-ONE.

— *Merle Haggard, "The Way It Was in '51"*

# SUBURBIA
## EXPLODES

Despite war restrictions, America's living standard is still the world's best —— thanks to U.S. industrial progress.

*As World War II drew to a close, Americans were ready for the good life. Opposite, clockwise from top left: GIs in New York celebrate victory in Europe with embraces, May 1945; Wall Street workers cheer the end of war; infantrymen head home on a French train, January 1946; troops arrive home on the* Queen Mary. *The war was hard on civilians, too, and posters, above, promised a brighter future.*

When the war in Europe ended on May 8th, 1945, after nearly six years of fighting, jubilant European crowds celebrated on home soil. American celebrations were more muted. The country was still reeling after the sudden death of President Franklin Delano Roosevelt less than a month before. As many as 200,000 people participated in "gay scenes of cheering and dancing in the streets of New York," but the *Washington Post* reported that "a feeling of 'one war down—one to go' yesterday quelled almost all signs of official VE-Day celebrations in the Nation's Capital." The Pacific war unofficially came to an end three months later, on August 15, 1945, about a week after President Harry S. Truman approved the Army plan to drop atomic bombs on the Japanese cities of Hiroshima and Nagasaki, decimating the cities' populations and buildings.

With victory finally achieved, Americans celebrated roundly. Around the nation, crowds came together in cities and towns to mark the end of the bloodiest conflict in world history. President Truman gave federal workers two days off with pay to thank them for their war efforts. An estimated 1.2 million people piled into New York's Times Square. In Boston, the *Christian Science Monitor* reported, "a long pent-up populace went wild the moment the first definite word of peace came over the radio from Washington.... Automobiles, jammed to their running boards with cheering, joyous throngs, streamed into the downtown area from every outlying suburb, their horns honking joyously, and cowbells and other noise-makers adding to the din." Just after the news broke, the nation's telephone

**225**

switchboards were jammed as people around the country placed millions of calls.

Life on the American home front during the Second World War had been difficult. Ordinary Americans across the nation had been coping for years with the side effects of a massive military undertaking. Rubber and gasoline rationing seemed to change almost every daily routine, even church: In 1943, attendance at Easter Sunday dawn services around the New York area dropped by half compared to that of years before. Women started carpooling to the grocery store. Rationing was so much on everyone's mind that the *Washington Post* mentioned it in a weather report. Unseasonably warm weather predicted in December 1943 would make for "a nice Sunday for a long drive in the country if it weren't for tire and gasoline rationing."

Gasoline and tires had been just the tip of the rationing iceberg. Fuel oil and food were also in short supply. Fuel oil was rationed, making winters difficult for the one-sixth of the nation who used it to heat their homes. Food was rationed as well: Sugar, meat, butter, coffee, and cheese were all in limited supply. Of the day before coffee rationing first went into effect, in 1942, the *New York Times* reported, "Housewives throughout the metropolitan area swooped down yesterday upon grocers, most of whom had little coffee even at the start of the last day, in an attempt to get enough coffee to carry them through the retail sales drought. Many, though they pleaded and threatened, went home empty handed."

Women were to consider preparing nutritious family meals a patriotic act: As *Good Housekeeping*

magazine editors told readers in 1943, "Food fights for freedom! That's not just a slogan.... You and your kitchen have a big job to do. And a proud one, too." Housewives all over the country referred to cookbooks like *300 Sugar Saving Recipes, Meatless Meals,* and *Cooking on a Ration: Food is Still Fun.* According to an April 1943 Gallup Poll, American families missed meat and coffee more than they missed unlimited gasoline.

That may have been because, despite the inconvenience to car owners, there were transportation alternatives. As rationing went into effect, urban public transportation systems experienced a renaissance. Americans in the cities either walked or went back to using their city's public transit systems to get to work. In Washington, D.C., when all the city's gas stations were closed—which meant buses and taxis were restricted—electric trolleys kept on running. City and suburban buses carried millions more passengers than they had before the war. By 1943, the Associated Press reported that "American bus, streetcar and rapid transit lines are carrying passengers at a rate of almost double 1934, but with slightly less than the total equipment capacity they had then."

In order to cope with the extra demand, some abandoned rail lines were brought back into service. Old rolling stock was kept on the streets. Trucks that had hauled cars to dealers before the war were converted to carry people instead. Thousands of school buses were drafted into performing double duty, transporting military personnel and war workers when they were not carrying children to and from

Women assemble the tail fins of a
Liberator bomber, above, in an aircraft
plant in Downey, California, in 1944.
Female workers supported the war
by helping to manufacture planes, bombs,
and other equipment. Some claimed
women excelled at riveting because it was
like doing needlework in metals.

school. Firms like the Washington, D.C., Capital Transit Company spent more money and parked their buses downtown, instead of on the city's fringe, to save gasoline and rubber. Buses stopped at fewer places along the lines to save gas and wear and tear on the tires. For a while, judging by the crowds of people using the systems, the future looked bright for transit. But vehicles were deteriorating and materials to build new buses, trolleys, and passenger railcars were scarce. The wartime resurgence in public transit turned out to be a temporary phenomenon.

World War II had also caused a housing crunch. America's construction industry had already tapered off in the 1930s, since it was one of the businesses hit hardest in the Depression. During World War II, construction ground to a standstill. The timing was bad. Residential needs during war were so different. The housing that was available was often in the wrong places. Hundreds of thousands of people moved to work in war factories in cities like Portland, Oregon; Richmond, California; Alexandria, Virginia; and Paterson, New Jersey. But existing housing could not meet the demand. The government tried to intervene, setting up temporary trailer parks and prefabricated housing to help alleviate the problems. People doubled up with their friends and family members and generally made do.

Despite all the day-to-day difficulties, war helped the nation's economy, solved unemployment problems experienced since the Crash of 1929, and pulled the nation out of the crippling Great Depression. As early as 1939, an army of American men and women went to work to feed the Allied war effort. Roosevelt's Lend-Lease program, signed into law in March 1941, focused American productivity toward the war effort and put people to work making planes and equipment for the Allied forces. After Pearl Harbor and the U.S. entry into the war in 1941, the home front economy geared up. Masses of new soldiers trained, then traveled and fought in the European and Pacific theaters, and unemployment fell nearly to zero.

After a decade of high unemployment—at the height of the Depression, one in four Americans was out of work—American businesses desperately needed workers during the war. Opportunities increased for African Americans, who joined industry in large numbers. Millions of women went to work in industry as well, encouraged by government and industry to consider heavy machine work as an extension of their domestic duties. A newsreel called *Glamour Girls of 43* showed women operating heavy machinery. "After a short apprenticeship, this woman can operate a drill press just as easily as a juice extractor in her own kitchen," declared the voice-over. "And a lathe will hold no more terrors for her than an electric washing machine."

.  .  .

Americans adapted to wartime, but with the sense that their sacrifices would be temporary. When the war ended, they celebrated, but they also felt anxious. They knew the future would be different from the prewar past—but how different? What would happen to the economy without the boosts of wartime demands? Americans who remembered World War I, and those who knew about the war

profiteering that had followed it, wondered whether the nation would plunge into another depression. What did the postwar era hold for American war workers and American soldiers?

On August 17, 1945, three days after the Japanesse announced their intention to cease hostilities, the *Wall Street Journal* reported that Detroit automakers would lay off 300,000 workers. That same day, the Army sent out "more than five thousand telegrams canceling millions of dollars in contracts on 168 different textile items." One hundred thousand workers were laid off in the New York–New Jersey area, reported the *New York Times,* and "the sudden transition to peace meant for them the loss of their jobs, either temporarily or permanently." On the West Coast, the situation would turn out even more bleakly for cities like Portland, which had grown exponentially to fill wartime needs. Half a million people lost their jobs on the Pacific Coast in the seven months after the Japanese surrender on September 2, 1945.

In the bigger picture, though, the United States suffered neither massive inflation, nor unemployment, nor economic collapse after World War II. In the immediate aftermath of the war, industries did close their doors. Many of the women who had been working in war industries were pushed out of their jobs. But after the initial adjustment period, a spirit of optimism and prosperity began to take hold throughout much of the nation. Spending skyrocketed. Americans had earned money while working hard during the war, but they had had very little to spend it on. Now consumers bought refrigerators, toasters, televisions, radios.

And they bought cars and houses—in record numbers. During the Depression and the war, on average, about one hundred thousand new homes were built each year. After the war, construction started up again to meet the demand for new housing—and it took place on the outskirts of cities. In 1950, for the first time in the nation's history, more than half of all Americans owned their own homes. Growing suburbs meant growing transportation demands. Quickly expanding housing patterns overleapt the reach of public transportation. Without streetcars or buses, American families began to consider the automobile something they couldn't live without. The family car and the house in the suburbs set the stage for Americans' expectations of what life would be like for decades to come.

The federal government fueled the move. Congress provided billions of dollars of mortgage insurance through the Federal Housing Administration (FHA), an agency set up as part of the New Deal, and the 1944 Servicemen's Readjustment Act, colloquially known as the G.I. Bill, which included a Veterans Administration housing program. Builders started a record 1,692,000 single-family houses in 1950.

New housing was favored over old, single-family housing over multi-dwelling units, and racially homogeneous white suburban locations over city neighborhoods. Although the Supreme Court ruled that racially restrictive covenants were unconstitutional in 1948, in the same year, Assistant FHA Commissioner W. J. Lockwood stated that his agency "has never insured a project of mixed occupancy," since "such projects would probably in a short period of time become all-Negro or all-white." All these changes, along with new federal support for building highways, made American suburbs spread in all directions, becoming both residential and commercial. By 1950, the suburbs were growing ten times faster than the cities they surrounded, altering the balance between the central core and the surrounding regions.

Tourist courts and small food stands had done business on the outskirts of cities for decades, but now new kinds of businesses moved out of America's downtowns. Relocating businesses could take advantage of cheaper land values. They lured ever-growing numbers of mobile customers by offering parking for shoppers. Commerce on the strip—and later, in the 1950s, at the shopping mall—became the norm. Automobiles started filling the American landscape.

. . .

Portland, Oregon, typified the change. Downtown Portland was located west of the Willamette River, on and around West Burnside Avenue. As in most early 20th-century cities, the main post office, fancy hotels, banks, and department stores clustered near the railroad's Union Station. Right in the heart of things, at Seventh and West Burnside, the Rothschild Building housed offices, printers, a commercial artist, and the Perfection Sportswear Company. By the mid-1930s, as Portland's population grew to over 300,000, car dealers lined the avenue. The Tarola Motor Car Company, Moore's Motor Company, Capital Motors, and their competitors offered customers the opportunity to get a glimpse of their products, and even to test-drive them. On the 1500 block of West Burnside, near George B. Wallace's Studebaker dealership, you could also shop for groceries; get your hair cut, your clothes pressed, your shoes repaired; and eat a sandwich at the Little Brick Lunch counter.

In 1949, Wallace moved his auto dealership across the river onto N.E. Sandy Boulevard, an address no one would have considered downtown. At the same time, he switched his product line to Buick, advertising from the new location as "One of the most modern, complete automotive sales and service plants in the west." The pea-green showroom, with its curved window and neon signs, attracted customers into the salesroom, where the business sold new and used cars, and into the repair shop, where the customers got warranty and repair service.

Wallace Buick wasn't the only new business on Sandy Boulevard. A few used car lots had opened there in the 1930s, but by 1950, shoppers could travel the strip and check out new Hudsons, Buicks, Fords, Studebakers, Plymouths, and De Sotos. They could get a car wash and wax at the East Side Sparkelize, which opened in 1950 and offered three-hour service, competing with the four-hour service customers would get at the Sparkelize Company over on Broadway. They could pick up a prescription at Owl Rexall Drugs; visit the West Furniture Company; and compare home appliances, including televisions, moving off shelves around the nation in record numbers that year. Millions of adults had watched the 1948 Democratic and Republican conventions, and now millions of children watched the *Howdy Doody Show* on their new sets.

Portlanders could do their grocery shopping on Sandy Boulevard, too, dropping into Louis Schwary and Sons, which claimed to be "Portland's most modern food market,"or parking for free on the roof of the two Fred Meyer stores, "complete shopping centers." For an evening out on the Boulevard, Portlanders could dine at Jim Dandy's or the Tick Tok Sandwich Shop, then go to see a movie at the ornate Hollywood Theater. They didn't have to go to downtown Portland at all. They could get all they needed in the strip on Sandy Boulevard.

. . .

After the war, Americans wanted cars. A hot-ticket item, at first automobiles remained in short supply. Gasoline became available quickly: Rationing was lifted immediately after VJ Day. But it took a while before automotive manufacturers began mass-producing cars again. The assembly lines had to be retooled from war products back to automobiles. Materials were in short supply. American factories actually produced fewer cars in 1945 than they had in 1909. Because of these delays, Studebaker could call its 1947 offering (advertised and sold in 1946) "America's first genuine post-war car."

In the fluid years after the war, independent automobile manufacturers like Nash and Studebaker grabbed a bigger market share than before.

*Sandy Boulevard in Portland, Oregon, top right, was a busy stretch of road lined by shops, gas stations, and, increasingly during the postwar era, car dealerships. By the mid-1950s, consumers visited Harold Kelley's Appliance Center, bottom right, on Sandy Boulevard, to choose among a number of television sets.*

*The 1955 Ford Country Squire, along with other period station wagons, became a symbol of postwar suburban life. Station wagons were so popular during the 1950s that by the end of the decade, they represented almost 17 percent of all cars built. Middle-class parents relied on them for commuting, carting the children, hauling household goods— and for the occasional family vacation.*

Studebaker brought out two 1947 models, the Champion and the Commander. Willys-Overland, the company that had designed and produced jeeps for the Army, began to make them for passenger use in the States, carving out its own market niche. Pent-up demand and short supply caused consumers to buy any and all varieties of automobile—even an offering from the new Kaiser-Frazer Company, which entered the automobile market after the war.

But the independents didn't fare well for long. By 1949, *Business Week* magazine was declaring that "The hard reality of competition has come back to the auto industry." In 1945, dealers sold just under 70,000 cars. They sold 6,000,000 cars in 1950 alone. General Motors, Ford, and Chrysler reasserted their market dominance, and by 1955, the Big Three sold 95 percent of America's new cars. General Motors alone produced about half of all new cars on the road.

In the late 1940s and '50s, American cars tended to be big, powerful, sleek, and ornamented to the nth degree with chrome. Annual style changes meant cars of the 1950s bore little surface resemblance to their predecessors. Studebaker's 1949 Land Cruiser, cashing in on established elegance by using the name of a yacht, declared itself to be among the "line of pacemaking post-war Studebakers—low-swung, flight-streamed new sedans, coupes and convertibles." Designers exaggerated the tail fins. Engineers powered up the motors, especially after General Motors adapted the V8 engine, used in cars since the 1930s, for its 1949 Cadillacs and Oldsmobiles.

*Radiator emblems decorated car fronts and declared commercial identities. In the late 1940s, independent companies like Nash still existed, but Ford, General Motors (which made Buicks and Chevrolets), and Chrysler dominated the market.*

Car companies emphasized styling, but some safety features crept in during these postwar decades, like the general adoption of directional turn signals. On the other hand, though, styling decisions often made cars less safe. Curved windshields distorted the driver's view. Tinted windshields made night driving more dangerous. Dashboards could be hazardous, especially since few Americans wore seatbelts. Dr. C. Hunter Sheldon contributed a journal article to the American Medical Association, pointing out that "The Cadillac has a prominent knife-like projection just above the instrument panel. It was designed to prevent reflection of the instrument lights onto the windshield. To accomplish this minor task, they [General Motors] have produced as lethal a device as is seen on any American passenger car."

Car companies stressed that they gave the public what they wanted. "The people of America, God bless them, design the cars. I just dance to their music," said one car designer in November 1948. The increasing monopoly of the Big Three meant that by and large, manufacturers decided what Americans would drive. Despite many brand names, cars were becoming increasingly similar under the hood. Still, America bought them in droves, placing orders for more than 6.6 million cars in 1950 alone.

Americans drove new cars from new suburban homes to new suburban shops. The opportunity to live outside the city but in the metropolitan area became increasingly available to white Americans of all classes in the postwar era. Housing was a huge social issue. Veterans were finding jobs, but "their hopes for places to live find bitter disillusionment as they bear the brunt of the national housing shortage." Families slept in their cars in San Francisco, in garages and coal sheds in Chicago. "The largest single opportunity for the rapid postwar expansion of private investment and employment lies in the field of housing, both urban and rural," President Truman declared. "The present shortage of decent homes and the enforced widespread use of substandard housing indicate vital unfulfilled needs of the Nation."

Low-cost housing was desperately needed. In 1949, the New York City Housing Authority reported, based on 50,000 applications for low-cost housing it received, that more than 8,000 people were living in rooming houses; about 1,500 families were split due to lack of accommodations that would hold them all; 20,000 families were doubled up in single-family residences; more than 30,000 lived in substandard housing; and nearly 4,000 faced eviction.

Ingenious Americans answered the housing problem by applying the principles of mass production. Levittown, New York, is the most famous example. The firm of Levitt and Sons began building houses in 1929 but came of age in the postwar era, when it sent out bulldozers to prepare the land for an enormous housing development on Long Island.

One of the sons, William J. Levitt, a Navy veteran, ran the firm. "Over the flat expanse of the western section of Long Island," wrote the *Christian Science Monitor*, "community after community of new homes is rising from vacant land and former potato fields." With a line of credit from the federal government, Levitt built thousands of houses for newly forming families looking for somewhere affordable to live. White veterans were first in line. When 350 Levittown homes went on sale in March 1949, lines started forming three days in advance. The veterans worked together, organizing themselves by giving each new arrival a number, so that the men in the line could go home and get some sleep but still keep their space in line. According to the *New York Times,* one man's wife gave birth to twins while he was waiting. "Unperturbed, he received the congratulations of his companions and kept right on standing in line." Lucky buyers paid $90 down and $58 a month for a house with a total price tag of $7,980.

Families moved into "small one-story, sometimes two-story, structures on comparatively small plots of land." Designed for cost efficiencies, the houses changed the landscape: "A potato patch of 1945 may now have 500 small homes exactly or nearly exactly alike, marching across it in parade-ground alignment." Levitt's development attracted young couples looking for a place to raise their growing families. "At the front door of a typical home stands a baby carriage or a kiddie car," reported the *Christian Science Monitor.* "More often than not, diapers and rompers hang from the line in the backyard." By the late 1950s, 60,000 people lived in Levittown.

Around the country, when builders tried to answer the postwar need for housing, they did it by building around the cities, not within them. Not everyone saw these new developments as beneficial. In *Colliers Magazine* in 1952, Thomas and Doris Reed, who described themselves as "roving doctors to sick cities," diagnosed America as suffering from

Mass-market novels like Hot Rod, above, glamorized speed and mobility even as they warned of the consequences of dangerous driving. Events like the 1955 Soap Box Derby competition in Akron, Ohio, right, introduced boys to the pleasures and pains of building and racing their own vehicles.

## PARK FOREST: A PLANNED COMMUNITY

AFTER WORLD WAR II, PLANNERS ALL OVER THE NATION PLOTTED OUT COMMUNITIES LIKE PARK FOREST OUTSIDE CHICAGO, FULFILLING—OR CREATING—THE SUBURBAN DREAM.

WHEN THE DEVELOPERS OF PARK FOREST SET ABOUT LOOKING FOR LAND, THEY BEGAN WITH A MAP OF CHICAGO, RIGHT. THEY MARKED THE LOCATION OF PARK FOREST IN RED, THEN PENCILED IN A SERIES OF CONCENTRIC CIRCLES, DETERMINING WHAT LAY 10, 20, AND 30 MILES AWAY FROM THEIR PROPOSED SITE.

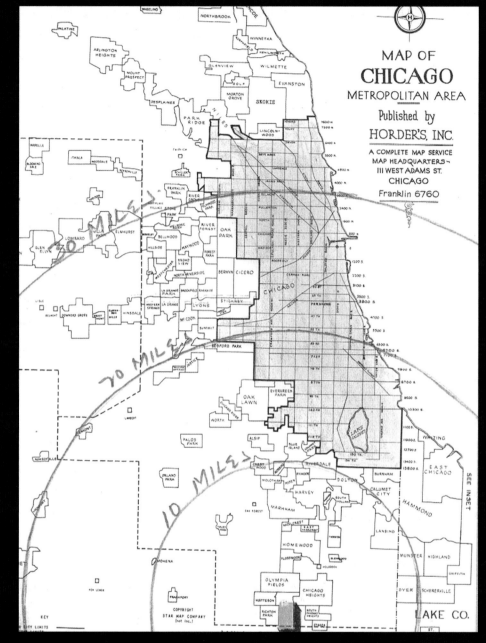

MAP OF
**CHICAGO**
METROPOLITAN AREA

Published by
HORDER'S, INC.

A COMPLETE MAP SERVICE
MAP HEADQUARTERS—
111 WEST ADAMS ST.
CHICAGO
Franklin 6760

THE DEVELOPERS–AMERICAN COMMUNITY BUILDERS (ACB)–COULD LOCATE PARK FOREST FAR FROM CHICAGO'S CENTER BECAUSE MORE PEOPLE WERE USING CARS FOR THEIR DAILY TRAVEL. RESIDENTS OF EARLIER SUBURBS, LIKE OAK PARK, LIVED CLOSER TO CHICAGO AND DEPENDED ON MASS TRANSIT. THEIR SUBURBAN PATTERNS LOOKED LIKE RIBBONS STRETCHING OUT FROM THE CITY'S CORE, INSTEAD OF CIRCLES AROUND IT.

ACB TRIED AND FAILED TO GET THE ILLINOIS CENTRAL TO BUILD A RAILROAD SPUR INTO PARK FOREST. BY THE 1960S, MANY SUBURBAN RESIDENTS WERE JOURNEYING INTO THE CENTER CITY BY AUTOMOBILE. THEY TRAVELED MILES FURTHER THAN BEFORE ON THEIR DAILY COMMUTES, ON HIGHWAYS BUILT THROUGH OLD CITY NEIGHBORHOODS.

"suburbanitis," which "kills cities by choking them off from further growth; by selectively thinning out the city's population—its lifeblood; and by bringing on a host of parasitical communities to feed on the already weakened city." The Reeds suggested annexation.

Whatever one's perspective, it was clear that change was afoot. The relationship between American cities and their outlying areas was changing.

. . .

Like other postwar cities, Chicago had to tackle the mismatch of a burgeoning metropolitan population with old housing and little new construction. As one observer put it, "Chicago's population right now is packed tight because of the housing shortage." One study estimated that returning veterans needed 120,000 more homes in Chicago. As elsewhere, most of the new homes got built in the surrounding countryside, not in Chicago itself—in places like Park Forest, a suburb nearly 30 miles south of the city. Planned by a single company, the American Community Builders (ACB), Park Forest first opened for business with rental townhomes in 1948, then offered houses for sale in 1951.

The suburbs filled some people's dreams. In 1945, a *Saturday Evening Post* survey showed that only 14 percent of Americans preferred an apartment or a "used" house to a new single-family dwelling. In 1947, 30-year-old Anthony Scariano read an article about a "dream city for veterans" being built outside Chicago. When he graduated from law school, he and his family decided to check it out. Tony's old neighborhood in the city was slated to be destroyed by public works—probably an expressway coming through—and the idea of moving into an all-new neighborhood appealed to the whole family. "Immediately we made plans to move in a planned community," Scariano recalled in 1980. "We liked the idea very much—growing with it, growing up with the town, being part of it, and starting from scratch."

Although some people genuinely wanted to live in the suburbs, others were less enthusiastic. Social commentator William H. Whyte, Jr., wrote in 1953 that "thanks to a shortage of moderate-cost housing for young couples with children, most of the people who moved to these places did so because they had to." Bernard G. Cunningham recalled that when his family moved to Park Forest in 1951, it was "the only place you could get an apartment."

Ross DeLue, a reporter for the *Chicago American* and another veteran who ended up in Park Forest, remembered that when he tried to find an apartment in Chicago, "everybody that I talked to was a real thief. The main gimmick was that there would be a battered kitchen table and a battered chair that looked like it had been picked up at the Salvation Army, and you would go in and if you said, 'Yes, I'd like this apartment,' (the landlord would say) 'Well you'll have to buy the furniture.' And they would point to the table and the chair and say, 'This will cost you fifteen hundred dollars, or two thousand dollars.' It was very obvious as to what was going on." With FHA backing, buying a house in a suburb like Park Forest was often, at first glance at least, cheaper than renting an apartment in the city.

Park Forest's boosters called it "a town that will provide a heap o' living and a 'good life' for families of the middle income group, particularly families with children." When the first families moved into Park Forest, though, the landscaping wasn't finished. Mud was everywhere. Residents had to use bottled water, furnished by ACB, for drinking and cooking. When Bernard Cunningham's family moved in, the rental units were completed but the rest of the development was still under construction. There were no trees and few sidewalks. People had to drive to Chicago Heights, three miles away, for doctor and dentist appointments. Despite these conditions, "Every day is moving day" in Park Forest, as an advertisement boasted. By 1950, more than 8,000 people lived in the two-year-old development. By 1960, Park Forest had nearly 30,000 residents.

Snobs tended to decry the suburbs in the 1950s. "For a quick twinge of superiority there is nothing quite like driving past one of the new Levittown-like suburbs," wrote William H. Whyte, Jr. "To visitors from older communities, the sight of rank after rank of little boxes stretching off to infinity, one hardly distinguishable from the other, is weird." After studying Park Forest, Whyte described it as a community where rootlessness and relentless conformity went hand in hand with suburban life. He also predicted that America's Park Forests and Levittowns were "not merely housing; they are a new social institution."

Suburban communities of the 1950s filled up with young, white, married couples with small children. Single women were barred from both Park

*A 1952 aerial view of Park Forest, opposite, shows how cars influenced design: Curving roads slowed traffic and provided safety for children riding bikes, like the 1953 Schwinn Panther, above. A decade after Park Forest opened, the first African-American family moved in, prompting a memo, inset, on integration. Following pages: In most postwar suburbs, younger children outnumbered older children and adults.*

Instructions to Village Employees
For Answering Questions With Respect to Local
Residence of Members of the Negro Race

These instructions have been issued with the approval of the Village President and every member of the Board of Trustees:

The Constitution of the United States and of the State of Illinois establish that there can be no question as to the policy of the Village Government in the event that a Negro family should make its home in Park Forest. However, in view of the questions sometimes addressed to Village personnel by individuals who are disturbed by rumors they have heard, this short statement has been prepared as a guide in replying to these inquiries.

It is probable that a variety of opinions on this subject are held by the individuals who make up the staff of the Village Government. It is important to remember that as public servants, it is absolutely necessary to support the policy of the Village Government even though it may not conform entirely with personal opinions.

The Village Government must extend equal services and protection of the law to all its citizens without any discrimination between them. The Village Government neither encourages nor discourages the residence in the Village of members of the Negro race. However, the Village Government carefully investigates all information which reaches it, so that preparations can be made to avoid any undesirable incidents. In the event that a Negro family should make its home in Park Forest, the Village Government will assure that family the same protection of the law that is afforded to any other resident or property owner in the Village.

July 27, 1959
Park Forest, Illinois

T-LOT

Forest and Levittown. Levittown excluded African Americans, even after the federal government threatened to take away its mortgage insurance because of the discriminatory policy. Park Forest did not discriminate in the same way, but preference was still given to white GIs and their families. The first African-American family moved into Park Forest in 1959.

Women who lived in the suburbs may not have felt as if they lived in the "comfortable concentration camp" described in Betty Friedan's 1963 polemical but influential book, *The Feminine Mystique*. Still, they were anchored to their homes by growing families of small children and by the distances they lived from public transport and social amenities, at least in the early years of postwar suburbia.

American family life was changing. People moved farther away from their extended families, and the single household dominated the definition of family. Men and women married younger and had larger families in a shorter period of time than their parents had ever experienced. The family unit became nuclear. "Today, the family clan, like the atom, is split," observed the *Christian Science Monitor* in 1958. "All that's left are Mother, Dad, and the youngsters." The new circumstances in the suburbs helped create

*Houses in the central city neighborhoods of Chicago, left, and other urban areas were condemned as expressways began to traverse American cities. Road building often displaced African-American and other minority communities. By the late 1960s, housing takes became a politically charged issue, as shown by a 1964 protest poster, inset, from Washington, D.C.*

a new definition of the American family. An editor of *McCall's* magazine wrote in 1954, "For quite a while now families have been living a new kind of life. It's more casual, easy going, and home is its pivot."

If home was the pivot, children and cars became the focus of a community like Park Forest. Houses looked out over playgrounds. Residents socialized at backyard barbeques and cocktail parties. They joined civic organizations together. But as even *McCall's* would admit, "it takes a certain knack to get the most of it. This life calls for a very special sort of woman, a 1954 model."

In Park Forest of the 1950s, that model woman was generally college-educated and a stay-at-home mother. Many such women met and talked together over coffee, attended self-improvement classes, and organized babysitting groups. Neighbors were friendly and often helpful: Even though Anthony Scariano's neighbors, Bob and Mary Dinerstein, had moved in just one day before the Scarianos, they still managed to bring their new neighbors lunch to welcome them to the community. According to William Whyte, Park Forest adults could join more than 60 community organizations.

But despite all the joining, communities like Park Forest were transient. Families often spent only a few short years in a subdivision before being transferred through work to a different region of the country—or before moving up in the suburban hierarchy to a pricier development with bigger houses.

While wives stayed at home in the suburbs, their husbands went to work in the cities. In the early 1950s, for example, the vast majority of Park Forest men worked in Chicago's central business district, the Loop. Every morning they either drove, took the bus, or boarded the Illinois Central train and headed downtown. In the early years, many residents preferred the train (leaving the car home for the wife and kids), but by 1960, more than half of Park Forest's commuters drove cars into the city.

Cars soon became a suburban necessity for both husband and wife. "Shopping centers have sprung up where billboards and hedges used to line the roads," a reporter wrote of Long Island. Levittowners claimed that "To attempt to live in Nassau or Suffolk county without an automobile is both foolish and impossible."

Park Forest was designed with a shopping plaza in its midst, and it drew customers from 30 miles around. The automobile culture drove Park Forest's design: Rental townhouses were organized around what architects dubbed "autocourts," and the streets curved in order to slow traffic.

. . .

City merchants worried that the surburbs were taking away their business. Park Forest entrepreneur Philip Klutznick claimed that suburban commerce would "merely take the pressure off the downtown centers by providing outlying areas with convenient buying facilities," but the statistics didn't seem to support his claim. Sales at Park Forest's shopping plaza climbed 216 percent between 1952 and 1953, while sales in downtown Chicago rose only 5.9 percent.

In the late 1940s, city planners still assumed that their central business districts would remain the primary focus of business and commerce. A *New York Times* survey in December 1945 reported that "automotive congestion has mushroomed" and that "a post-war traffic and parking problem of primary magnitude confronts municipalities throughout the United States." Road-building programs, like housing and car manufacturing, had stalled during the war. Meanwhile, there were more cars on the roads. Bigger, heavier, faster, and more powerful, all those cars put existing roadways under a lot of strain.

City planners believed that if they could get people into the city and get them parked, they could revitalize their downtowns, washing away the years of decay that depression and war had inflicted on the city's infrastructure, commerce, and housing. When the *New York Times* surveyed spokesmen for 27 cities in the immediate aftermath of the war, most cited more parking lots and more parking meters as their answers to congestion problems. No more significant mass transportation planning than that seemed to be on their minds.

Once results from the 1950 census were publicized, though, increasing pessimism crept into the rhetoric about the future of cities. "The Suburbs are Strangling the City," read one headline in the *New York Times*. Too many suburbanites worked in the city without paying taxes for metropolitan services. They were "living on the life-blood of the central city without contributing the nourishment so necessary to sustain it." A structural change in American living patterns—and, by extension, working, shopping, playing, and traveling patterns—was underway, and cities had to figure out how to respond.

Chicago, the second largest city in the nation, faced challenges typical of those faced by many

**A GLEAM IN THE CHROME**

AUTOS AS IMAGE-MAKERS

WRITERS OF A 1949 AD, RIGHT, ASSUMED HUSBANDS MADE THE DECISIONS, EVEN THOUGH THEY PITCHED THE DODGE AS A "WOMAN'S CAR." THE KAISER TRAVELER AD, LEFT, PLACED ITS PRODUCT IN A CONTEXT OF MASCULINE OUTDOOR PURSUITS.

most prestigious and expensive car, the Cadillac. Where Cadillac led, others followed, and tail fins grew, literally and figuratively, into the biggest style trend of the 1950s.

Automotive styling became important once simply owning a car was no longer a sign of status. Car advertisers tried to create market niches. They sold the postwar car as a symbol of whatever variant of the American dream might engage a customer's fancy. As satirist and novelist John Keats wrote in 1958, "Detroit believes and operates on the theory that Americans don't buy automobiles, but instead buy dreams of sex, speed, power, and wealth." Americans bought cars by the millions every year through the 1950s, and the nation's roads, garages, and driveways filled up with "dreams" bedecked with chrome trim and tail fins, exaggerated chassis, and two-tone color combinations.

Automobile advertisements show in text and image how marketers tried to sell cars by appealing to certain personalities. A 1949 Willys ad called the Jeepster a "a daring, fun-loving dream, realized in steel and chrome." A 1950 Chrysler Town and Country Newport ad promised a car with the "most dramatic, most exciting,

most daring styling. A classic of long, low and lovely— with the most luxurious trim and new nylon fabrics ever available." Glamorous and urbane women, men sharing leisure activities in the great outdoors, and happy suburban families—all these images found their way into advertisements as marketers turned the car into more than a mode of conveyance.

In the words of a 1955 Packard ad, cars brought "Pride of possession—a gleam in the owner's eye … ardent admiration—a gleam in other eyes." That gleam — or at least the chrome reflecting that gleam—diminished as the excesses of the 1950s were replaced by the economies of the 1960s and '70s and as Americans projected a new self-image in the cars they chose to buy.

IN 1949 NASH, RIGHT, HIGHLIGHTED THE VALUE OF THE AIRFLYTE MODEL'S AERODYNAMIC LINES, CURVED WIND- SHIELD, AND SMOOTH RIDE. BY THE MID-1950S, IMAGE PLAYED A LARGER PART IN ADVERTISING. CADILLAC TAIL FINS AND CHROME, LEFT, IMPLICITLY PROMISED A LIFE OF BEAUTY, GLAMOUR, AND ROMANCE, ADORNED WITH FUR AND JEWELS.

American cities. In 1946, David Graham Hutton wrote, "The problems of Chicago, as of the other big cities and towns in the Midwest and everywhere else, are left at or near the center: the 'inner ring' of solid and densely settled residential areas, where the manual workers live, the areas of slums, dilapidation, or overcrowding, and these are linked with the level of incomes and the grading of jobs. That leaves the problems with the city fathers while the satisfied suburbanites go free." As more people could afford to move into new housing outside the city—and as more people did just that—the migration out of Chicago had the effect of lowering the city's tax base.

A number of contemporary commentators connected the increasing poverty and decay in America's cities with changes in the racial complexion of their populations. When the Chicago Housing Authority built public housing, for example, Philip G. Sadler, a Public Housing Administration official, described the process in terms that simplistically connected poverty, slums, and African Americans. "We have had this concentration of public housing on the South Side of Chicago and in many instances this public housing has been used for clearing the slums," Sadler told the U. S. Commission on Civil Rights. "You find the slums, as is usually the case, in highly concentrated Negro areas."

*Following pages: In 1954, suburbanites rode the commuter train to Chicago and returned in the evening to stations like the one in Park Forest, left. In the city, many traveled by elevated train, or El, right. Despite competition from the auto, Chicago public transit provided a vital link in the region's transportation system.*

The situation was somewhat more complicated than Sadler conveyed. Squeezed by racial prejudice into segregated neighborhoods, Chicago's growing black population lived on the city's traditionally African-American South Side as well as in a more recently settled area on the West Side. When photographer Gordon Parks moved to Chicago, he "started poking around the south side," he wrote in his autobiography. "I knew more than anything else I wanted to strike at the evil of poverty. And here it was, under my feet, all around and above me ... this landscape of ash piles, garbage heaps, tired tenements and littered streets was worse than any I had seen."

Some families had the means to escape the overcrowded and expensive housing, but they often faced virulent opposition. When Harvey Clark and his family rented in Cicero, west of Chicago, in 1951, white residents burned down the apartment building rather than allow a black family to move into it.

City planners believed that urban blight and congestion could be solved in one fell swoop, by urban renewal. Some cities' efforts included transportation system improvements. By giving people quicker and more convenient ways to travel between downtown and outlying areas, planners believed, they could revitalize city centers. Chicago provides an example of how city planning worked—and how it didn't.

. . .

Soon after World War II—and years before the federal government funded an interstate highway system—Chicago city planners dusted off a 1940 superhighway planning document. Calling for the design and construction of "a radial system of five

expressways converging on downtown Chicago," the plan, it was hoped, would meet the demands of the growing car culture and stem the flow of people and investments out of the city center. Chicago's expressways were designed to provide "more efficient access to the business district."

Ironically, the expressways also helped people travel out of the city more efficiently, and so they reoriented traffic and commerce away from the city's center. Better roads encouraged automobility, which in turn made public transit less appealing, hence less profitable, hence less available. It was a vicious cycle in which the private convenience and public funding support provided to automobility bore down on the success, profits, and progress of the various modes of public transportation.

Many cities put their hopes, and their tax dollars, into new expressways. As early as 1953, though, a *Washington Post* reporter noticed the deleterious effect of new highways on public transit. "All too late, perhaps, we are beginning to realize that a serious mistake has been made in designing express highways without adequate provision for rapid transit in the largest urban areas. Enthusiasm for construction of expressways for motor vehicles has obscured our vision as to the over-all transportation needs of the modern city."

The numbers argued for public transit. In 1958, Chicago Mayor Richard Daley reported that 95,000 vehicles used Chicago's Congress Street Expressway (renamed the Eisenhower Expressway in 1964) and two million people used the transit system. Even the newest, widest roads couldn't compete with a mass

transit system for carrying capacity, and city planners around the country knew it. But the powerful highway lobby, born out of the traditional rivalry between rail- and road-related businesses, urged federal funding in their direction. Federal highway money came available for cities. They could use it to build expressways, but they couldn't use it to build more or better railways.

In Chicago, as it happened, the path of the Congress Street Expressway usurped existing railway rights, so in exchange a rapid transit lane was built right down the center of the new expressway. The combination of road and rail was hard to come by in other places, though. Philadelphia, for example, could get no state or federal support to build rapid transit lines in the median strip of its proposed superhighways. Planners argued that a "total transportation solution" was a necessity, but money and political support rarely seemed forthcoming. A 1956 article in the *New York Times* analyzed the problem as the lack of a systematic transportation plan. While expressways offered "both better methods of moving and higher standards of living," cities could not cope with the problem of what to do when the "irresistible car meets the immovable metropolis."

The article urged community planning and zoning "that reflect the needs of a motorized society" and argued that otherwise, "we are creating new congestion and blight in the suburbs faster than we can hope to remedy downtown errors." Transit ridership fell off precipitously in the decade between 1946 and 1956, and half of the nation's straphangers stopped riding the nation's buses, trolleys, streetcars, elevated railways, and trains. Between the late 1950s and the early 1970s, over 170 transit companies in the United States ceased operations.

In Chicago, the proportion of people using public transportation to get into the city fell below 50 percent in the 1940s. But Chicago's mass transit system, one of America's oldest and most extensive, was in better shape than most and was an important part of the city's transportation scene.

Many of Chicago's privately owned bus, rapid transit, and streetcar companies were approaching bankruptcy by the end of World War II, but the city was committed to keeping public transportation alive. The Chicago Transit Authority, created in 1945, consolidated and ran all the city lines. City government stepped in to help, purchasing the lines but keeping them under CTA control. Fares alone were expected to finance operations and pay off the bonds that helped set up the system in the first place. The CTA struggled to balance the needs of its riders with limited funds, rising expenses, and changing patterns of use. Benefits for suburbanites were achieved at the cost of quality of life for those still living in Chicago's inner city.

Between 1948 and 1956, two hundred fifty buildings, up to ten and twelve stories tall, were destroyed in the Loop during the construction of the 67-mile-long Congress Street Expressway, built at a cost of 6.2 million dollars a mile. More than 6,000 Chicago families lost their homes to municipal repossession of land, or "highway takes." Most of the new expressways went through poor neighborhoods, like the community around 45th and Wentworth, which was demolished for a 14-lane expressway.

•  •  •

The urgent transportation needs of American cities became a national concern. President Lyndon B. Johnson, in his 1964 State of the Union address, pledged to "carry forward the plans and programs of John Fitzgerald Kennedy—not because of our sorrow or sympathy, but because they are right." President Johnson declared an "unconditional war on poverty," an initiative for which he came to be well known. He also announced an intention to improve systems of public transportation. "We must help obtain more modern mass transit within our communities," said Johnson, "as well as low-cost transportation between them."

Under President Johnson's leadership, Congress passed the Urban Mass Transit Act in 1964. It was, as *Time* magazine said when its editors named LBJ Man of the Year, "a $375-million mass-transit program that had been stalled in a House committee for two years." That same year, Johnson pumped significantly more money—billions of federal dollars—into roads.

By the 1970s, aid to mass transit was one of the fastest-growing federal programs. It helped fund new high-profile rapid transit systems, like Washington D.C.'s Metro and San Francisco's Bay Area Rapid Transit (BART). Ridership still remained low, though, as cities continued to sprawl. Public transit still couldn't beat the car for convenience. Amid falling ridership and revenue in the 1980s,

one official with the Chicago Transit Authority official declared mass transit "no longer relevant to the American way of life."

. . .

Mass transit had fueled suburbanization at the beginning of the 20th century. But by the century's end, even transportation professionals were calling it irrelevant. The footprint of a planned suburb like Levittown, Long Island, seemed like a tiny speck on the map compared to the automobile-powered sprawl that had developed around the cities in the American West and Southwest.

Take Los Angeles, for example.

In 1880, it was a sleepy little town, but by 1924, it had grown to one million residents, and they had spread out all over Los Angeles County. Fewer than 60 percent of those who called Los Angeles home actually lived within the city limits. All lived in the metropolitan region. By 1990, Los Angeles had grown to a five-county region with a population of over 14 million and an economy matching that of many countries. Hollywood, home construction, and the aerospace industry all helped fuel the city's enormous growth.

Los Angeles was predominantly a white, native-born, Protestant city in the 1920s, despite California's Hispanic heritage. By the 1990s, the city's airport, LAX, had become a latter-day Ellis Island. Millions of

*By the end of the 20th century, as cities sprawled, more Americans drove farther and longer every day. Clockwise from upper left: Traffic intensified on Los Angeles freeways; downtown Los Angeles grew up as well as out; some L.A. commuters still chose public transit; and other commuters found their own alternatives to the automobile.*

newcomers flew into America via LAX from all around the world. Immigrants also traveled into California by crossing the border from Mexico. The Cold War and the Vietnam War made refugees among Asian populations, and they emigrated to the United States as well. Immigration legislation in 1965 ended racially based quotas and helped open up the United States to immigration from all over the world. At the end of the 20th century, as one scholar put it, Los Angeles had "the largest Korean metropolitan district outside Korea, the largest Mexican metropolitan area outside Mexico, the largest Filipino district outside the Phillipines and the largest Vietnamese district outside Vietnam."

California's public transit tradition—streetcars and inter-urban railway networks—dated back to the 19th century. Angelenos took to the automobile with great enthusiasm, though, making the city a low-density automobile metropolis. As early as 1920, more cars traveled on the roads and byways of Los Angeles than in any other city in the United States. And, perhaps as a result, more single-family houses could be found in Los Angeles than anywhere else in the nation.

As Los Angeles grew, city fathers wanted to keep its density low, along the lines of the vision of "the city of the future" described in 1926 by the Los Angeles City Club as "a harmoniously developed community of local centers and garden cities." The small central business district of the 1920s rapidly became just one of many business districts within the city. As Los Angeles's 1941 master plan proudly declared, "this region can and should remain one in which single-family dwelling predominates."

. . .

The sprawling and road-dependent city structure of Los Angeles prefigured the direction taken by other cities across the nation. Its early decentralization of office space did, too. City officials tried to keep offices in central business districts, because office space was a high-rent use of the land. But as more middle-class Americans moved to the suburbs, offices followed. Often a corporate headquarters relocated within easy commuting distance of the chief executive officer's chosen home location.

In 1954, General Mills moved its headquarters out of Manhattan and into White Plains, New York—the first big corporate move out of that city. Soon the same thing was happening in cities all over the country. Business locations spread, just as residences and commerce had. By 1987, the suburb of Tysons Corner, just outside Washington, D.C., was helping the nation's capital undergo its own version of Los Angelization. As the *Washington Post* calculated it, "Only a crossroads general store as recently as the 1950s, Tysons is now bigger in terms of office space than all but 15 downtowns in the country."

Commentators of the 1960s, 1970s, or 1980s began to use Los Angeles as a symbol of the trend in American cities to become increasingly congested and sprawling, auto-dependent and smog-ridden. At the same time, as historian Robert Fishman has

pointed out, "If other great cities have come more and more to resemble Los Angeles, Los Angeles in turn has begun to resemble them." And the city with the reputation of having the "world's most dedicated motorists"—the city that rejected bond issues for subways downtown, even in the 1920s—built mass transit rail lines in the 1980s.

Still, whether you lived in Los Angeles, Detroit, Washington, Chicago, Miami, or any of the other great metropolitan areas, regardless of government support of mass transit, regardless of the conscientious efforts of the environmental movement, more and more families became multicar owners during the second half of the 20th century. America's older cities, its newer edge cities, and its great breadth of suburbs all depended on the automobile.

By 1990, just under 10 percent of households had no car. More than 60 percent had two or more. All told, Americans owned one car for every licensed driver. And Americans drove those cars more each day than they had in previous years. Compared to their parents' generation in 1950, drivers in 1991 owned twice as many cars and drove 2.5 times as far. In 2000, the Federal Highway Administration estimated that transportation costs represented the second largest American household expenditure, exceeded only by housing.

As the 20th century came to an end, America's relationship with the automobile—whether for glamour or utility or both—was still going strong.

THERE THEY GO, IN THE FAMILY CAR,
A WHITE PONTIAC BONNEVILLE SEDAN—
THE FAMILY CAR!—
A HUGE CRAZY GOD-AWFUL-POWERFUL
FANTASY CREATURE TO BEGIN WITH,
327-HORSEPOWER, SHAPED LIKE TWENTY-
SEVEN NIGHTS OF LUBRICIOUS LUXURY
BROUGHAM SEDUCTION—YOU'RE ALREADY
THERE, IN FANTASYLAND...

EDGE CITY...

— *Tom Wolfe*, **The Electric Kool-Aid Acid Test,** *1968*

# SUPERHIGHWAYS:
# THE PACE
# PICKS UP

*The 1939 New York World's Fair celebrated technology's power. Opposite, clockwise from upper left: Visitors view 1960 in GM's Futurama; the diorama included city highways of the future; Sparko the mechanical dog was an endearing machine; and fairgoers stroll the walkway near "The World of Tomorrow." Above, the fair's poster spotlights stunt planes in flight.*

Nearly 28,000 people visited the General Motors Building on a typical summer day at the 1939 New York World's Fair. They waited in line for hours to enjoy the fair's most popular attraction, the 15-minute Futurama ride at the "Highways and Horizons" exhibit. Once inside the building they sat, 322 at a time, in partially enclosed, blue velour easy chairs that moved along a track and gave the illusion of flying over the United States in the amazing year of 1960.

A recorded voice in the darkened room told the riders they were on a "magic, Aladdin-like flight through time and space." Optimism burst from the audio speakers as the voice promised "new horizons in many fields, leading to new benefits for everyone, everywhere." Visitors saw 50,000 teardrop-shaped toy cars below them, moving along tiny 14-lane highways that crisscrossed a 35,000-square-foot diorama. The narrator promised abundant sunshine, fresh air, and air-conditioned skyscrapers providing all the necessities of city life. A million tiny trees made of copper wire and Norwegian moss forested the high-tech world in emerald green.

Futurama visitors witnessed the future promise of speed. "Speed is the cry of our era," the exhibit's designer, Norman Bel Geddes, had said, and the diorama demonstrated his vision. Cars would zip along the pavement at 50, 75, and even 100 miles per hour and exit seamlessly, at high speed, into a web of connecting roads. Future commuters could live six times farther from work, thanks to superhighways. The disembodied voice spoke of cars crossing the whole country in a day, never slowing down for intersections or railroad crossings.

**259**

It impressed the ten million who visited Futurama. "Cars were regulated by remote control, the drivers didn't even do the driving!" gasped Edgar, the child narrator of E. L. Doctorow's 1985 novel, *World's Fair,* based on the 1939 extravaganza. "And we passed bridges and streams, and electrified farms and airports that brought up airliners on elevators from underground hangars.... In the cities of the future, pedestrian bridges connected the buildings and highways were sunken on tracks below them. No one would get run over in this futuristic world."

"Strange?" the recorded voice asked. "Fantastic? Unbelievable? Remember, this is the world of 1960!" As visitors left the building, they received a button that declared, "I Have Seen the Future." Walking out, they turned a corner—and there was a real-life intersection that exactly matched the street scene they had just been watching at the end of Futurama. There was the future, "right where you were standing," Edgar observed.

Futurama whetted American appetites for fast roads. It acquainted the public with the potential benefits of superhighways and got people thinking along the lines of the autobahns that already sliced through Germany. And what were highways without cars? If Futurama made Americans want to buy the most modern cars to exploit those roads, so be it.

Speed would rule the future, in 1960 and far beyond. But with each advance would come a price. In that year of 1939, little did World's Fair visitors know, nor did GM executives envision, the air pollution, traffic jams, and safety problems destined to attend the coronation of the highway system as king

*A construction crew working in 1935, above, tears up pavement to widen a street. Street, road, and bridge projects such as this proceeded all over the nation, funded by the federal Works Progress Administration, a relief program in President Franklin Roosevelt's New Deal.*

of transportation. There were aspects of the future that 1939 visionaries did not foresee: Widespread, affordable jet travel, for example, brought flight path and airport highway congestion, security risks, and cabins that packed travelers like eggs in a carton. New benefits! New speed! The future!

. . .

As World's Fair visitors drooled over the prospect of superhighways, federal government officials were contemplating how to build them. Two key questions had to be answered: Where would the roads go, and how would they be paid for?

President Franklin Roosevelt's Works Progress Administration had built roads and bridges in the 1930s, primarily to make work for the unemployed. Now Roosevelt had grander plans. In 1937, he sketched six transcontinental lines on a crude highway map, presented it to U.S. Commissioner of Public Roads Thomas H. MacDonald, and asked how to turn the lines into reality. The President suggested building highways on "excess right-of-way." A new national agency would rent and eventually sell the land to private enterprises and local governments to help pay the costs.

Roosevelt's idea sounded like big-government bureaucracy to opponents of his New Deal. Some in Congress thought it smacked of socialism. The Federal-Aid Highway Act of 1938 gave MacDonald's Bureau of Public Roads a congressional mandate to examine the possibility of a toll-financed superhighway system. The bureau's report, *Toll Roads and Free Roads,* suggested that a plan along the lines of Roosevelt's sketches could be built for just under three billion dollars. Thinking even bigger, the bureau reported that a superhighway system totaling 29,300 miles, twice the size of Roosevelt's plan, could realistically be built for six billion. MacDonald's staff rejected tolls as a way to finance the highways: Tolls would never provide enough income, they believed, because Americans would never drive the highways in sufficient numbers.

*Toll Roads and Free Roads* mirrored some aspects of GM's vision of "Highways and Horizons" at the 1939 World's Fair. In both plans, highway pavement snaked through, around, and between cities. The prospect of urban highways cheered Studebaker Corporation President Paul Hoffman, who also was head of the Automobile Safety Foundation, a lobbying group. He believed superhighways in the cities would erase congestion, which he called the modern version of the mud that had once slowed rural traffic. Writing in the *Saturday Evening Post,* Hoffman shared the highway data gathered by the Bureau of Public Roads. Only one percent of traffic on coast-to-coast highways actually was en route from one ocean to the other, and trips of one hundred miles or more accounted for barely two percent of traffic. "We use highways, then, chiefly for short trips," Hoffman wrote. "And where do we go? We go to town."

American cities, wrote Hoffman, should accommodate automobiles better, especially through access to new highway grids. "Many of our cities are almost as antiquated, trafficwise, as if they had medieval walls, moats, drawbridges," he elaborated. "If we are to have full use of automobiles, cities must be remade. The greatest automobile market today,

the greatest untapped field of potential customers, is the large number of city people who refuse to own cars, or use the cars they have very little, because it's such a nuisance to take them out.... Chief MacDonald insists that we must dream of gashing our way ruthlessly through built-up sections of overcrowded cities, in order to create traffic ways capable of carrying traffic with safety, facility, [and] reasonable speed."

Hoffman and MacDonald articulated the fundamental vision of the interstate system: Highways crisscross the nation, carrying a lot of traffic from country to city and from city to city. No one, though—not Hoffman, not MacDonald, not even a string of mid-century Presidents—foresaw how widely urban housing would have to be sacrificed to make way for central-city highway corridors.

Like the GM exhibit, neither MacDonald's report nor Hoffman's article offered many specific recommendations. Those came later, after Roosevelt appointed a National Interregional Highway Committee in April 1941. Its report, issued in 1944, proposed a "National System of Interstate Highways." The committee envisioned 33,920 miles of interstates, including 4,400 miles of city pavement. Additional urban miles extended the total over the next few years. By 1947, a 37,800-mile ribbon of land

*Cars pass through the Buffalo tollbooth at the end of the 427-mile New York State Thruway in 1956. For one cent a mile, drivers could reach New York City from Buffalo in just over seven hours. New York State's was the nation's longest toll superhighway system. The federal government chose to build tax-supported interstate highways instead.*

had been designated for interstate highways. Maps of the system appeared in a Bureau of Public Roads publication called the *General Location of National Systems of Interstate Highways,* also known as the "Yellow Book." A modern reader perusing the book's maps would find familiar highway patterns. Beltways usually encircled cities' downtown areas, with spokes moving outward. In some cities, a second beltway ring pierced through the suburbs. A superhighway that approached a city usually divided into one route that went downtown and another that circled around.

Mapping the entire system proved politically astute. It created a package deal that simplified congressional approval. All that was needed to complete the picture was money, or at least a method to finance construction.

Not long after MacDonald's office issued *Toll Roads and Free Roads,* the Pennsylvania Turnpike opened and promptly disproved his dismal predictions about toll road revenue. Hundreds of drivers lined up on opening day, October 1, 1940, eager to drive America's first superhighway. MacDonald had predicted that only 715 drivers a day would pay to travel the turnpike connecting Harrisburg and Pittsburgh. The reality was closer to 10,000.

The roadway's four wide lanes and limited access became a model for interstates. At first, no speed limits were posted along the 160 miles of smooth, hard surface, which cut drive time between the two cities in half. Straightaways amounted to almost 70 percent of the turnpike, designed so cars could travel one hundred miles per hour.

Besides the benefits of swift travel through the

state's industrial region, Pennsylvania hoped that the turnpike would create jobs and boost the state's economy. To pay for construction, the state set up a private agency that could issue bonds, which were to be retired through toll income. The financial formula proved successful, so much so that after World War II, New York, New Jersey, and other states set up similar turnpike authorities.

Drivers gladly paid tolls to reduce road time. The first section of the New Jersey Turnpike opened in November 1951. Once all 118 miles were completed, by January, drivers could pay $1.75 to drive from New York to Wilmington, Delaware, and cut the trip from five hours to two. New Hampshire made a quick profit on its tiny 15-mile toll road. To travel the state's short coastline from Massachusetts to the Portsmouth traffic circle, drivers paid 15 cents. Pennsylvania doubled the length of its turnpike, nearly spanning the state, and produced a cash surplus of $5.6 million by 1948.

Toll roads hastened travel regionally, but until the mid-1950s, no national oversight agency linked them. By then, 19 states had formed toll road authorities. It worried the federal government, and the automobile and highway lobbies, that private road authorities had such autonomy and influence. *Engineering News* editorialized that the toll agencies could "become just as pernicious an evil as the privately owned toll road of a century or more ago." The federal government wanted not a state-by-state system of arterials, but rather a fully integrated national highway system. Ultimately, toll roads did not interfere with national-level designs as an interstate

system slowly incorporated the postwar turnpikes. Today, much of the Pennsylvania Turnpike forms part of Interstates 70 and 76.

While toll roads were spreading across the Northeast, federal officials focused their efforts in other directions. Harry S. Truman, who succeeded to the Presidency upon Roosevelt's death in 1945, routed steel and concrete not to highway construction but to the construction of homes for returning war veterans and their families.

MacDonald, a continuing force in the road industry, advocated a transportation system that would promote mass transit, such as passenger trains, in balance with highways. Long-distance luxury diesel trains—such as the *California Zephyr*, traveling between Emeryville, California, and Chicago, Illinois—attracted record numbers of passengers in the late 1940s and early 1950s. Railroads aggressively marketed their travel advantages, including the beds and dining cars that automobiles could not duplicate. But highways and their convenience proved more attractive as consumers bought record numbers of cars after World War II. Passenger trains suffered huge financial losses in the early 1950s and abandoned unprofitable routes. The number of intercity rail passengers dropped from 913 million in 1944 to 352 million by the end of the 1950s. Intercity

*The Santa Monica Freeway, part of Interstate 10, dominated some of the most heavily populated sections of Los Angeles and its suburbs in 1965. President Dwight D. Eisenhower, who signed the 1956 bill creating the interstate system, did not foresee the impact superhighways would make on the urban landscape.*

# THE U.S. INTERSTATE SYSTEM, 1959

PAVING THE WAY FROM COAST TO COAST, INTERSTATE HIGHWAYS TOOK SHAPE IN THE 1950s.

THE LARGEST CONSTRUCTION PROJECT IN WORLD HISTORY WAS BARELY UNDER WAY WHEN THIS 1959 AMERICAN AUTOMOBILE ASSOCIATION "MAP OF THE INTERSTATE SYSTEM" WAS CHARTED. INITIAL PLANS CALLED FOR 41,000 MILES OF PAVEMENT AT LEAST FOUR LANES WIDE—A MONUMENT OF CONCRETE THAT COULD HAVE BUILT SIX SIDEWALKS TO THE MOON.

MAP OF THE INTERSTATE SYSTEM
AND TURNPIKES
As of February 1, 1959

HIGHWAY CONSTRUCTION CONTINUED AT A RAPID PACE UNTIL THE MID-1970s, WHEN THE EMPHASIS SHIFTED TO MAINTENANCE. AS THE LEGEND AT LEFT REVEALS, CARTOGRAPHERS CONSTANTLY UPDATED MAPS TO INDICATE SECTIONS OF INTERSTATE COMPLETED, UNDER CONSTRUCTION, OR PROPOSED. WITH GAS CHEAP AND SPEED LIMITS HIGH, MILLIONS OF DRIVERS TRAVELED THE INTERSTATES EACH DAY, PUSHING USAGE RATES FAR ABOVE FEDERAL FORECASTS.

THE MILEAGE TABLE, AT RIGHT, SHOWS THE DISTANCES ONE COULD TRAVEL ON LONG SECTIONS OF LIMITED-ACCESS SUPERHIGHWAYS. THE NEW ROADS MOVED TRAFFIC EFFICIENTLY BUT LACKED THE AESTHETICS OF OLDER ROADS LIKE U.S. ROUTE 66. "THANKS TO THE INTERSTATE HIGHWAY SYSTEM," CBS JOURNALIST CHARLES KURAULT CONFIRMED STEINBECK'S 1960s PROPHECY, "IT IS NOW POSSIBLE TO TRAVEL ACROSS THE COUNTRY FROM COAST TO COAST WITHOUT SEEING ANYTHING."

bus ridership took a similar tumble. MacDonald told a national highway association in 1947 that if the emphasis on privately owned automobiles could not be reversed, "the traffic problems in the larger cities may become well nigh insoluble."

Symbolizing the ascendancy of the automobile in the 1950s, Dwight D. Eisenhower, newly elected President, demanded MacDonald's resignation and pushed vigorously for interstate highways. Eisenhower had witnessed the deplorable state of America's roads during the Army's cross-country trek of 1919 and, in contrast, the efficiency of the German superhighways during World War II. "The obsolescence of the nation's highways presents an appalling problem of waste, danger and death," he told a newspaper reporter even before the 1952 election. He was willing to make a huge capital investment to improve America's highway system. Construction would stabilize employment and help bolster national defense, he believed.

Disagreements about funding delayed interstate construction during the first years of Eisenhower's Presidency. He appointed retired Army General Lucius Clay to sort out the issues. Clay had organized the Berlin Airlift in 1948, carrying food to West Berliners whose road access to the West had been cut when Soviet forces occupied East Germany. Thus Eisenhower's choice of Clay hinted at the interstates' link to the Cold War, a link that became crystal-clear after Clay and his committee reported their findings in 1955. They recommended a construction plan costing $27 billion over ten years, designed to improve internal transportation for defense, among other goals. After public hearings and input from the highway lobbies, the administration won congressional approval. With the Federal-Aid Highway Act of 1956, the National System of Interstate and Defense Highways began to take shape.

The bill expanded highways to a total of 41,000 miles and ensured that the federal government would pay at least 90 percent of the construction bill, using funds raised primarily by taxing gasoline and diesel fuel. Tax dollars were funneled into a Highway Trust Fund, and one year's receipts paid for the next year's work.

Eisenhower's highway system proved to be the largest construction project in world history. Earth-movers pushed enough dirt to bury Connecticut knee-deep. The paving that began in late 1956, if placed edge to edge, would cover all of West Virginia. Interstates affected where and how people lived, worked, shopped, vacationed—nearly every aspect of life. The huge investment in car culture precluded substantial subsidies for mass transit out of federal and state transportation budgets. Lucrative chain enterprises concentrated their growth patterns at the exit and entry ramps of the new limited-access highways, while independent mom-and-pop stores on the old highways withered. Amarillo's Big Texan, for example—the Route 66 steak house that served a 72-ounce steak dinner free to anyone who could eat it in an hour—lost all its business when I-40 opened in November 1968, but stood tall again after relocating on the interstate. Workers traveled into cities that had been beyond the reach of a daily commute, and suburban communities along the interstates

Guenther and Siewchin Yong Sommer
of Queens, New York, saw America in this
1967 Pontiac Grand Prix. Between 1967
and 1999, they visited all 49 continental
states. The Grand Prix was one of Detroit s
new, luxuriously sporty  performance
cars  of the 1960s, designed for Americans
spending more time in their cars on
the growing network of first-class roads.

flourished. Families considered buying a second car. If one parent drove the first car into the city or took business trips down the interstate, the other needed a second car to do daily chores and haul the kids.

The Interstate Highway System wound a key and then released a perpetual motion machine. Planners had not reckoned how strongly such roads would attract traffic. More roads invited more travel, creating more demand for cars and gasoline, begetting more taxes to pay for more roads. New urban highways quickly clogged with cars, especially during rush hour. Funding began in 1957 and was forecast to end in 1972, when the system was to be complete. Additional miles and cost overruns extended the job. Finally, in 1976, the Federal Highway Administration, successor to the Bureau of Public Roads, acknowledged that its emphasis had shifted from building to maintaining interstate highways.

At first, states received highway funding according to population. Allocation adjustments after the first few years of construction paid the states by proportion of interstate miles instead. States such as Texas and Florida benefited. Their highways, and that revenue, contributed to the Sun Belt boom in population and industry during the late 20th century.

Arlington, Texas—a trading post that became a stop along the Texas and Pacific Railroad—stood between Dallas and Fort Worth along a turnpike that became part of Interstate 30. Arlington had fewer than a thousand residents at the start of the 20th century. It grew to 45,000 in 1960 and topped more than 330,000 by century's end. Many residents drove to work in the big cities to the east and west, using

*Protest buttons spoke the minds of those who, during the 1970s, reacted against the dominant car culture, its contribution to air pollution, and its dependence on the corporate oil industry.*

either I-30 or I-20. Arlington's two east-west interstates fed into I-820 around Fort Worth and I-635 around Dallas, as well as other interstate highways heading north and south. Arlington's location just south of the sprawling Dallas/Fort Worth Airport made the once-sleepy town convenient for air travel. Drivers within a few hundred miles, as well as air travelers, could easily visit. Small wonder that Arlington became an entertainment mecca, home of the Texas Rangers and Six Flags Over Texas. Both baseball park and amusement park sit right on Interstate 30.

. . .

Critics slammed the urban interstates. Beltways spread affluence in the suburbs, neglected the urban cores, and carried high price tags. "Our great urban centers have been subjected to the busy concrete mixers and asphalt rollers in the guise of progress," wrote Washington, D.C., journalist Helen Leavitt, who sued to keep freeway construction from knocking down her townhouse. She said urban highways were "strangling automobile traffic, adding to the already dangerous air pollution levels and displacing the city's residents with still more cars." By the 1960s, the sounds of bulldozers in low-income city neighborhoods called to mind a Marine's classic quotation from the Vietnam War: "It becomes necessary to destroy the town in order to save it." Between 1967 and 1970, interstate construction displaced nearly 169,000 people, three-fourths of whom lived in cities. Opposition to urban interstates, particularly from minority groups whose homes stood in the way, marked the first significant rejection of highways in American history. Protesters scored some victories. San Francisco halted construction on a twin-level Embarcadero Freeway and opted instead for public transit. Bostonians killed the plan for an eight-lane highway through a historic part of town. It would have displaced 1,300 households.

Interstate highway driving invited new automobile designs. Interiors became more comfortable. Car engines produced more and more horsepower. "Muscle cars" married powerful eight-cylinder engines with standard auto bodies. GM's Pontiac division and the Ford Mustang Mach I epitomized the style. Pontiacs displaying "a new approach to styling" won major NASCAR races in the early 1960s. In the company's amazing year of 1961, Pontiacs won 30 of 52 Grand National stock car races and ranked third in new car sales. By 1964, Pontiac buyers could choose the Tempest compact, the Grand Prix, or the GTO, cars built for the interstate. While not as performance-oriented as sports cars or as comfort-oriented as luxury vehicles, their powerful, smooth rides made the most of the engineered surfaces of superhighways. And they looked good. The Grand Prix had a sleek shape, rakish fenders, and an optional 428-cubic-inch engine.

Guenther and Siewchin Yong Sommer of Queens, New York, bought a 1967 Grand Prix convertible and spent 32 years driving it around the 49 continental states. They visited 251 national parks, monuments, memorials, forests, and recreational sites. As the main driver, Siewchin christened the vehicle "Tiger," taking the name from television commercials of the 1960s that compared the car to a jungle cat, "all nimble, all tiger." Their Grand Prix—soon nicknamed "Tig Tig"—proved to be the only vehicle that could handle black ice conditions in the Tennessee mountains. The Sommers were never disappointed in any of the places they visited. They enjoyed the stark beauty of Bryce Canyon and Zion National Parks in southern Utah, accessible to tourists thanks to Interstates 15 and 70.

Not all auto designs deserved such congratulation, though. Consumer advocate Ralph Nader's 1965 book, *Unsafe at Any Speed: The Designed-in Dangers of the American Automobile,* exposed flaws in the early models of another General Motors car, the Chevrolet Corvair. Debuting in 1959, the Corvair featured the first modern swing-axle independent rear suspension and a rear-mounted, air-cooled engine. It was a small, light car that got good gas mileage, carried six passengers, and gave a good ride, marketed as a sexy beast that could "purr for the girls." But its design put more than 60 percent of the car's weight on the back wheels. The heavy push from the rear caused the car to oversteer and go out of control on turns, even at relatively slow speeds. Rollovers and skids resulting in injury and death were common. Television comedian Ernie Kovacs was one of the many killed in one-car Corvair accidents. By the time Nader's book appeared, GM had substantially corrected the design flaws, but not until after death tolls had risen and sales had fallen. The last Corvair rolled off the GM assembly line in 1969.

Next, Nader broadened his attack and addressed America's auto safety flaws in general: illegible control panels, steering wheels that impaled drivers upon impact, inadequate passenger restraint systems. "From instrument panels to windshields, the modern automobile is impressive evidence that the manufacturers put appearance above safety," wrote Nader. His voice led a rising chorus that called for design changes to lessen the risks of injury and death in car accidents. Congress passed the National Traffic and Motor Vehicle Safety Act and the Highway Safety Act in 1966, creating an agency that evolved into the National Highway Traffic Safety Administration.

Gradually, the federal government forced safety regulations upon the sometimes reluctant auto industry as well. Seat belts became standard equipment. Padded dashboards, air bags, collapsible steering wheels, children's car seats, and other improvements followed. As a result, while more than 50,000 Americans died in traffic accidents in 1966, that number fell to 46,000 two decades later, although during the same interval the number of miles driven by Americans doubled.

Automobile safety depended just as much on the driver as on the vehicle. In the 1930s, high schools began offering driver education programs. In 1960, after years of studies into the effects of alcohol consumption on driving ability, the National Safety Council and the American Medical Association jointly urged laws that defined intoxication while driving and proposed a blood alcohol content of .10 percent as the limit. With the Breathalyzer, a machine invented in 1952 to calculate blood alcohol content from a single breath, police officers could confirm intoxication as soon as they stopped a suspect driver.

As 13-year-old Cari Lightner was walking to a church carnival in 1980, a car swerved off the road and hit her so hard, her body landed 120 feet away. The driver was inebriated, out on bail after his fourth drunken-driving arrest. He pleaded no contest to a single charge of vehicular manslaughter and served two years' time in a work camp and halfway house.

Cari's mother, Candy Lightner, a Sacramento real estate agent, vowed to fight what she called the "needless homicide count" caused by drunken drivers. She formed Mothers Against Drunk Driving (MADD), and the grassroots movement soon spread to all 50 states. MADD supporters tied red ribbons to their vehicles to announce their sobriety and solidarity. The group endorsed law enforcement crackdowns, including traffic sobriety checkpoints, a .08 percent blood alcohol limit for drivers, and bans on open containers of alcohol in vehicles. It also pushed California to pass the nation's toughest drunken driving law. America's alcohol-related traffic deaths dropped from 25,000 per year in the mid-1980s to 17,000 at the end of the century.

Nader and others also blasted the automobile for causing air pollution. In Los Angeles, for example, heavy traffic spewed out exhaust fumes day and night. Topography and weather concentrated the toxins. In 1966, California introduced emission standards in an effort to reduce cities' perennial smog. Automakers designed exhaust systems that chemically neutralized most pollutants, and petroleum engineers developed unleaded fuels, a boon to the environment and a necessary formulation for the new catalytic converters.

Then, in 1975, a Japanese automaker introduced a revolutionary engine that ran smoothly on a lean mixture of air and fuel and drastically reduced hydrocarbon and carbon monoxide emissions. The Honda CVCC—which stood for "compound vortex controlled combustion," the innovative engine design—traveled more than 40 highway miles on a gallon of gas, an attractive alternative to gas-guzzling American cars, which averaged less than 20. By the 1990s, both foreign and domestic new cars incorporated computer controls, fuel injection, and other recent technologies that reduced auto exhaust pollution even further.

While cars improved, superhighways stayed the same. Focused on function instead of form, they maximized traffic flow along nearly perfect pavement with minimal roadside distractions. Drivers became accustomed to reliable, swift highways and measured travel in hours rather than miles. On old, scenic, two-lane highways, drivers had chuckled at Burma-Shave signs, planted along the roads since the 1920s. Each sequential sign contributed a phrase to the jingle: "On curves ahead ... Remember, sonny ... That rabbit's foot ... Didn't save ... The bunny ... Burma-Shave." But the Minnesota company stopped erecting signs in 1963. Superhighways meant speed. Big billboards were in, little road signs were out.

As the world beyond the windshield became less interesting (or at least less distracting), drivers enjoyed greater comforts inside. Radios, power steering, air-conditioning, automatic transmissions: Once luxuries, now all these features became standard. By the 1970s, drivers could switch on the AM-FM radio, play their own choice of music on eight-track and cassette tapes, or talk on their CB radios to other travelers, miles away. You could travel from city to city and barely think about the actions of driving. If your car offered the feature, you could switch on cruise control and ease on down the highway at 60 miles per hour without even pressing the accelerator.

. . .

As the experience of travel changed, so too did the travel narrative. Jack Kerouac's 1957 novel, *On the Road,* may well have started a new genre, the road- trip novel. Kerouac fictionalized his journeys around America and Mexico with his friend, Neal Cassady. His novel crackled with the free-form jazz of life as the narrator, Sal Paradise, barreled across the Midwest, eating apple pie and ice cream, meeting truck drivers and fellow hitchhikers, and whoopeeing at the thrill of it all. Paradise had the "greatest ride in my life" in the back of a flatbed truck as he and a half dozen other hitchhikers passed a bottle and watched the great, blazing stars emerge over Nebraska. Fellow Beat writer William Burroughs said that *On the Road* "sold a trillion levis and a million espresso machines, and also sent countless kids on the road." Behind Kerouac's jazzy prose, however, lay feelings of alienation, restlessness, and dissatisfaction with postwar conformity. Perceptive reviewers said Kerouac's long journey carried him inward, not outward.

By the 1960s and 1970s, other writers explored the spiritual component of the road trip, emphasizing the mental landscape over the physical one. Ken Kesey, high priest to the hippie generation and author of *One Flew Over the Cuckoo's Nest,* bought a 1939 International Harvester school bus in 1964, intending to take a consciousness-expanding trip to New York. He and his friends, calling themselves the Merry Pranksters, painted the bus in psychedelic colors—as if, according to Tom Wolfe's book, *The Electric Kool-Aid Acid Test,* "somebody had given Hieronymous Bosch fifty buckets of Day-Glo paint." High on LSD and other drugs, the Pranksters lived up to their name on their cross-country trek. They played tricks, boomed out music from an onboard sound system, joked with people they met, and filmed 40 hours of their antics. Their destination was always "Furthur"— the word they painted above the windshield. Driving the bus was Neal Cassady, a link to Kerouac and the past.

Hunter S. Thompson's *Fear and Loathing in Las Vegas,* another LSD-fueled American odyssey, told of the writer's adventures attending an off-road race and law enforcement convention. Thompson explicitly connected the drug-altered consciousness and the pleasures of driving. "Every now and then when life gets complicated and the weasels start closing in, the only real cure is to load up on heinous chemicals and then drive like a bastard from Hollywood to Las Vegas," the gonzo journalist wrote in 1971. "To relax, as it were, in the womb of the desert sun." Upon arriving in Vegas, Thompson and a companion took in the town from a convertible. "Turn up the radio. Turn up the tape machine. Look into the sunset up ahead. Roll the windows down for a better taste of the cool desert wind. Ah yes. This is what it's all about. Total control now. Tooling along the main drag on a

BUCKLE UP ...

EVEN IN THE BACK SEAT

## SAFETY BECOMES STANDARD

**LET THE DRIVER BEWARE**

A 1984 SEAT BELT POSTER, ABOVE, PROMOTES AUTO SAFETY IN A CAMPAIGN TO BUCKLE UP. BY THEN, WAIST BELTS WERE STANDARD FEATURES IN EVERY NEW CAR. THE LAW, HOWEVER, DID NOT REQUIRE INDIVIDUAL SEAT BELT USE.

HIS DETRACTORS CALLED him "Seat Belt Roberts." The Chamber of Commerce in his state's largest city scoffed at the "do-gooder." Democratic Congressman Kenneth Roberts of Alabama, a lawyer known for persistence, kept working nonetheless and eventually won an auto safety law, first step toward federal laws requiring safety devices on all new American cars.

Roberts began pondering auto safety during his 1953 honeymoon. A vehicle rammed the back of his car, where he and his bride had carefully packed their wedding crystal. They opened the boxes and found nothing broken. "If you could do a better job of packaging people in a car," said Roberts, "you could save a good many lives." He created a subcommittee in 1957, which filed a report endorsing seat belts.

Congress chuckled, then ignored it. Even though Cornell University demonstrated in the mid-1950s that ejection from a car multiplied a passenger's risk of death by five, popular myth held that seat belts caused more injuries than they prevented. Roberts introduced a bill giving the General Services Administration oversight of safety standards for federally purchased cars. Roberts had to cut a deal with a powerful senator, and finally his bill was enacted in 1964. The GSA listed 17 safety features, including padded instrument panels, safety door latches, and a uniform sequence for automatic transmissions (P-R-N-D-L). It also mandated anchors where seat belts could be installed but not the belts themselves.

In the mid-1960s, crashes ranked as the fourth most common cause of death. Yet automakers resisted safety regulations, arguing that the new features would increase costs and compromise styling, thus hurting sales. They blamed accidents on "the nut behind the wheel."

Lobbyists and pro-business bureaucrats began watering down the GSA's regulations. Roberts's law might have had little impact if not for events in 1965. First, grassroots groups joined his cause. *Consumer Reports* magazine berated sloppy production and listed specific safety problems. Thirty doctors picketed the New York International Auto Show to demand safer designs. Second, a Senate subcommittee headed by Connecticut Democrat Abraham Ribicoff held hearings on auto safety and invited automakers to testify. GM's representatives, when pressed, admitted that their company spent an amount representing less than 0.1 percent of its profits on safety. Third, Ralph Nader published his landmark book, *Unsafe at Any Speed*. GM hired private investigators to shadow Nader, who was a consultant for Ribicoff's committee. A guard at the Senate Office Building tipped off federal officials about the surveillance, and that revelation helped President Lyndon Johnson decide to support an auto safety bill.

The newly established National Highway Traffic Safety Administration set safety standards for new cars. It adopted the GSA's list and said all cars built after 1967 must have seat belts. As predicted, safety equipment added about $300 to the sticker price of a new car by 1974, but crash fatalities dropped 20 percent.

Installation of belts did not automatically result in their use, though. Most Americans resisted buckling for reasons ranging from wrinkled clothes to the fear of getting stuck in a burning or submerged car. A 1972 Department of Transportation education pamphlet quizzed readers as to which was safer, ejection or restraint. "No, no, no," it scolded readers who checked "ejection." Such education campaigns, coupled with state "click-it-or-ticket" laws beginning in 1984, did have an impact. Seat belt use rose from 11 percent in 1980 to 68 percent in 1997.

Roberts lost his 1964 bid for re-election, but he stayed active by serving as a highway safety advisor. He died in 1989—but he lived long enough to see his mission fulfilled.

"FOR OVER HALF A CENTURY THE AUTOMOBILE HAS BROUGHT DEATH, INJURY, AND THE MOST INESTIMABLE SORROW AND DEPRIVATION TO MILLIONS OF PEOPLE." SO BEGINS *UNSAFE AT ANY SPEED*, THE LANDMARK 1965 BOOK BY HARVARD-EDUCATED ATTORNEY RALPH NADER, BELOW. NADER TESTIFIES BEFORE CONGRESS AND URGES AUTO SAFETY REGULATIONS.

Saturday night in Las Vegas, two good old boys in a fireapple-red convertible ... stoned, ripped, twisted."

. . .

Perhaps it was no coincidence that the hedonistic counterculture of the '60s and early '70s lost energy figuratively as America was literally experiencing the same thing. Americans' appetite for fossil fuels had grown explosively after World War II. The world's largest oil fields lay under the sands of North Africa and the Middle East, granting those regions raw power far exceeding their political or military might.

That became apparent in the fall of 1973, when the United States supplied weapons to Israel during its Yom Kippur War against Syria and Egypt. The Arab-dominated Organization of Petroleum Exporting Countries (OPEC), formed in Iraq in 1960, controlled more than half the world's oil supply and took advantage of the war to demonstrate its clout. Enflamed by America's pro-Israeli actions, OPEC Arab members initiated an oil embargo against the United States that lasted from October 1973 until March 1974. Then they boosted oil prices. In 12 months, the price of OPEC oil nearly quadrupled, from $3 to $11.65 a barrel. At American service stations, gasoline prices began a steady rise toward a dollar a gallon by decade's end, up from 36 cents a gallon in 1972.

Although skeptics doubted that OPEC's actions would mean a real, broad-based fuel shortage, spot shortages did hit Oregon and the Northeast in late 1973 and early 1974. Drivers in the Northeast waited in three-hour lines to get their turns at the gas pumps. States including California adopted a gas-rationing plan: Cars with odd-numbered license plates could buy gas on odd-numbered days of the month; those with even, on even. To save energy, Congress compelled the states in 1974 to lower the maximum highway speed to 55 mph. There the limit stayed for 13 years, squeezing some of the thrill out of the road trip but lowering the fatality rate on highways.

The oil crisis hurt airlines at least as hard as it hit the automobile industry. Cheap oil during the 1950s had created a boom in air travel for business and pleasure. Once jet fuel prices rose, airlines canceled and merged flights. Hardest hit were the long-distance carriers, such as Pan American, which flew exclusively to foreign destinations. In the auto market, manufacturers targeted various audiences, but in the airline business, all offered a fairly uniform product. One trip inside a jumbo jet was much like any other. Fares were regulated by the Civil Aeronautics Board (CAB) and tended to be uniform for each city-to-city route, regardless of airline. Advertisements, therefore, tried to distinguish companies by focusing on image and in-flight services.

By the 1970s, the extreme regulations imposed on airlines struck many industry observers, including CAB Chairman John Robson, as wasteful and unnecessary. Lifting the federal government's restrictions on fares and routes would bring real competition, advocates of deregulation argued. That, in turn, would raise efficiency and profitability for the carriers and lower ticket prices for passengers. Skeptics focused on the risk: Cutthroat competition might kill off the small and weak airlines. Survivors would gain a greater market share, increasing the likelihood of higher fares and lower service. Congress sided with those favoring an end to most federal controls and, in 1978, passed the Airline Deregulation Act. As the law took effect over the next six years, free-market forces began reshaping the economically troubled airline industry. By the end of the century, it looked a lot different than it had 50 years before.

Before 1938, government regulation of the airline industry addressed only matters of safety. Any entrepreneur with a scheme to make money could start an airline service. Success was assured by securing a contract to carry the mail. In 1927, an airline charged $150 to fly a passenger from New York to Chicago, while for carrying the same weight in air freight, 200 pounds, it could charge as much as $600. The DC-3, first flown by American Airlines in June 1936, broke the pattern by carrying more passengers at a higher speed than previous airplane models.

After the Civil Aeronautics Act of 1938, airlines had to obtain a "certificate of public convenience and necessity" from an aeronautics board. The law allowed government officials to compare and coordinate routes and schedules between cities. It grandfathered in the routes of existing airlines, thus locking in the dominance of existing major airlines for decades to come. However, the law also favored competition.

Four major domestic airlines had emerged before World War II: American, Eastern, TransWorld Airlines (TWA), and United. Pan American flew to Latin America. Early airplane travel was glamorous—and expensive. Each of the 22 passengers who flew the first Pan Am Clipper from Long Island to Lisbon in June 1939, for example, paid $375. The flight took 22 hours. Every seat was first-class. The cabins were roomy. The pilots circulated among the passengers, much as ship's officers would do.

Passenger demand exploded after the war. Airlines flew 1.2 billion revenue-generating passenger miles on American domestic and international routes in 1940. The number increased to 10.6 billion in 1950. Each decade, the total rose higher, so that in 1990 Americans flew nearly half a trillion miles.

On October 26, 1958, the first commercial jet rolled out onto the tarmac in New York: Pan Am's *Clipper America,* bound on an eight-and-a-half-hour flight for Paris. "In one fell swoop we have shrunken the earth," crowed Juan Trippe, Pan Am's founder. He considered it the biggest advance in aviation since 1927, when Charles Lindbergh flew solo to Paris. Domestic airlines followed suit some months later.

Unlike piston-driven propellers, the jet engine's spinning turbines created a lot of thrust but little vibration. They operated by sucking in air at the front, combining it with fuel, and igniting it. The engine channeled the explosive force to the rear, pushing the jet forward. Jet engines devoured huge amounts of fuel and generated great heat, but they flew faster and higher than piston planes, which

*In the late '60s and early '70s, the road trip became an inward journey for hippies aboard psychedelic buses, right. The Merry Pranksters, a band of counterculture oddballs, set off on a cross-continental adventure like no other aboard a similar bus in 1964. They drove from the West Coast to New York and back again, playing tricks, music, and mind games along the way.*

meant a swifter journey and a smoother, safer ride above any turbulent weather.

Seattle's Boeing Airplane Company pioneered American jet prototypes in the mid-1950s. Test pilot Alvin "Tex" Johnston gave a daring demonstration of the sturdiness of the Dash-80, Boeing's experimental commercial jet, during Seattle's Seafair Gold Cup hydroplane races in August 1955. Johnston's 160,000-pound jet performed two barrel rolls (technically, aileron rolls) 400 feet above Lake Washington at 400 miles per hour. William Allen, president of Boeing and one of thousands of lakeside witnesses, was so nervous that he asked a guest who suffered from heart problems for some of his medicine.

Juan Trippe provoked more gasps two months later, at a meeting of the International Civil Aviation Organization. Trippe announced that Pan Am planned to invest heavily in jets, the first commercial airline to do so. He had already placed an order, he said, for 45 Boeing commercial jets. "You could have heard a pin drop; it caught everybody by surprise," recalled Pan Am's technical vice president, Sanford Kauffman. Investing in jets was a gamble on a new technology. If they proved safe, day after day, they would revolutionize air travel.

"What kind of airplane is that?" asked air traffic controllers in 1958, as the first Boeing 707s flew across the continent and into Pan Am's New York terminal. "I can't keep you on the radar, you're going so fast. I picked you up in Topeka, and now you're already in Wichita! Are you flying a meteor or something?" By 1950s standards, the 707 truly zoomed along, cruising faster than 550 mph, and at

*A 1960 United Air Lines ad emphasizes convenience: the expressway to Chicago's O'Hare airport and the company's many jet routes. Before Congress let free-market forces loose upon the industry in the late 1970s, airlines were highly regulated. Rates varied little, prompting competition over intangibles, such as the promise of "Extra Care."*

the same time nearly doubled the passenger capacity of the biggest propeller airplane, the DC-7C.

. . .

Airplanes had already overtaken ocean liners in 1957 as the largest passenger carriers crossing the Atlantic. Special tourist fares attracted armies of sightseers onto planes bound for Europe, doubling the volume of the trans-Atlantic air traffic every five years. Now passengers could plan on six-and-a-half-hour flights from New York to Europe, forty hours to circle the globe completely. Jet travel seemed to support Trippe's hyperbolic claims.

Jet speed altered the experience of travel. "Don't know when I'll be back again," Peter, Paul, and Mary sang in the chart-topping hit of 1969, "Leavin' on a Jet Plane." The song by John Denver, son of an Air Force pilot, expressed romantic longing and suggested that air travel took loved ones far away, fast. Functional jet airports lacked either the atmosphere of train stations or the earthiness of bus depots. What they missed in ambience, they made up for in intensity of emotion. A jet would materialize out of the ether and unload its passengers, many of them arriving to joyful cries and hugs of reunion. More passengers would line up, ready to board the same jet, channeling through the same checkpoints, giving loved ones tearful good-byes.

Jets distorted and discolored the experience of travel. A new phrase, "jet lag," entered the lexicon, describing the physical discomforts caused by rapidly entering a different time zone and extending or compacting the hours in a day. Temporal displacement wreaked havoc on the body's internal rhythms,

including the sleep cycle. Bodies ached from confinement, minds ached from boredom. Airlines shoehorned seats into the planes, then filled as many seats as possible. Many passengers could not see out a window, limiting their world to piped-in music and movies, drink carts, and packaged meals. In 1962, historian Daniel Boorstin described his air travel experiences as "the most insulating known to man." He left a New York airport at 6:30 p.m. and arrived the next morning in the Netherlands. "The flight was routine, at an altitude of about 23,000 feet, far above the clouds, too high to observe landmark or seamark. Nothing to see but the weather; since we had no weather, nothing to see at all. I had flown not through space but through time. My only personal sign that we had gone so far was the discovery on arrival at Amsterdam that I had lost six hours.... The plane robbed me of the landscape."

Demand for air travel rose into the 1960s, and the initial glamour wore off. Airline executive Eddie Rickenbacker and others spoke of putting "bums on seats." The introduction of wide-bodied jets in the 1970s—the Boeing 747 Jumbo Jet, the Lockheed L-1011, and the McDonnell Douglas DC-10—seemed a logical extension. The new wide bodies could seat 200 to 500 passengers: more seats, more bums to park in them. Pan Am's Kauffman said the new planes made sense because aviation was becoming too popular for its own good. Airports were getting too crowded. "You could be as late as an hour landing in New York, and you would see twenty planes lined up ready to take off," said Kauffman. Even the 747s quickly filled up as jet travel boomed.

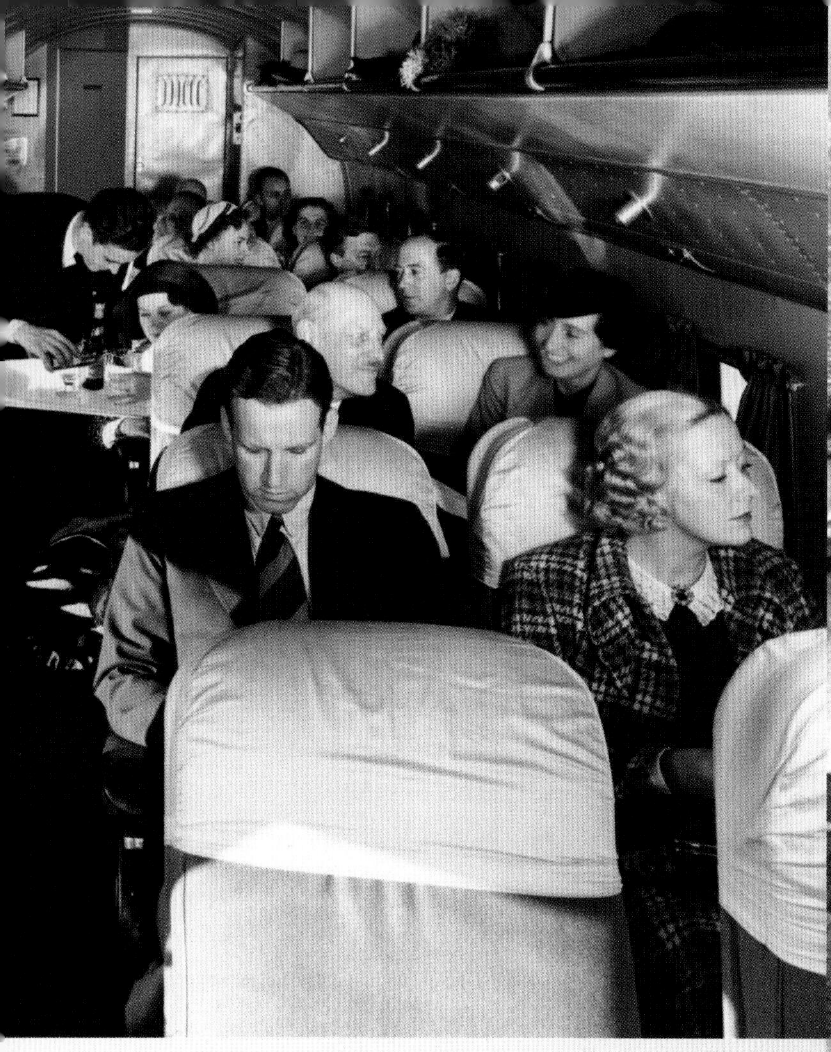

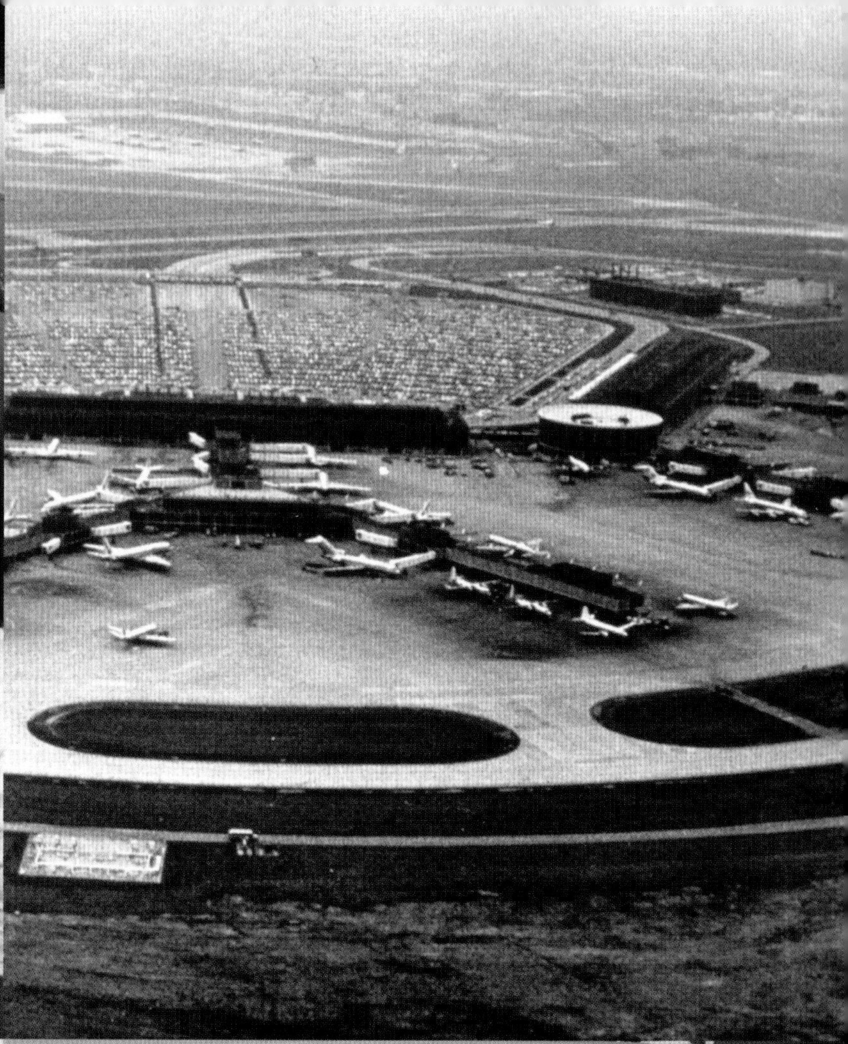

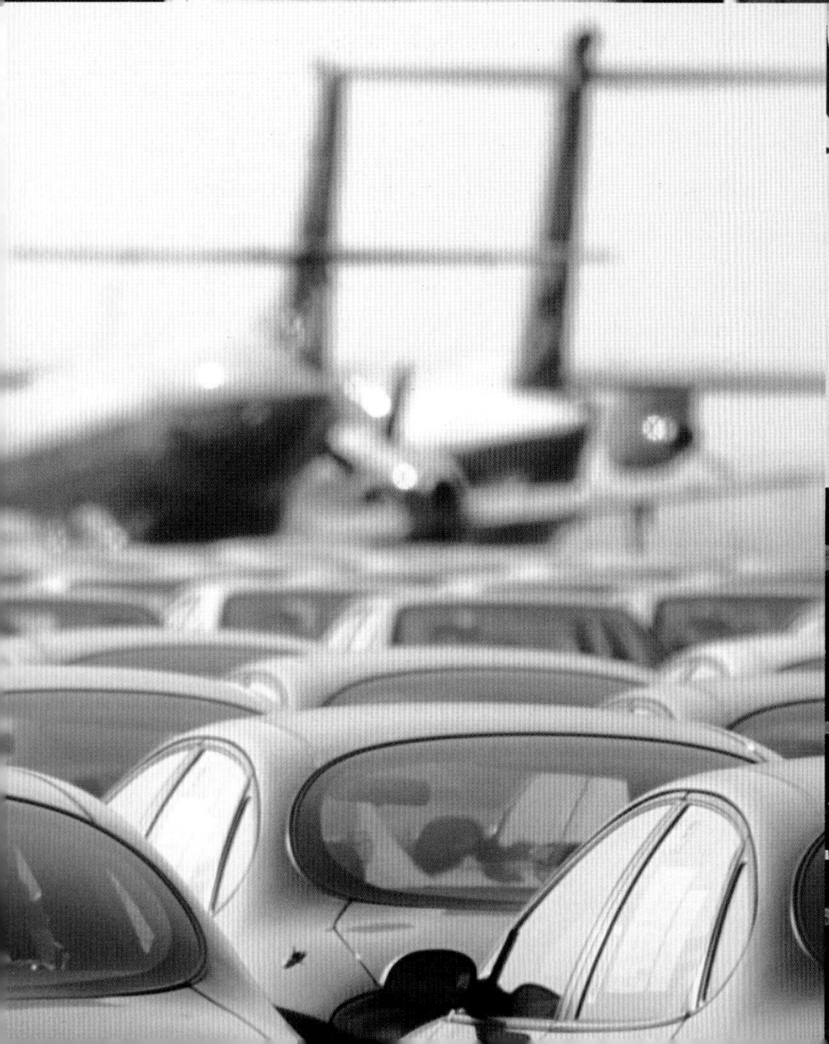

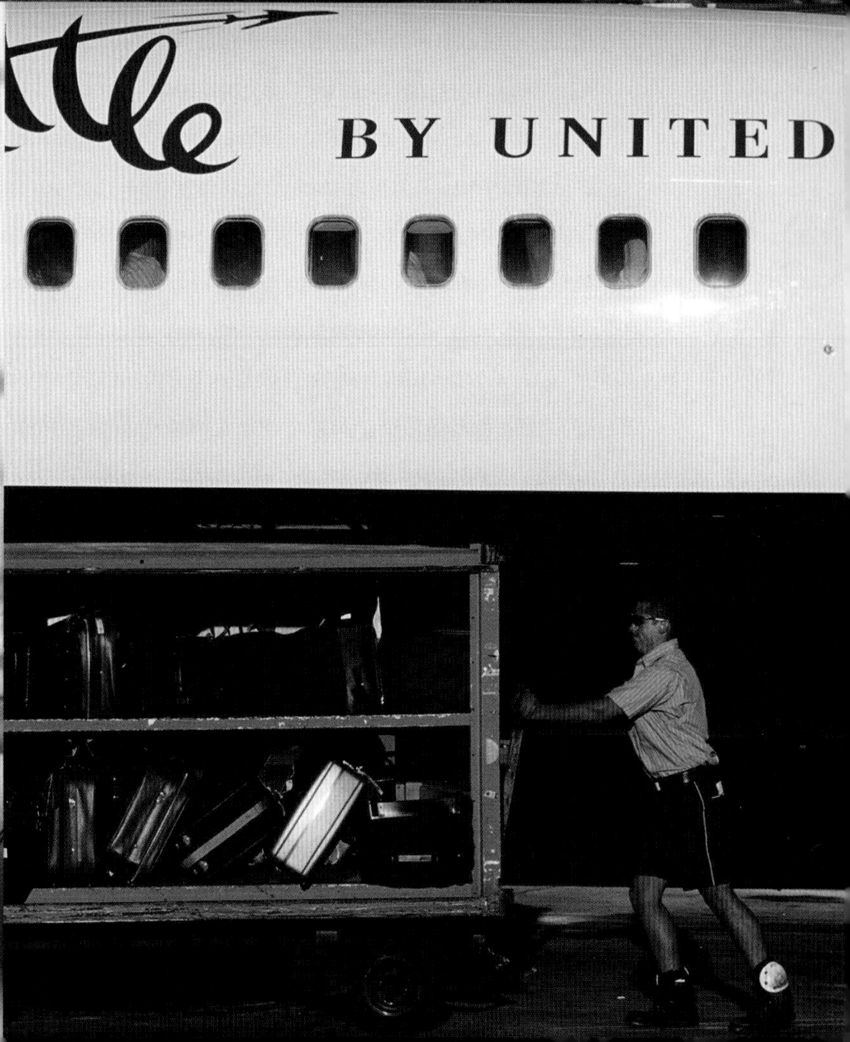
BY UNITED

While crowding made cold, economic sense, it did not please passengers. "Air travel has become less and less pleasant, as more and more passengers are being crammed into planes that appear to have been configured to transport bait," wrote syndicated newspaper columnist Dave Barry. "This is why there is talk of an Air Travelers' Bill of Rights, which would require airlines to determine their fares on some basis other than lotto drawings, and serve food that is not made from the same material as flotation devices, and provide seats that allow for the possibility—however remote—that some passengers might have both arms and legs."

At least the wide-bodied jets transformed airports in attractive ways. Large jets required runways at least 10,000 feet long. Fat fuselages naturally took up more space at the gate. These new dimensions forced small airports to renovate and stretch out. Terminal designers took the opportunity to rethink human traffic flow, and they clustered services in pods: ground transportation, baggage, restaurants, newsstands, bars, etc. In the late 20th century, airports began to look like shopping malls, or even little cities. Chicago's O'Hare Airport employed 50,000 people and handled 185,000 passengers daily.

On a typical day in the late 1990s, two million Americans took to the air, booked on more than 20,000 flights. Some flew to vacation destinations, Las Vegas or Miami. Others flew for business. In the globalized economy, many large multinational corporations scattered operations such as manufacturing and research around the planet, taking advantage of natural resources, high technology, and cheap labor wherever it was found. While the new way of doing business kept prices low for the consumer, it required continual travel by business representatives to keep the global web together. Even in an age of sophisticated communication, executives wanted face-to-face discussions. Many took portable offices with them and worked in the air. When Delta Air Lines surveyed passengers on its Boston-New York-Washington shuttle in 1998, more than half said they took 21 or more business trips per year. For a select few, jet travel allowed a bicoastal lifestyle: Work on one coast, then fly home to the other coast for the weekend. One professor who shuttled between classes in New York and family in California described the experience as a "bizarre dream of someone else's life."

With deregulation, things got more surreal. The law gradually transferred the functions of the Civil Aeronautics Board to the Department of Transportation and removed most of the regulations on domestic routes. Gone, for example, were the CAB's airline fare controls, which it had exercised case by case, asserting authority as well to set a price range for a particular route. Free-market forces brought many niche airlines into existence—such as People's Express, which scaled back to no-frills service and no reservations in exchange for low fares—but they also

*During the second half of the 20th century, air travel evolved from elegant privilege to mass habit. Clockwise from upper left: A steward serves passengers on a Douglas DC-3 in the 1950s; Chicago's O'Hare Airport was already bustling in 1963; a ground crew member pushes luggage from jet to terminal in San Francisco, 1995; and cars jam an airport parking lot, 1998.*

caused a string of mergers and bankruptcies. Both Pan Am and Eastern, two of the original Big Five, failed. Pan Am suffered a staggering blow in 1988 when terrorists blew its Flight 101 out of the skies over Lockerbie, Scotland. A long labor dispute forced Eastern's decline. A third airline, United, filed for bankruptcy in 2002 but kept on flying.

From 1979 into the first years of the 21st century, the United States saw a 70 percent growth in the number of scheduled commercial airline flights. Industry growth was lumpy, though, complicated by fierce competition. At the start of the 21st century, 80 percent of all flights flew into only 50 of America's thousands of airports. Airlines adopted "hub" airports, network centers where many routes converged. Passengers disembarked and in many cases boarded connector flights bound for non-hub destinations served by smaller, regional airlines. Delta positioned its hubs in Salt Lake City and Atlanta, TWA in Kansas City, American Airlines in Dallas/Fort Worth. Atlanta became such a mixmaster of human beings and planes, people started joking that "When you go to heaven, you must change planes in Atlanta." While the hub system did keep down the cost of travel into hub cities, flights to smaller, out-of-the-way destinations generally became more expensive.

Despite the drawbacks of deregulated air travel, the airline industry enjoyed record profits in the late 1990s. After surviving a bankruptcy filing in 1991, America West Airlines earned $301.9 million in aggregate net profits from 1997 through 1999. Southwest Airlines enjoyed nine consecutive years of record-setting profits, with 2000 its biggest year ever. An economic downturn cut into the industry's earnings early in the new century. The profitable times ended dramatically on September 11, 2001, when fundamentalist Muslim terrorists armed with box cutters hijacked four American jets and crashed them into the two World Trade Center towers in New York, the Pentagon in Washington, and a field in Pennsylvania. All U.S. flights were grounded for two days. Soon most airports reopened, but fearful passengers still stayed away.

Security became much tighter at American airports. In November 2001, President George W. Bush signed the Aviation and Transportation Security Act, transferring the responsibility for aviation security from the airlines to the federal government. New steps to protect planes included tougher screening of airport and airline employees, air passengers, and luggage. Random searches and increased use of explosive detection equipment helped make airports safer, while installation of stronger cockpit doors and a significant increase in the number of federal air marshals boosted the security of planes in the air. "Americans have long known that 'eternal vigilance is the price of liberty,'" Jane F. Garvey, head of the Federal Aviation Administration, told an air security technology conference two-and-a-half months after the terrorist attacks.

"Now, we know, it is the price of mobility as well."

AS PROPOSED, THE EXPRESSWAY IS TO CURVE
AND WIND ITS WAY ACROSS AN AUDUBON
BIRD SANCTUARY AND OLMOS CREEK, ... FORCE
AN ELEMENTARY SCHOOL TO CLOSE, PASS
THROUGH THE ZOO, BLOCK OFF THE PUBLIC
GYMNASIUM, FOLLOW THE EDGE OF THE SUNKEN
GARDENS, PAST THE OUTDOOR THEATRE ...
AND LIMP HOME THROUGH A WOODED PORTION
OF THE SAN ANTONIO RIVER'S NATURAL
WATERCOURSE, ONE OF THE FEW REMAINING
WILDERNESS AREAS LEFT IN THE CITY.

THIS IS A CLASSIC EXAMPLE OF
HIGHWAY PLANNING.

— *Helen Leavitt*, **Superhighway—Superhoax**, *1970*

# ENTERPRISE IN A
# GLOBAL AGE

*Dock work changed during the 20th century. Opposite, clockwise from upper left: Longshoremen used slings to hoist bulk shipments; barrels, bags, and boxes came off freighters; workers packed items on pallets to come off a vessel; new ships like the* Hawaiian Progress *were loaded by longshoremen using cranes to lift pallets. Air travel sped up world communications, as suggested in the 1948 poster, above.*

General Motors' Futurama in 1939 was neither the first time nor the last that Americans predicted the future. In 1950, the pundits again looked beyond the present day and imagined the world in 2000.

They did so in an era wracked with tensions. Alliances between the Soviet Union, Britain, and the United States fell apart in the postwar world. Between 1945 and 1950, the Soviets blockaded West Berlin, the North Atlantic Treaty Organization (NATO) formed, and China became a Communist country. The so-called Cold War really started heating up when, on August 29, 1949, the Soviet Union first tested its atomic bomb. On June 25, 1950, North Korea invaded South Korea, and the United States entered another war. The nation had achieved wealth and world-recognized power, but its future in the atomic age was uncertain. You wouldn't know that from the future forecasters, though. In 1950, many of them blithely ignored geopolitical realities and painted a picture of a society where technology guaranteed prosperity to every American.

The February 1950 issue of *Popular Mechanics* ran a typical article on the promise of the future. Titled "Miracles You'll See in the Next Fifty Years" and written by the *New York Times* science editor, Waldemar Kaempffert, the article described the mythical Dobson family, living in the mythical town of Tottenville in the year 2000. In the future Kaempffert envisioned, cities were clean, and solar power fueled stoves. Americans shopped from the comfort of home, using interconnected televisions and telephones. Gender roles didn't change much. Men went to work and women stayed home. Some things had evolved, though: The average American housewife cleaned her house with a hose and tossed her family's plastic plates down the drain. Chemical factories converted the family's used "paper table 'linen' and rayon underwear" into candy.

Changing transportation systems were central to the 2000 scenario. The airport was at the "heart of the town," and air travel dominated American life. Rich travelers jumped onto supersonic planes and crossed the Atlantic in under three hours. The family helicopter carried people wherever they wanted to go. Commuters traveled to the city, "a hundred miles away, in huge aerial busses that hold 200 passengers." Roads and cars still existed, but flying vehicles fulfilled most travel needs. Our relationship with the automobile—a streamlined vehicle that ran on cheap denatured alcohol—would change dramatically.

In some respects, the 1950 predictions had come true by the year 2000. Americans did indeed take more and more to the skies. But in many respects, cars, trucks, and trains still closely resembled their 1950 predecessors. Our transportation systems still depended on oil, although by 2000, the U.S. no longer could claim to be the world's largest producer. Changes unforeseen in 1950 did go on, though—a quiet transportation revolution behind the scenes, fueling economic and political transformations so vast that commentators could declare at the end of the 20th century that we lived in a newly global age.

. . .

The postwar transportation revolution started on the nation's docks, with the seemingly mundane idea of packing goods into large, standardized steel boxes.

As early as the 1930s, some railroads were hauling loaded truck trailers and their chassis. But it was Malcolm McLean, a trucking executive turned ship owner, who took the idea and made it a full-fledged transportation system.

McLean got his start in the 1930s, "hauling empty tobacco barrels in a clunker of a truck" in Depression-ridden North Carolina. Waiting in line for his truck to be unloaded onto a freighter, McLean apparently asked himself, "Wouldn't it be great if my trailer could simply be lifted up and placed on the ship without its contents being touched?" To test the idea, he converted a World War II surplus oil tanker—called by one *Washington Post* reporter "an old bucket of bolts"—into a container ship.

To enter the shipping business, McLean had to leave the family trucking business, since ICC rules didn't allow companies to own interests in more than one mode of freight transportation. He also had to broker a deal with the teamsters and the longshoremen, and, as the *New York Times* put it, "he persuaded the Port of New York Authority" to build new docks with "elbow-room for truck maneuvering." The newly configured *Ideal X* made the maiden voyage from Newark to Houston with 58 boxes aboard. McLean was on his way to becoming, as he was called when he died in 2001, "the father of containerization."

On the West Coast, a long-established shipping firm, the Matson Navigation Company, took the lead. Swedish immigrant William Matson started the company in the 1880s, servicing the Hawaiian Islands. By the mid-1950s the Matson Company had what *Washington Post* columnist George E. Sokolsky

In this 1950 Popular Mechanics *article,*
New York Times *science editor Waldemar Kaempffert predicted that people's daily lives would be shaped by technological conveniences yet to be invented. The typical U.S. city would be clean, and people would commute by airbus.*

called a "virtual monopoly" on the Hawaii trade, even though Randolph Sevier, Matson's president in 1955, repeatedly told the House Merchant Marine Committee that shipping was a "sick industry." He blamed the sickness to no small degree on labor disputes. Jumping on the container bandwagon helped the struggling company become more profitable.

Matson analysts discovered that moving goods between ship and pier accounted for almost half the total transportation costs. Container ships could alleviate that problem. Matson's first container ship, the *Hawaii Merchant,* sailed from San Francisco to Honolulu in August 1958 with 20 containers "filled with everything from beer to baby food." Within two years, the company's freighter, *Hawaiian Citizen,* had been converted into the Pacific's first all-container ship. It carried 436 containers in the hold.

Containerized operations looked very different from the hook-and-hoist workplaces they replaced. Loading a ship by hand took days. Teams of workers used cargo hooks and the strength of their backs, as well as their spatial skills, to stow a wide array of goods tightly into the ship's hold. Workers handled crates, packages, bags, bales, and larger items. They packed them in to use all space available and make sure the cargo didn't shift en route.

By contrast, cranes lifted containers, already packed with goods, off trucks and stacked them inside a ship's hold. Dockworkers no longer had to concern themselves with their contents or the pattern in which they were stacked. Containers didn't conform to the shape of a ship's hull, so they did tend to waste space, but after the initial investment in

## AIR TRAFFIC CONTROL COMES OF AGE

**A FOUR-DIMENSIONAL CHESS GAME
KEEPS HUMAN LIVES IN THE BALANCE.**

IN 1930, THE CLEVELAND, OHIO, AIRPORT WAS THE FIRST
IN THE UNITED STATES TO USE RADIO–IN ADDITION TO
TARMAC FLAGS AND LIGHTS–TO ENHANCE COMMUNICATIONS
BETWEEN AIRPORTS AND PILOTS WHO WERE TAKING OFF
OR LANDING. RADAR INSTRUMENTS THAT HAD BEEN
DEVELOPED FOR WORLD WAR II HELPED TRACK INCOMING
AND OUTGOING PLANES.

WITH THE HELP OF COMPUTERS, RADAR DATA REVEALING
A PLANE'S IDENTITY, ALTITUDE, AND SPEED READ OUT
ON THE SCREEN ABOVE. "AIR TRAFFIC CONTROL IS SIMILAR
TO THE GAME OF CHESS," SAID ONE CONTROLLER IN THE
LATE 1980S. "YOU PLAN, YOU SCHEME, AND YOU ANTICIPATE
THE NEXT MOVE. BUT IN ANY GIVEN MOMENT THE GAME
PLAN CAN CHANGE."

AIR TRAVEL BOOMED IN THE LATE 20TH CENTURY. IN 1999,
AIRLINES EMPLOYED OVER 700,000–MORE THAN DOUBLE THE
NUMBER IN 1970. THE FEDERAL AVIATION AUTHORITY (FAA)
EMPLOYED ABOUT 13,000 AIR TRAFFIC CONTROLLERS,
LIKE THOSE ABOVE, TO COORDINATE THE COMPLEX FLOW OF
AIRCRAFT. TAKEOFFS AND LANDINGS THAT YEAR TOTALED
MORE THAN EIGHT AND A HALF MILLION.

containers and equipment, they saved money and lowered turnaround time. Austin J. Tobin, the head of the Port Authority of New York, called containerization "the greatest technological revolution since steam furled the sails."

Perhaps it is counterintuitive to think of a steel box as a technological revolution, but the container system linked transportation modes together in new ways. It took a while for the new system to reach full potential. The capital costs of converting to containers were high, and the ICC's archaic regulatory structure made intermodality more difficult to achieve. It was clear, though, that when the same container could stack on a ship, a train, or a truck interchangeably, the innovation would profoundly change the way transportation modes worked with one another.

. . .

Containers first changed the nation's waterfronts. Relationships between dockworkers and employers had a history of contention and conflict. As in so many other early 20th-century businesses, managers originally would not recognize the right of their workers to join a union. The issue came to a head on the San Francisco waterfront in 1934.

Dockworkers had staged a strike in 1919 but had failed to reach their goals. A decade and a half later, West Coast longshoremen tried again. New Deal legislation (declared unconstitutional a year later) gave workers the right to join together. A wave of organizing activity across the country involved coal miners in several states, rubber factory workers in Ohio, steelworkers in Ohio and West Virginia, garment shop workers in New York and California,

and autoworkers in Michigan. Longshoremen on the West Coast—including a fiery young radical named Harry Bridges—rebuilt their union, calling it the International Longshoreman's Association.

Pacific Coast locals met in February 1934 and decided to push for a dollar an hour, a 6-hour day, a 30-hour week, $1.50 overtime, and a union hiring hall. "We shouldn't take any notice of what the shipowners think or say about us," said rising star Bridges. "They would shoot us if they had the chance or could get away with it without being discovered. We are putting them on the block and we should keep them there." In March 1934, the longshoremen voted overwhelmingly to strike if necessary. On May 9, they did put the shipowners on the block—and kept them there for 82 days.

The 1934 Pacific Coast waterfront strike reached its apogee on July 5 when, as reporter Royce Brier put it in the *San Francisco Chronicle*, "Blood ran red in the streets of San Francisco." A pro-business association had hired strike breakers to move freight. On July 3, "police used their clubs freely and mounted officers rode into milling crowds. The strikers fought back, using fists, boards and bricks as weapons." Two men were shot and wounded, trucks were overturned, and, as the *San Francisco Daily News* reported, "The police used so much tear gas that Chief Quinn asked the Department of Justice to rush him more gas equipment from Alcatraz Island."

The city quieted down for the Fourth of July, but the next day, things got worse. On a day remembered by longshoremen as Bloody Thursday, "police revolvers cracked into mobs of howling, cursing

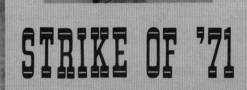

STRIKE OF '71

strikers. Tear gas guns sent off blinding fumes; hand grenades exploded. Riot sticks cracked upon scores of heads," according to the *San Francisco Daily News*. By the end, two men—a longshoreman and a Marine cook—lay dead on the sidewalk.

Their deaths drew sympathy for the union. City workers called a general strike that lasted four days. Longshoremen continued theirs through July, then agreed to arbitration. After the strike, the balance of power shifted and the Longshoremen's Union became a fact of life on the waterfront.

The union made a difference, but the work of filling ships' holds didn't change until the 1950s, when mechanization altered the nature of dock work. As Harry Bridges, President of the International Longshoremen's and Warehousemen's Union (ILWU), put it in 1963, "Machines when they came appeared as merciless monsters, more deadly by far than slack times, because jobs swallowed never came back."

Trade through the docks had fallen off. Workers and their bosses both had a stake in moving more cargo through the docks. Relationships between the longshoremen and industry began to change, bringing about one of the oddest alliances imaginable, between Harry Bridges, union leader, and J. Paul St. Sure, management expert.

*Harry Bridges, the charismatic leader of the West Coast longshoremen, rose to leadership in his union in the 1930s. He was best known for his radical politics and his tough negotiating style, but this image shows a relaxed young Bridges on a sailing ship. The fist and cargo hook logo, inset, was adopted when longshoremen voted to strike in 1971, despite Bridges' disapproval. Since then, the logo has been widely used as a symbol of the International Longshoremen's and Warehousemen's Union (ILWU).*

The two men seemed like opposites. Alfred Renton Bryant Bridges was born in a suburb of Melbourne, Australia, in 1901. He started working as a sailor when he was 16 and, in 1920, jumped ship and stayed in the United States. In 1922, he went to work on the San Francisco docks. A charismatic leader, the "dapper, hawk-faced" Bridges had been exposed as a child to radical ideas by a favorite uncle. He was briefly a member of the International Workers of the World, known as the Wobblies. Tall and skinny, with wild hair and flashing eyes, Bridges helped revitalize the waterfront's union movement with his powerful oratory and his attention to bread-and-butter issues like pay and working conditions. During the turmoil in 1934, Bridges was elected head of the strike committee and thus thrust into the limelight and a leadership role.

Bridges became head of the ILWU in 1937 and remained in power for 40 years. "I'm just a member of the working class of the world," he modestly claimed just before he retired. "These honors just come to me as their representative." Then, in typical Harry Bridges fashion, speaking before an audience of government, industry, labor, and church leaders, he said, "I still believe in that old Marxist slogan: 'From each according to his ability, to each according to his need.'"

In earlier years, Bridges had struck fear and revulsion into the hearts of shipowners with his outspoken radicalism. Fighting for workers' rights, he antagonized San Francisco's business elite. In 1938, a conservative publication claimed, "Bridges is as insidious as a cancer. He reaches his goal through the use of soft, dulcet tones and velvet touches." One shipping company vice president admitted, "I used to think he had horns and a tail and long fangs."

His politics and verbal bravado got him in trouble with the law. From the late 1930s until 1955, government officials targeted Bridges. The House of Representatives passed a bill in 1940 to deport him to Australia because he was a "hurtful" presence in the United States. Officials imprisoned Bridges on Angel Island during World War II. At the beginning of the Korean War, they called him a "menace" and locked him up again. He was repeatedly charged with being a member of the Communist Party.

The political climate of the early 1950s was colored by the beliefs and actions of Senator Joseph McCarthy. Being fingered as a Communist was a serious threat to one's liberty, and Bridges would have been imprisoned, then deported, if his connections to the Communist Party had been proven. Into the 1950s, as fellow longshoreman Bill Ward put it, Bridges "took all the flack and all the heat that could be mustered by the richest government in the world." The Supreme Court finally stopped the unending legal actions against him in 1955. When Harry Bridges retired from union leadership in 1977, the *New York Times* recalled that for "millions ... he was an apocalyptic herald of revolution."

If Harry Bridges seemed born to get into trouble with the law, Joseph Paul St. Sure seemed born to uphold it. His family moved from Wisconsin to California in the 1860s. Joseph Paul was born in 1902 in Alameda, a thriving island city outside San Francisco. His father was a judge, appointed to the

*Cartoons from the ILWU newspaper,* The Dispatcher, *during the 1960s humorously reflect the anxieties of long-shoremen facing job mechanization.*

federal bench by Republican President Calvin Coolidge. St. Sure studied law at the University of California at Berkeley, graduated in 1924, and became assistant district attorney for Alameda County under Earl Warren, who later became a U.S. Supreme Court justice.

Although J. Paul St. Sure was a respectable lawyer and not a longshoreman, the 1934 dockworkers' strike was an important moment in his life. As Harry Bridges was leading maritime workers in their struggle, St. Sure was working in Oakland, California. He served as counsel for the East Bay Defense Association for Business and Labor, a group set up by local entrepreneurs to monitor the strike and keep Oakland's businesses running. The events of 1934 made St. Sure "acutely aware of the great areas of potential social conflict which I had not realized existed," he said later. "Personally, these events changed the course of my professional life."

St. Sure continued working as a labor negotiator, believing that the 1934 strike and the New Deal had "brought about a rather complete change in the relationship between management and labor and certainly brought about a very real organizing drive on the part of the unions." In the 1930s and '40s, he advised a range of businesses and, as he said later, "on several occasions I advised disbelieving managements that their encouragement of inside unions amounted to a violation of the law." St. Sure became head of the Pacific Maritime Association (PMA) in 1952, and by then he had more than a decade of experience in labor-management relations.

Beginning in the early 1950s, the man representing the workers and the man representing the managers began interacting, and in the process they created a friendship that helped peace reign on the West Coast docks. Together, the ILWU and the PMA changed the ways ports did business, but they did so by negotiation and agreement rather than by strike and strife. Both men came to recognize that mechanization and modernization, including the use of freight containers, was the wave of shipping's future. "Whether you or I, or the union, or the steamship operators, like it or not," St. Sure told Bridges, "pressures are going to mount to the point where either we are going to have a show down battle, or we are going to have to find some way to bring about a correction, or adjustment." Bridges and St. Sure pursued the adjustment rather than the battle. They convinced their memberships that change was going to come, no matter what, so the best approach was to reach agreements on how to work mechanization into the future they shared.

Moving a steel box between dock and hold required a different kind of worker. Traditional longshoring gangs used skill, strength, tools, and ingenuity to heave massive weights of cargo. Now different skills were needed. "When you climb about the *Hawaiian Citizen,* remarked a visitor to the Matson container ship, "you are no longer entering the swaying world of the seafaring man. It has become an ingeniously designed mobile warehouse floating between the states of Hawaii and California and rapidly filled and emptied at either end."

Labor and management, working together, paved the way for these mobile warehouses. On October 18,

1960, in a swirl of publicity, mostly positive, Harry Bridges and J. Paul St. Sure signed a Memorandum of Agreement on Mechanization and Modernization, nicknamed M&M. Most papers declared the agreement "epochal" and "historic," but not everyone agreed it was a good thing. A *Wall Street Journal* editorial called it a "payoff" and said the union had "every reason to be jubilant at the fat price they got for something that never really belonged to them." Some employers thought it undermined managerial prerogatives, since it tacitly acknowledged the workers' right to be compensated for job losses.

St. Sure threatened to resign from the PMA if he didn't get a unanimous vote in favor of the memorandum. Some longhoremen, a minority, didn't like it either. Eric Hoffer—the longshoreman-philosopher whose first book, *The True Believer: Thoughts on the Nature of Mass Movements,* was published in 1951—thought the union had sold out. "This generation has no right to give away, or sell for money, conditions that were handed on to us by a previous generation," he wrote. Other longshoremen thought that the union deserved even more money for giving up their time-honored work rules.

Still, the longshoremen passed the M&M agreement by a vote of two to one. Employers were to pay five million dollars a year into a fund for longshoremen, to hedge against cases of unemployment or mandatory retirements caused by increased mechanization. Workers would gain a share of the profits, and managers could reorganize work as they saw fit.

The M&M agreement paved the way for a dramatic increase in containerized cargo. In 1960,

freighters carried 494,000 tons in containers; by 1970, nearly 9,000,000 tons. By 1995, 95 percent of shipping line cargoes were containerized.

As the shipping industry changed, so did the ports. The port of San Francisco had served California since the gold rush, but the port of Oakland, just across San Francisco Bay, was more easily transformed to receive container cargo. By 2000, the port of Oakland handled 98 percent of the containerized cargo coming into the Bay Area. The terminal stretched four miles along the waterfront and covered more than 600 acres.

Around the world, new seaports rose to prominence, once they converted to receiving container-loaded freighters. Britain's traditional maritime strongholds, London and Liverpool, faced competition from Felixstowe, northeast of London on the North Sea. Bangkok's port became overwhelmed by traffic, so the new port of Laem Prabang was built. Trade through Hong Kong and Singapore grew rapidly in the 1980s, as they became the world's two largest container ports. New York had since colonial days been the nation's maritime trade center, but with the increase of trade coming from Asia, Los Angeles became the nation's preeminent port by 1990.

Containerization was a global phenomenon. By 1981, the top five container companies—from America, Germany, Denmark, Britain, and Japan—

*A container ship at dock, right, receives cargo from a mechanized lift in 1966. Container ships, and the cranes that loaded and unloaded them, became increasingly common sights in the nation's ports during the 1960s.*

Heavy-duty trucks moved cargo on the nation's highways as the interstate highway system developed. Peterbilt, founded in 1939, became the standard. In 1980, trucks hauled 555 billion tons per mile traveled.

were spread around the world. By 1994, the port of Hong Kong was processing the world's largest volume of containers, and five out of six of the world's busiest container ports were in Asia. Container shipments traveled around the world, contributing to the development of a global, intermodal transportation system that served multinational corporate interests.

. . .

The effects of containerization rippled through the United States's other transportation systems and, over time, helped breathe new life into the nation's ailing railroads. During World War II, railroads had carried more people and freight than ever before, but once the war was over, railway companies started struggling.

Trucks cut into the freight business. More and more people were driving cars or, for longer travel, flying. In 1944, railways were responsible for some three-quarters of the miles Americans traveled from city to city, but by 1960, the railway's share had plummeted to less than a third. In the late 1950s, David P. Morgan, the editor of *Trains Magazine,* could claim without hesitation in the late 1950s that railroad travel "renders the competition nothing less than barbaric by comparison," considering the "package of space and mobility and luxury" that

*Containers whiz by on a rail journey near Carrizozo, New Mexico. As containers made the leap from sea to rail, they helped create an integrated transportation system where different modes of transportation road, rail, and waterborne worked together to create a fast, cheap, and reliable network.*

trains could promise. Those features no longer seemed to attract passengers in the 1960s.

Once railroad companies started losing passengers, they concentrated on freight. There they also faced steep competition from roadway vehicles. Manufacturers often preferred the adjustable schedules and door-to-door service that trucks provided. Some companies purchased their own trucks, saving costs and turning them into mobile billboards. Railroads sought economies at every turn. By 1962, they had cut their workforce nearly in half. New technologies made change possible. Diesel engines, easier to operate and maintain, required fewer workers on the trains and in the shops. Despite these changes, by 1962, as historian William Withuhn put it, "freight ton-miles in railroads skidded to their lowest level since the Great Depression." Miles of track fell out of use. Railroad companies merged or went bankrupt. The once proud and mighty Pennsylvania Railroad Company and the New York Central merged in 1968 to form Penn Central, but the new company went bankrupt in 1970.

Eventually America's railroads came back to life by assuming a critical role in the international transportation system. Shippers began to talk about a "land bridge" from Asia, across the U.S. to Europe, but as Larry Kramer wrote in the *Washington Post,* the term was a marketers' creation, and "to everyone else, it is known as the railroad." Asian products, destined for stores and factories throughout not only the United States but Europe as well, came by container ship into West Coast harbors. Railroads retooled so that their cars could carry containers.

Shipments arriving on the West Coast from Asia would be loaded onto trains. The technique cut several days off the time it took goods to travel from Asia to Europe, and it eliminated the costly trip through the Panama Canal. By the mid-1990s, reported the *New York Times*, "a fully loaded container train can now take the place of 200 tractor-trailers." No longer the force they once were in American transportation, the railroads still performed their stalwart duty, maintaining commercial links from coast to coast.

. . .

As the waterfront revolution began to improve American shipping and the railroads joined the move to containers, bulldozers had been carving the all-new interstate highway system into the American landscape. Trucking companies appreciated the benefits of the new highways. They were engineered to such high standards that trucks could pull more weight—and they were 90 percent paid for by the federal government. The number of trucks on American roadways grew at an exponential rate after World War II. In 1944, trucks carried 58 billion ton-miles (tons per mile traveled) of intercity freight; by 1960, they carried 285 billion. Meanwhile, freight carried annually by rail fell by more than 150 billion tons.

As federal and state governments poured money into building more and better roads, trucking businesses could handle long-haul freight, the kind that traveled far and fast across the country—like fruit from California. By 1970, truckers spent half their drive time on interstates. Long-haul drivers roared along the nation's highways, day and night, sometimes for days or weeks at a time, now able to drive from coast to coast in three days. Truck manufacturers started building sleeper cabs into their large rigs, back behind the driver's seat, so drivers could pull over and sleep without veering far from the highway.

But truckers needed places where there was room to park the truck, buy diesel fuel, get a meal and a shower, and enjoy a few of life's other amenities before hitting the road again. They needed truck stops. *New York Times* reporter J. Anthony Lukas rode with Barker Keith in his "barn-red International Harvester tandem tractor" in the spring of 1970. After a couple of hours in that "Monster of the Pavement," they stopped at the Tichard Stockton Service Area near Bordentown, New Jersey, to get coffee and a blueberry muffin at the Howard Johnson's there. When Barker pulled into the parking lot, he told the reporter, "Trailermen stop here because they got this lot. Let me tell you, when you got 115-feet of rig like we do, you look twice before you pull in some places. Some places you can get in all right, but you can't get out."

Barker took a second break at another truck stop at one o'clock in the morning. There, along with a dozen other truckers, wrote Lukas, Barker and a friend "chat about a trucker they know who dropped dead at the wheel" while Barker "downs a hamburger and onions, a slice of cherry pie, and two cups of coffee."

In 1951, 2,000 truck stops already dotted American highways. Many early ones were in California, the fruit basket of the nation, where good roads and the need to ship fresh and frozen produce quickly made trucks, not trains, the transportation

## NEXT-DAY AIR
### PACKAGES FLY IN THE INFO AGE

WORKERS PREPARE A UPS PLANE FOR TAKEOFF OUT OF THE COMPANY'S WEST COAST HUB IN ONTARIO, CALIFORNIA, IN 1997. WHEN A PLANE LANDS AT A HUB, FREIGHT IS SORTED AND RELOADED ONTO ANOTHER, OUTBOUND FOR AN ULTIMATE DESTINATION.

TO "FED EX": It has become the verb used to describe sending an overnight letter, whatever carrier actually delivers the letter. E-mails, faxes, and phones have all helped create a world in which nearly instantaneous communications are possible, but the growth of the overnight delivery business shows how important physical transportation systems remain in the electronic age.

Federal Express led the way into a world where we can put a letter in a mailbox in Washington, D.C., at 8 p.m. and expect it to be in San Francisco before 10 a.m. the next day. Founded in 1971, Federal Express struggled for its first few years, but by 1991, it delivered 1.5 million packages a day. In the same year, the overnight delivery business was an eight-billion-dollar-a-year industry. Its success began with a brilliant, unlikely innovation. As a *Washington Post* article put it in 1982, "The key to Federal Express' rapid rise is the unlikely sounding,

highly original and nongeometric notion that the fastest way to move cargo between two points in the United States is through Memphis."

FedEx's origin myth claims that Fred Smith, the son of a Tennessee transportation entrepreneur, came up with his "nongeometric notion" for a paper he wrote as a Yale undergraduate. As the story goes, Smith got a C on the paper—but the FedEx founder later recanted that part of the story, saying, in an article in *Fortune* magazine, "I was asked what grade I got on it, and I stupidly said, 'I guess I got my usual gentlemanly C.' ... To be honest, I don't really remember what grade I got. I probably didn't get a very good one, though, because it wasn't a very well-thought-out paper."

Regardless of the grade he received on his paper, Fred Smith had a multimillion-dollar idea. Like Malcolm McLean, the father of containerization before him, he thought about delivery in a synthetic way. As he put it,

"I did something else a little bit unusual, which was to combine the airplanes and trucks into one delivery system. This didn't seem to me to be so controversial, but all the traditional people felt that it was highly iconoclastic." As "just-in-time" manufacturing became a way of life in American industry, overnight deliveries became more essential for business and industry. To stay competitive, existing freight carriers followed Federal Express's lead.

One of those companies had started out in the first decade of the 20th century as a small, local business. In 1907, James Casey, a 19-year-old in Seattle, started the American Messenger Company, a fleet of delivery people on foot and bicycle who hand-delivered packages for businesses. In 1919, the company expanded to Oakland, California, and took a new name. The United Parcel Service (UPS) began buying planes and offering air freight service in 1929, but the Great Depression put an end to that endeavor.

UPS stayed in business through the Depression by providing customer delivery service for department stores. It returned to the air freight business in the 1950s, and by 1978, the company could deliver packages to every address in the United States. Most were driven by freight trucks across the country on the U.S. interstates, then up to the customer's door in familiar brown panel trucks.

As FedEx's business grew phenomenally, though, UPS opted to offer next-day service as well, in 1982. By the beginning of the 21st century, both UPS and FedEx had grown into global operations.

In 2003, for $92.71, a letter could travel by FedEx from Washington, D.C., to the Mariana Islands in the South Pacific, arriving in six days. In the words of Mike Esckew, Chairman and CEO of UPS, "We want to make it as easy for you to reach your customers from Illinois to India as it is from Illinois to Indiana."

A FEDEX TRUCK MAKES AN AFTER-DARK PICKUP FROM A BROADWAY AVENUE ADDRESS IN MANHATTAN. IN THE LATE 1990S, OVERNIGHT DELIVERY TRUCKS BECAME PART OF THE FABRIC OF EVERYDAY, AND EVERY-EVENING, LIFE IN BUSINESS CENTERS AROUND THE NATION.

mode of choice. The Mayflower Diner and Truck Stop, located in Milford, Connecticut, opened in 1938. By the 1960s, it had grown so that it covered 16 acres and stayed open 24 hours a day. Truckers could "park and sleep in their cabs or in a 96-room motel, shop at a store that stocks everything from aspirin to hiking boots and truck lights, get service and fuel their trucks and even purchase a new one."

In 1971, Long Islander Emmie Peek decided to train to become a truck driver. It sounded to her like a good way for a woman to earn a living. "You also get to see a lot of the country," she said. Despite Peek's romantic view of it, long-haul trucking on the interstates was monotonous, stressful, and lonely. Drivers found ways to make their cabs homey. Radios, televisions, and, in the 1970s, CB radios became common accoutrements to life on the road. Some husband-and-wife teams drove rigs together, mitigating the loneliness and strain that the trucking life put on marriages. "I was tired of never having a husband at home," said Mrs. Ed Startt, so when her husband asked her to go along, she answered, "If you're willing to take me, I'm willing to go."

. . .

By the late 1970s, long-haul trucking and containerized shipping had changed the nation's transportation system and set the stage for world competition. Other changes in American business followed.

In its quest for workers at lower wages, for example, RCA moved its television factory from Camden, New Jersey, to Bloomington, Illinois, in 1940. Then, in 1998, RCA closed the Bloomington factory and shifted production to Ciudad Juarez,

Mexico. In 1989, a manufacturer of fluorescent light ballast literally moved machinery out of its Paterson, New Jersey, factory to a new plant across the Mexican border, leaving assembly line workers unemployed after decades of work. New Jersey factory worker Mollie James had earned $8 an hour. When a woman in Matamoros, Mexico, took the same job, she began at about 65 cents an hour.

The forces of global competition and production had a similarly profound effect on the fortunes of American auto manufacturers. Historically, Americans have owned more cars than have the citizens of any other nation in the world. Between 1969 and 1995, the number of cars in the United States rose by more than a hundred million. During the 1960s and 1970s, cars became individual, rather than family, possessions, and the average American garage grew to hold more than one car. By 1990, in fact, most households had two or more, while the proportion of American households without a car fell below 10 percent.

All that automobile ownership didn't translate into profits for American automobile manufacturers, though. When Americans put their keys into their ignitions, they increasingly heard the hum of a foreign car's engine. In 1977, reported the *Wall Street Journal,* the United States exported vehicles worth 5.7 billion dollars and in the same year imported vehicles worth 10.2 billion. "Obviously the American auto industry is no longer king of the road," commented the reporter. It was a change that happened quickly, and it took Detroit by surprise.

Immediately after World War II, the world saw the

United States as "the cornucopia of manufactured goods," dominant as producer and consumer. Plants all over the country churned out washing machines, televisions, and automobiles. By 1947, American production represented half of the entire world's goods. "The world revolution of our times is 'Made in the USA,'" declared management consultant Peter Drucker in 1949. "The true revolutionary principle is the idea of mass production." But as other countries, notably Japan, rebuilt their infrastructures, the economic balance of power began to shift. Imports joined American merchandise on store shelves. Even after shipping costs, merchandisers often could sell imported products at prices competitive with, and sometimes lower than, those of American products.

At first, things looked good for Detroit. In the 1950s, General Motors, Chrysler, and Ford dominated the U.S. auto market, and the United States dominated the world auto market. In 1950, for example, over two-thirds of the cars in the world had indeed been made in the U.S.A. As the '60s turned into the '70s, social and economic forces challenged the once mighty Big Three, in the form of new cars made by upstart manufacturers in other countries.

Imports, notably German Volkswagens, had begun to show up on America's roads in larger numbers in the late 1950s. But Japanese cars really changed the automotive playing field in the next two decades. It all happened fast. In 1950, auto manufacturers in Japan produced a total of 32,000 motor vehicles. Just 15 years later, in 1965, they produced 1.8 million. Honda began manufacturing cars in 1962 and in 1968 introduced its first car for

sale in the United States, at the International Auto Show. The N600, a two-door four-seater, weighed 1,213 pounds and cost $1,300.

The first Hondas didn't sell very well. As a *New York Times* reporter summarized it, in 1980, "Honda's first efforts in the passenger car field were little short of disastrous. In the late 1960s, the company turned out a small sports car that sold slowly and a tiny passenger car, the N-360, that had a habit of turning over at high speed." In 1970, the company sold just 1,387 cars in the United States. But during the 1970s, Honda's fiery maverick owner, Soichiro Honda, patented the CVCC engine, which met emission standards without an expensive catalytic convertor. By 1977, the *Times* reported that Honda's "gasoline sipping Civic and Accord models are enjoying mushrooming sales."

The oil crisis of the 1970s, and the government's introduction of higher emission standards, created a larger market for reliable, fuel-efficient cars. Japanese manufacturers provided both. It was a shift in global perceptions. "Until the 1960s Japanese products were an international joke," a 1983 article in the *New York Times* stated. "Japanese heads of state did not ride in Japanese cars until 1968." When postwar Americans read "Made in Japan," they thought "poor quality," but when postwar baby boomers, then their children, came of age, they bought Hondas and other Japanese cars marketed toward them.

In the first two months of 1977, America's three top-selling imported cars came from Japanese companies: Toyota, Datsun, and Honda. Honda's Accord was "the hottest of the hot-selling little

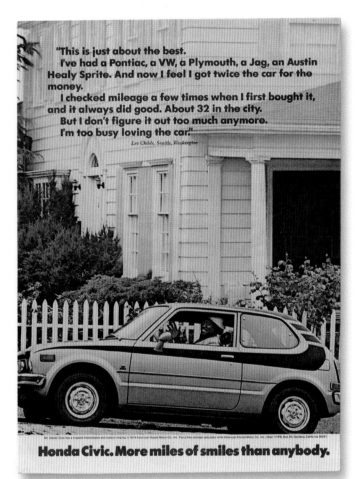

"This is just about the best.
I've had a Pontiac, a VW, a Plymouth, a Jag, an Austin Healy Sprite. And now I feel I got twice the car for the money.
I checked mileage a few times when I first bought it, and it always did good. About 32 in the city.
But I don't figure it out too much anymore.
I'm too busy loving the car."

Lee Childs, Seattle, Washington

**Honda Civic. More miles of smiles than anybody.**

*In 1976, Honda advertising touted the fuel efficiency and the quality of the Civic. By choosing to picture an African-American driver, Honda seems to have been appealing to baby boomers, whose political consciences led them to support both civil rights and environmentally friendly vehicles in the 1970s.*

Japanese autos that have taken the import-car market by storm." The momentous news in the 1979 automobile industry was that "imports pushed their way into the No. 2 spot in the American automobile sales rankings, surpassing the Ford Motor Company and trailing only the General Motors Corporation in a market that was once dominated by domestic producers," as reported in the *New York Times*.

By the early 1980s, it was clear that the U.S. auto industry was in trouble. Imports took a larger share of the U.S. market. Between 1978 and 1983, 300,000 American autoworkers lost their jobs. The Chrysler Corporation lost 261 million dollars in the first half of 1979. With about 130,000 workers in seven states, Chrysler received bail-out funds totaling 1.5 billion dollars from the federal government. The United States—home to Ford's mass-production techniques, central tenets of modern capitalist productivity—was faltering in the world market. In 1980, Japan became the world's leading car manufacturer, upsetting the United States's hold on the market. By the late 1980s, the Honda Accord was America's top-selling car. The United States was importing one hundred Japanese cars for every car it exported. The American dream suddenly seemed to belong to the Japanese.

Japanese companies began to set up shop on U.S. soil. Honda was the first, announcing in 1980 that it would begin making cars in Marysville, Ohio. Honda managers were motivated in part by unofficial import quotas imposed by both the Japanese and American governments, intended to let the reeling U.S. auto industry reorganize itself. "Honda Plant

Brings a Touch of Japan to Ohio," read the headline when the new auto assembly plant opened up amid cornfields. Ohio lured the company by offering, as the *Wall Street Journal* reported in 1982, "a package of government-paid benefits that included the construction of a main sewer line from the plant to Marysville's waste-water treatment plant, an expansion of a two-lane highway leading from Marysville to the assembly plant and a 15-year tax abatement."

Marysville had been losing jobs—companies like Nestle had been leaving the area—but not everyone was happy that Honda was opening a plant in their small town. "Why the hell are we doing all this for a foreign company?" asked one resident. Another, reacting to a Columbus, Ohio, newspaper photograph that showed a Japanese flag over Marysville, said, "That didn't sit too well around here. We're pretty conservative around here and we've got people living in this town who were in the Bataan death march." A Honda advertisement called Marysville the capital of the "good ol' U.S. of H." "They didn't need to do that," said Mayor Tom Nuckels, who was in favor of Honda's move. "They're trying to put the American flag over Honda, and I remember something my daddy once told me: If you have to stop and tell people what you are, you probably aren't."

But two years later, when the first American-made Honda Accord rolled off the assembly line in 1982, the superiority of Japanese-made goods had become a cultural norm. Ironically, car dealers worried that they would have to persuade reluctant American consumers that a Honda made in the U.S.A. would be just as good as a Honda made in Japan.

Despite all the grumbling, the Marysville experiment was a success, and other Japanese companies followed suit during the 1980s. Nissan built a plant in Tennessee. Toyota set up a joint venture with GM in California and opened a factory in Kentucky. Most cars were assembled from parts made in Japan, but in 1987, Honda announced what the *New York Times* called "a daring U.S. step" and set up a factory in Anna, Ohio, near the Marysville plant, to manufacture engine components.

Japanese-style auto factories were successful for a number of reasons. Japan established trade barriers, limiting imports from America and elsewhere and restricting foreign capital investments. At the same time, Japan's business practices—which operated without contracts and were based on long-term relationships—made it hard for foreign companies to break into the country's economy.

. . .

But that was only part of the story. While American auto companies followed the principles of Fordism, Japanese auto companies devised a new manufacturing philosophy, bringing success at home and sending ripples of influence throughout industry and management in the U.S. and around the world. Newspaper articles with titles like "The Company that Stopped Detroit" and books like *The Machine that Changed the World* (which sold 150,000 copies in two years) popularized the notion that Japan had performed an economic miracle.

Japanese practices turned many of the commandments of mass production upside down. Under the guiding hand of Taiichi Ohno—born in Manchuria and raised in Nagoya, a self-taught engineer—Toyota grew from a tiny, struggling operation in the late 1940s to the world's third largest automaker in 1990, when Ohno died.

Short on capital after World War II and coping with the country's physical destruction, Toyota established practices in the 1940s now characterized as "lean production" techniques. They streamlined the production process, occupied less factory space, and tied up as little capital as possible in inventory. They used employee time more efficiently, too. Employees worked where they were most needed instead of being assigned to a single task. Japanese firms also guaranteed their workers jobs for life, so that workers never felt threatened by the prospects of smarter automation or increased efficiency. In the Japanese work setting, managers actually encouraged workers to innovate and suggest improvements.

The Japanese model challenged the long-respected logic of American mass production. Traditional American assembly line production had followed the thinking of Frederick Winslow Taylor, a turn-of-the-century industrial engineer, who believed that managers should break down jobs to their smallest parts for workers. Remove the brain work from the factory floor, and jobs will be done faster and more uniformly. Taylor's influential book, *The Principles of Scientific Management,* published in 1911, argued that for the highest productivity, "the management must take over and perform much of the work which is now left to the men." The managers of American auto factories by and large did just that.

Traditional American assembly lines created an environment in which workers were not expected to be inventive. As the son of an autoworker put it, "My father worked in auto for thirty-five years and he never talked about the job. What's there to say? A car comes, I weld it; a car comes, I weld it; a car comes, I weld it. One hundred and one times an hour."

In a mass-production car factory, parts were manufactured and purchased in large quantities, then stockpiled on the assumption that economies of scale improved cost efficiency. Improving the process or conceiving of new ways to piece a car together was done on the drawing board, by engineers and managers, not by the workers themselves. It could take days to switch over the assembly line to a different model, during which time many workers were idle, since only some were trained to switch the dies that stamped out the parts.

According to Rick Madrid, who worked at the Fremont GM plant, "an elephant is a mouse designed by an engineer. These people knew nothing about the operation. They knew nothing about what the grunts actually did, ... so they would change, they would deisgn, they would install, and the grunt had to adapt, whether it was right or not." The system depended on workers keeping the line moving, regardless of the quality of the end product. As one worker put it, "at GM, if you stopped the line, you'd get fired."

The Toyota system reversed the conventional wisdom. Workers were expected to contribute feedback, make suggestions, improve operations, and solve problems on the line. Japan's lean producers called this idea *kaizan*—roughly translated, "continuous improvement." Workers were rewarded for new production solutions. Rocky Kelly, a dairy-farmer-turned-Honda-associate in Marysville, was given a 60-dollar savings bond for "figuring out how to straighten a matchbook-sized tab of sheet metal to keep it from jamming a robot welding process farther down the line." Kaizan worked to improve the end product, to give workers a personal sense of control and value, and to increase plant efficiency.

Japanese cars seemed to prove its effectiveness. In *The Machine that Changed the World,* based on a five-year MIT study of the future of the automobile, the authors charted the difference between a mass-production and a lean-production factory. In 1986, at GM's Framingham plant, it took 40 hours to assemble a car, and there were 130 defects for every 100 cars that rolled off the line. At Toyota's Takakoa plant, assembly took 18 hours, with 45 defects per 100 cars. Furthermore, while American companies were stockpiling different models and variations, hoping that inventory would match consumer demand, the Japanese were running a flexible assembly line. Toyota workers built cars to order.

Thanks to improved transportation systems, the Japanese system included one more economy, called "JIT," for just-in-time management. Toyota ordered supplies and materials in smaller quantities than American car manufacturers ever had. "Twenty-one times a day, around the clock, trucks are dispatched from the shipping areas with loads of alternators bound for the Toyota Motor Corporation's Kamigo

and Shimoyama engine plants in nearby Toyota City," the *New York Times* reported in 1983. "Each truck carries just enough parts to keep the production lines running for an hour." The arrival of an empty shipping container at the supplier's company triggered the next delivery. JIT inventory management made large stockpiles of parts and materials a thing of the past.

Even advocates agreed that the new pace of work was hard. Rich Madrid worked for New United Motor Manufacturing, a General Motors–Toyota joint venture that opened in 1984, taking over an old mass-production building in Fremont, California. He called the Toyota production system "harder than the American system," but at the same time he and others were more satisfied with their jobs. Regardless of what you do, "you're important in the system, and I think this is what gives people a positive attitude."

Other workers were less positive: Jane Slaughter and Mike Parker thought lean production should be called "management by stress," that it pushed workers to breaking points. Don Preston, who worked at the Marysville Honda plant, said, "They can really put pressure on you here, and it can really mess with you." He favored unionizing. But like the dockworkers of the 1950s and the railroad workers of the 1960s, many autoworkers felt they had to choose

*A New York City taxi cab driver uses hands and voice to release his tensions in crowded traffic. As more Americans got behind the wheel, cars jammed up cities and created frustrations. By the end of the 1990s, "road rage" was the subject of articles, books, and television reports.*

between hard-won union rules and a job. In the late '70s and early '80s, the *New York Times* reported, "The union has given billions of dollars in concessions to the auto industry." After decades as one of the most unionized groups in the country, with the power to shut down the entire industry, the United Auto Workers (UAW) struggled to gain a toehold in new factories as the forces of global production and competition took over. When Owen Bieber, a "big quiet man from North Dorr, Michigan," addressed members for the first time as president of the UAW in 1983, he said, "We've given all we're going to give."

But in Japanese-owned, American-based factories, despite strenuous organizing campaigns, the UAW got no management recognition whatsoever. Many workers resigned themselves to the new world order. Walt Bird, chairman of the local bargaining committee at the Grand Blanc, Michigan, GM stamping plant, told the *New York Times* in 1988, "We've seen enough plant closings. Most people realize we have to do better now before our backs are to the wall." But some resisted. In 1990, Ohio UAW member Pamela Richards wouldn't accept a Honda she won in the state lottery because it wasn't union-made. Meanwhile, many other American consumers were buying new Accords, Civics, Camrys, and Corollas.

While Japanese manufacturers made permanent inroads into the American market, the fortunes of

*As city congestion created gridlock, some people took to moving about cities using bikes, in-line skates, skateboards, and scooters, like this messenger delivering packages around Los Angeles.*

American car companies improved in the 1980s. They adopted some Japanese methods of production and introduced new, popular models—taller, roomier, but definitely less fuel-efficient than Japanese cars. As the specter of the 1970s oil crises faded, and Reaganomics put social responsibility and environmentalism on the back burner, minivans and sport utility vehicles (SUVs) replaced station wagons and family sedans in many American driveways. This trend back toward big vehicles helped Ford and other American car manufacturers claw out a new market position. Still, the influence and threat of the Japanese auto industry had lasting effects. American managers found ways to incorporate lean production and just-in-time inventory into their factories as well, trying to level the playing field between the Big Three and their Japanese competition.

Distinctions between American and foreign cars began to blur. In 1992, St. Louis–based Monsanto encouraged its employees to buy American by offering them one thousand dollars to do so. In the same year, filling station owner Bill Chartrand of Edwardsville, Illinois, sold gas at a discount to customers driving American cars. "I didn't do it to punish foreign-car owners," he said. "I did it to reward the American-car owner." But in fact, the Ford driven by a customer paying two cents less per gallon was possibly no more American than a Honda. In 1985, General Motors bought nearly a million engines and transmissions from manufacturers in Brazil, Japan, and Mexico. In 1987, Ford imported trim, engines, and transmissions, and made plans to import over 100,000 Mercury

Tracers from Mexico. GM bought bumpers and radio parts from Mexico. Chrysler imported over 150,000 cars from Japan and Mexico and was designing cars jointly with the Italian company, Maserati.

In contrast, in 1990 more Hondas were assembled in Marysville than the total number of autos produced at any other single American plant. *New York Times* reporter Doron Levin informed readers that the Honda Accord station wagon—designed and assembled in the United States—was "another step in the Japanese company's drive to become the first foreign company to create a self-sufficient United States auto maker."

International merger mania struck at the end of the 20th century, affecting banking, communications, entertainment—and the automobile industry. Having survived earlier misfortunes, Chrysler was acquired by Germany's Daimler-Benz in 1998. Volkswagen bought the English aristocrat, Rolls Royce. Sweden's Saab Motor Company became a part of General Motors. Cars with names like Yugo, Kia, and Hyundai appeared on the American market, marking the entrance of new nations, like Serbia and South Korea, into the international auto arena. But the general move toward international consolidation seemed the name of the game. In 1999, Hiroshi Okuda, the president of Toyota, predicted that "In the next century, there will be only five or six auto makers."

. . .

Changing transportation systems have created and damaged, shaped and influenced American life for centuries. Wagon trains set out across the vast expanse of America and helped forge the links that created a new continental nation. H. Nelson Jackson, Sewall Crocker, and Bud went on a 63-day cross-country road trip, establishing the automotive version of an American rite of passage. Nineteenth-century Rochester, New York, grew because of the Erie Canal, and Watsonville and Santa Cruz were transformed by their rail connections. Twentieth-century Washington and LeDroit Park, Chicago and Park Forest were transformed by streetcars and automobiles. And tiny Marysville, Ohio, became a node in the global business community when Honda opened a factory there.

Individuals such as Frederick Hihn, Cyrus Avery, Charlotte Hawkins Brown, and Harry Bridges made a difference to those around them and to the course of history. So, too, did the policies of cities like Oakland and Chicago, of states like Ohio and Kentucky, and of the federal government. As individuals and communities embarked on a quest to affect and improve the ways Americans traveled, they profoundly changed the culture and character of the American nation. Although history shows that it is foolish to predict the future, it does seems clear, as we move into a new chapter of American history, that transportation will continue to shape our lives.

THERE IS SOMETHING TO BE SAID
FOR THE BALM OF PAVEMENT
MOVING UNDER YOU,
MILES GLIDING BY
WITHOUT DESTINATION
BENEATH YOUR WHEELS.

SOMETHING LIFTS.

— *Marsha Moyer*, The Second Coming of Lucy Hatch, 2002

# ENDNOTES

**Endnote format:** After each page number, a brief phrase from the text identifies material being referenced, then a short citation follows. Semicolons separate citations.

**Chapter 1:** 20 "Civilization has reached out": "Fourth: The Day We Celebrate," *Santa Cruz Sentinel*, July 8, 1876; 27 "at the edge of the unknown": Duncan Dayton and Ken Burns, *Lewis & Clark*, 61; 29 "Merchants in Boston": Paul E. Johnson, *Shopkeeper's Millennium*, 16; 32 An early guide: Lansford W. Hastings, *Emigrants Guide to Oregon and California*, 143; 41 "Within a little more": George Rogers Taylor, *Transportation Revolution*, 79; 42 "And the Iron Horse": "Statistics and Speculations Concerning the Pacific Railroad," *Putnam's*, Sept. 1853; 47 "the first railroad war": James D. Dilts, "The Early Days," in Withuhn, ed., *Rails Across America*, 24; 47 "The railroad stations along our route": John E. Clarke, Jr., *Railroads in the Civil War*, 177.

**Chapter 2:** 60 "the state's largest corporation": William Deverell, *Railroad Crossing*, 41; 60 "All agreed": "Railroad," *Santa Cruz Sentinel*, Oct. 16, 1869; 63 Construction commenced: Rick Hamman, *California Coast Railways*; 69 "Thriving, busy, rustling": M. E. Gilbert, *Santa Cruz County*, 100; 70 "Life at Santa Cruz": E. S. Harrison, *The History of Santa Cruz County, California*, 156; 71 "growers found": Watsonville Chamber of Commerce, *Watsonville: The First Hundred Years*, 29; 73 Residents of South China: Ronald Takaki, *A Different Mirror*, Chapter 8; 73 Despite its fairly small: Sandy Lydon, *Chinese Gold*, 119; 74 "vigorous Japantown": Sandy Lydon, *Chinese Gold*, 190.

**Chapter 3:** 78 a week before: C. Vann Woodward, *Reunion and Reaction*, 7-8, 64-67; 78 "a puff of the waste smoke": C. Vann Woodward, *Reunion and Reaction*, 69; 79 "fierce-throated beauty": Walt Whitman, "To a Locomotive in Winter," *Leaves of Grass*, 80; "A railroad in a town": Matthew Hale Smith, *The Old Colony Railroad*, 10; 84 "You come here": James Thorpe, *Henry Edwards Huntington*, 177-179; 86 "One well-regulated institution": Walter Licht, *Working for the Railroad*, 79; 90 "Cut it up": William Cronon, *Nature's Metropolis*, 237; 94 "It is not surprising": W. J. and M. B. Bryan, *Memoirs of William Jennings Bryan*, 220; 97 "the tocsin that sounded": Samuel Gompers, *Seventy Years of Life and Labor*, 106; 102 He projected the cost: Drake Hokanson, *The Lincoln Highway*, 6-12.

**Chapter 4:** 106 Preparing for her own: Emily Post, *By Motor to the Golden Gate*, 6-7; 110 "Often the trail narrowed": Curt McConnell, *Coast to Coast by Automobile*, 69; 113 Ramsey said the seed: Alice Huyler Ramsey, *Veil, Duster, and Tire Iron*, 7; 116 "We were not sure": "The 1919 Transcontinental Motor Convoy," *OverView* (Eisenhower Foundation Newsletter), vol. 10, no. 3 (Fall 1984); 116 "huge, clumsy, unwieldy affairs": Theodore Dreiser, *A Hoosier Holiday*, 25, 93; 118 "Two of us chartered": August Mencken, *The Railroad Passenger Car*, 155-56; 120 "I proposed to stay": Ida B. Wells, *Crusade for Justice*, 18-19; 125 "We got up a handsome speed": Stephen B. Goddard, *Colonel Albert Pope and His American Dream Machines*, 9-10; 129 Unhurt, Daniels later boasted: Tom D. Couch, *The Bishop's Boys*, 265-69; 134 Of all these ships: Melvin Maddocks, *The Great Liners*, 69-70.

**Chapter 5:** 137 eight-year-old Rose Schneiderman: Annelise Orleck, *Common Sense and a Little Fire*, part 1; 138 "When the steerage is full": "Steerage Conditions," Reports of the United States Immigration Commission, 1911, 29-39; 140 "For what reason": Him Mark Lai et al., *Island*, 84; 141 "extra money to live on": Chad Berry, *Southern Migrants, Northern Exiles*, 22; 145 "From a mixed neighborhood": Keith Melder, ed., *City of Magnificent Intentions*, 202; 145 Americans even invented: Robert M. Fogelson, *Downtown*, 10-12; 146 Starting in 1827: John Anderson Miller, *Fares, Please!*, 1-2; 156 "Washington is like": Mary Church Terrell, *A Colored Woman in a White World*, 113.

**Chapter 6:** 167 "The chain system you have": Ray Batchelor, *Henry Ford*, 52; 169 organizing a unique demonstration: Keith Sward, *The Legend of Henry Ford*, 8; 172 A timesaving breakthrough: David A. Hounshell, *From the American System to Mass Production*, 247-48; 177 allowed farmers to receive: Cecil C. Hoge Sr., *The First Hundred Years Are the Toughest*, 98-102; 178 Stations relied on: John A. Jakle, *The Tourist*, 168, John A. Jakle and Keith A. Sculle, *The Gas Station in America*, 59; 181 A different type of traveler: Lucille Hamons, *Lucille, Mother of the Mother Road*, 5-9; 182 "I let 'em all go": Dorothea Lange & Paul Schuster Taylor, *An American Exodus*, 68; 182 The Haggard family: Merle Haggard and Tom Carter, *Merle Haggard's My House of Memories*, 11; 185 At a pea pickers' camp: Bill Ganzel, *Dust Bowl Descent*, 30; 186 The last commercial steam engines: William L. Withuhn, ed., *Rails Across America*, 154-60; 189 The Spencer freight yard: Duane Galloway and Jim Wrinn, *Southern Railway's Spencer Shops*, 18-19.

**Chapter 7:** 196 "When I sit again": James Tobin, *Ernie Pyle's War*, 33; 196 Auto travel provides: Ernie Pyle, *Home Country*, 468; 199 Mystery novelist: Roger B. White, *Home on the Road*, 51, 57; 200 "An Ideal Vacation": Cindy S. Aron, *Working at Play*, 240-44; 204 "comprehensive system": Michael Wallis, *Route 66: The Mother Road*, 7-8; 204 In 1932, their ad: Quinta Scott with Susan Croce Kelly, *Route 66*, 37; 208 America's melting pot: Warren James Belasco, *Americans on the Road*, 96; 213 To encourage bus trips: Margaret Walsh, *Making Connections*, 24, 75-80; 218 But for African Americans: Kathleen Franz, *Narrating Automobility*, 131-36; 219 She slept in a Pullman: Charles W. Wadelington and Richard F. Knapp, *Charlotte Hawkins Brown & Palmer Memorial Institute*, 91, 139; 222 Walkers took inspiration: Catherine A. Barnes, *Journey From Jim Crow*, 116-22.

**Chapter 8:** 225 "gay scenes": Anne Hagner, "VE-Day Gets Staid Greeting in Washington," *Washington Post*, May 9, 1945; 229 "has never insured": Kenneth T. Jackson, *Crabgrass Frontier*, 209; 235 "The Cadillac has": Joel W. Eastman, *Styling vs. Safety*, 198; 235 "their hopes for places": "Homeless veterans," *Wall Street Journal*, Nov. 15, 1945; 239 "Chicago's population right now": Grace Miller, "Satellite Town Designed for 30,000 Persons," *Christian Science Monitor*, Aug. 10, 1948; 240 "For a quick twinge": William H. Whyte, Jr., "The Transients," *Fortune*, May 1953, 113; 246 Sales at Park Forest's shopping plaza: John S. Cooper, "Downtown's Reply," *Wall Street Journal*, Sept. 28, 1954; 249 "We have had this concentration": Hearing before the U.S. Commission on Civil Rights, Housing, vol. 2, June 10, 1959, 38; 252 Calling for the design: David M. Young, *Chicago Transit*, 255; "the largest Korean": Charles Jencks, "Hetero-architecture and the L.A. School," in Edward W. Soja and Allen J. Scott, *The City*, 49.

**Chapter 9:** 259 A recorded voice: Phil Patton, *Open Road*, 119-20, David J. St. Clair, *The Motorization of American Cities*, 121-22, 146; 261 He believed superhighways: Stephen B. Goddard, *Getting There*, 17; 270 Funding began in 1957: Christopher Finch, *Highways to Heaven*, 337; 277 Fares were regulated: William E. O'Connor, *Introduction to Airline Economics*, 5; 280 a daring demonstration: S. B. Kauffman, *Pan Am Pioneer*, 106; 281 "the most insulating": Anthony Sampson, *Empires of the Sky*, 113; 283 "Air travel has become": Mark Gottdiener, *Life in the Air*, 101.

**Chapter 10:** 289 "filled with everything": William L. Worden, *Cargoes*, 143; 291 "the greatest technological revolution": David R. Francis, "Containers Revolutionize Freight," *Christian Science Monitor*, Nov. 15, 1966; 293 "I still believe": Harry Bernstein, "Old left winger of ILWU, Harry Bridges, is honored," *Washington Post*, April 8, 1977; 295 J. Paul St. Sure: Jennifer Marie Winter, *30 Years of Collective Bargaining*; 305 RCA: Jefferson Cowie, *Capital Moves*; 305 Mollie James: William M. Adler, *Mollie's Job*; 306 "the cornucopia of manufactured goods": Vermont Royster, "Thinking Things Over," *Wall Street Journal*, Jan. 31, 1979; 309 Rick Madrid: New United Motor Manufacturing, Inc. Session One, Smithsonian Videohistory Program, Sept. 25-26, 1990, 67.

## FURTHER READING

David Haward Bain, *Empire Express: Building the First Transcontinental Railroad*, Viking, 1999. Catherine A. Barnes, *Journey From Jim Crow: The Segregation of Southern Transit*, Columbia U. Press, 1983. Warren James Belasco, *Americans on the Road: From Autocamp to Motel, 1910-1945*, Johns Hopkins U. Press, 1979. John Bodnar, *The Transplanted: A History of Immigrants in Urban America*, Indiana U. Press, 1985. Alfred D. Chandler Jr., *The Railroads: The Nation's First Big Business*, Harcourt, Brace & World, 1965. Robert M. Fogelson, *Downtown: Its Rise and Fall, 1880-1950*, Yale U. Press, 2001. Henry Ford with Samuel Crowther, *My Life and Work*, Doubleday, Page & Company, 1923. Kathleen Franz, *Narrating Automobility: Travelers, Tinkerers, and Technological Authority in the Twentieth Century*, Ph.D. dissertation, Brown University, 1991. Stephen B. Goddard, *Getting There: The Epic Struggle Between Road and Rail in the American Century*, Basic Books, 1994. David A. Hounshell, *From the American System to Mass Production, 1800-1932: The Development of Manufacturing Technology in the United States*, Johns Hopkins U. Press, 1984. Kenneth T. Jackson, *Crabgrass Frontier: The Suburbanization of the United States*, Oxford U. Press, 1985. Benjamin W. Labaree et al., *America and the Sea: A Maritime History*, Mystic Seaport, 1998. Tom Lewis, *Divided Highways: Building the Interstate Highways, Transforming American Life*, Viking, 1997. Curt McConnell, *Coast to Coast by Automobile*, Stanford U. Press, 2000. Clay McShane, *Down the Asphalt Path: The Automobile and the American City*, Columbia U. Press, 1994. August Mencken, *The Railroad Passenger Car: An Illustrated History of the First Hundred Years With Accounts by Contemporary Passengers*, Johns Hopkins U. Press, 1957. Phil Patton, *Open Road: A Celebration of the American Highway*, Simon & Schuster, 1986. David J. St. Clair, *The Motorization of American Cities*, Praeger, 1986 Quinta Scott with Susan Croce Kelly, *Route 66: The Highway and Its People*, U. of Oklahoma Press, 1988. Ronald Takaki, *Strangers From a Different Shore: A History of Asian Americans*, Little, Brown, 1989. George Rogers Taylor, *The Transportation Revolution 1815-1860*, Holt, Rinehart and Winston, 1951. Michael Wallis, *Route 66: The Mother Road*, St. Martin's Press, 1990. Roger B. White, *Home on the Road: The Motor Home in America*, Smithsonian Institution Press, 2000. William L. Withuhn, ed., *Rails Across America: A History of Railroads in North America*, Smithmark, 1993.

## AUTHORS

Historian **Janet Davidson** is co-curator of "America on the Move," the Smithsonian Institution's new exhibition in the National Museum of American History. A native of Wales, Davidson received a B.A. from the University of East Anglia in Norwich, England, and an M.A. and Ph.D. in history from the University of Delaware. She was named a National Historical Publications and Records Commission Postdoctoral Fellow in Historical Editing by the National Archives and Records Administration and worked on the papers of Samuel Gompers at the University of Maryland. She lives in Washington, D.C, with her husband, Brian Kerrigan. Her favorite transportation memory is flying in a small plane from Phoenix to Flagstaff, Arizona, on the way to the Grand Canyon, listening to "Shotgun" by Junior Walker and the All Stars.

**Michael Sweeney** is an associate professor of journalism at Utah State University. He has written two other books: *Secrets of Victory*, a history of World War II American censorship, named 2001 Book of the Year by the American Journalism Historians Association; and *From the Front: The Story of War Featuring Correspondents' Chronicles*, published in 2002 by the National Geographic Society. Sweeney worked as a reporter and editor at newspapers in Missouri and Texas, then earned a Ph.D. in journalism at Ohio University, where he studied at the prestigious Contemporary History Institute. He lives in Logan, Utah, with his wife, Carolyn, and their son, David. He prefers to drive cars small enough to get good gas mileage but large enough to hold bicycles, golf clubs, a Labrador retriever, and a basenji. His favorite transportation memory is motoring along the Columbia River gorge during an August sunset.

## ILLUSTRATIONS CREDITS

We thank Smithsonian Institution photographers Harold Dorwin, Joe Goulait, Eric Long, Richard Strauss, Hugh Talman, and Jeff Tinsley for superb object photography.

SI = Smithsonian Institution, National Museum of American History—History of Technology Collections (unless numbered); LC = Library of Congress

Cover Neil Rabinowitz/Corbis; 1 State St Bank & Trust; 2-3 SI#P-63164; 4-5 SI #2003-6549; 6-7 SI; 8 With permission of the O.Winston Link Trust and the O. Winston Link Mus, Roanoke; 10 SI #2003-11618; 14 Studebaker Natl Mus; 18 (up both) U. of Wash Lib; (lo le) Southern Pacific Co; (lo rt) Idaho Hist Soc; 19 (both) SI#2003-19284; 20 Yale U; 21 Bettmann/CORBIS; 22-3 LC; 25 LC; 26 (le) LC; (rt) Hulton Archive/getty; 28 Cincinnati Hist Soc Lib; (inset) Hulton Archive/getty; 31 Joe Bailey; 34-5 LC; 36 (up) NY Pub Lib; (lo) LC; 37 (all) SI#2003-19230; 38-9 SI#86-9636; 41 Wells Fargo Ntl Bank; 43 SI; 44 St. Joseph Mus; 46 (top, both) LC; (lo le) 7th Regiment Army Fund/Victor Boswell; (lo rt) Henry Huntington Lib; 50 (up le) SI#38416-C; (up rt) Minnesota Hist Soc; (lo le) California State Lib; (lo rt) Santa Fe Railroad System; 51 State St Bank & Trust; 52 Hihn House; 53 California Hist Room, California State Lib; 54 Palo Alto Hist Assoc; 56 (up) Charles Ford Co Coll; (lo) Santa Cruz Mus of Art & His; 58-9 SI#99-40014; 61 LC; 62 LC; 65 SI; 66-7 Shades of Watsonville Arch, Watsonville Pub Lib; 68 LC; 71 Breton Littlehales; 72 (up le) Special Colls, UCSC, (up rt) Sandy Lydon Coll; (lo le) Shades of Watsonville Arch, Watsonville Pub Lib; (lo rt) Pajaro Valley Hist Assoc; 76 (up le) Kansas State His Soc; (up rt) *Southern News Bulletin*, February 1929; (lo le) LC; (lo rt) LC; 77 (le) NY Hist Soc; (rt) Henry Huntington Lib; 78 SI#2003-19287; 81 (up) The Granger Coll; 81 (lo) LC; 82-3 Pennsylvania Hist & Mus Commission; 85 NY Pub Lib; 88 (both) SI; 89 LC; 91 SI#2003-11613.6; 92 Chicago Hist Soc; 93 USDA; 95 & 96 Pennsylvania Hist & Mus Commission; 98-9 SI#2003-11614; 100 (up le) SI; (up rt) SI, Arch Ctr; (lo le) SI Libraries; lo rt) SI, Arch Ctr, 104 (all) U of Vermont, Special Colls; 105 (both) SI; 106 SI#2003-19022; 107 Hulton Archive/getty; 108-9 SI#2003-15516.5; 111-112 (all) SI, Arch Ctr, 114 American Auto Manufacturers Assoc; (inset) *NYT* April 7, 1916; 117 (all) SI#2003-11616; 119 (both) The Dwight D. Eisenhower Lib & Mus; 120 SI, Arch Ctr; 121 LC; 122 Peter Newark's American Pictures; 124 (up) SI#2003-19250; (lo) SI#2003-19246; 125 (both) SI, Arch Ctr, 126-7 LC; 129-130 (all) SI; 131 Carnegie Lib of Pittsburgh; 132 (all) SI; 136 (up le) Maryland Hist Soc; (up rt) American Heritage Coll; (lo le) Ntl Arch; (lo rt) Bettmann/Corbis; 137 LC; 139 The Newberry Lib; 142-3 LC; 144 SI; 147 Special Colls, Boston U; 148 (le) SI, Archives Ctr; (rt) Bettmann/Corbis; (lo rt) SI#2003-15513.10; 153 LC; 154 Chicago Hist Soc; 156 SI Libraries; 157 (up) LC; (lo) Historic Takoma, Inc; 158-9 (both) SI#2003-19252; 160 (up le) Oakland Mus of California; (up rt) getty; (lo le) Bettmann/Corbis; (lo rt) Hulton Archive/getty; 164 (up both) The Colls of Henry Ford Mus & Greenfield Village; (lo le) Packard Motor Car Co; (lo rt) Goodyear Tire & Rubber Co; 165 (both) SI; 166 SI; 169 SI Arch Ctr; 170-1 Brown Brothers; 174-5 (all) SI#2003-19239; 176 Robert M. Lightfoot II; 178 (foreground) Corbis; (background) John Margolies Coll; 180 Carolyn Ringe Miele; 184 (both) American Auto Assoc; 186 (both) Lillian Haggard Hoge; 188 LC; 190 (up le) *Pullman News*, Dec 1925; (up rt) Hulton Deutsch Coll/Corbis; (lo le) Bettmann/Corbis; (lo rt) SI#78-13870; 191 (all) *Pullman News*, May 1924; 194 (all) Tracy Fitzwater, Teri Fink and the estate of Ethel M. Bellisine; 195 (top-bottom) SI#2000-4604.6; #2000-4604.1; #2000-4602.1; #2000-4597.10; 196 U of Virginia Lib; 198 LC; 201 Photo by Ferenz Fedor, ctsy Mus of NM, neg #102015; 202-3 (all) Pete Koltnow, 205 Alexander Wiederseder; 206 J. Baylor Roberts; 208 (up) Virginia C. Gove; (lo) The Colls of Henry Ford Mus & Greenfield Village; 212 (inset) Lake County Mu/Corbis; 214-5 SI#94-13399; 216 (up) John Margolies Coll; (lo) SI, Arch Ctr; 219 NY Pub Lib, Schomburg Ctr. for Rsch in Black Culture; 220 (all) LC; 224 (up, both) Bettmann/Corbis; (lo le) Corbis; (lo rt) U.S. War Dept; 225 SI#91-2454; 230 (up) Gerald Riseberg; (low) Oregon Hist Soc. #CN0223759; 232-3 SI#2003-15796; 234 (all) SI#2000-4597.5; 236 SI; 237 Akron Beacon Journal; 238 Ctsy Park Forest Pub Lib; 240 SI#2003-19249; 241 Chicago Hist Soc; (inset) Natl Arch & Records Admin; 242-3 LC; 244 Chicago Hist Soc; (inset) D.C. Community Arch, D.C. Pub Lib, by Sammie Abbott; 247 (le) SI; 247 (rt) Daimler Chrysler Corp; 248 (le) G M Corp; (rt) SI; 250 LC; 251 Chicago Hist Soc; 254 (up le) Corbis; (up rt) Mark L. Stephenson/Corbis; (lo le) William Gray/Corbis; (lo rt) Lake County Mus/Corbis; 258 (up le) Bettmann/Corbis; (up rt) Corbis; (lo le) Hulton Archive/gettyimages; (lo rt) Bettmann/Corbis; 259 Swim Inc/Corbis; 260 Corbis; 262 Robert F. Sisson; 265 California Dept of Trans Lib; 266 American Auto Assoc; 268-9 SI#2003-15514.4; 270 SI, Science, Medicine & Soc; 275 David James/Mike McCune photo, ctsy Auto Club of So. California Arch; 276 Bettmann/Corbis; 279 Lisa Law; 280 SI, Arch Ctr; 282 (up le) Hulton-Deutsch Coll/Corbis; (up rt) Chicago Hist Soc; (lo le) Mark Gamba/Corbis; (lo rt) David Burton/Corbis; 286 (up, both) Ctr for Creative Photography; (lo le) Matson Navigation Co; (lo rt) Ctr for Creative Photog; 287 Swim Inc/Corbis; 289 SI; 290 Taxi/gettyimages; 292 ILWU Arch, Anne Rand Rsch Lib, Int'l Longshore & Warehouse Union, San Francisco; 294 (both) ILWU Archives, Anne Rand Rsch Lib, Int'l Longshore & Warehouse Union, San Francisco; 297 Port Authority of NY & NJ; 298-9 Werner Enterprises; 300 Steve Jay Crise/Corbis; 303 David Butow/Corbis; 304 Alan Schein Photo/Corbis; 307 Honda Motor Corp; 310 Jim Erickson/Corbis; 312 Jose Luis Pelaez, Inc/Corbis.

# INDEX

*The National Museum of American History gratefully acknowledges these sponsors for their support of the "America on the Move" exhibition*

General Motors Corporation
The History Channel
U.S. Department of Transportation
State Farm Companies Foundation
AAA
ExxonMobil

American Public Transportation Association
American Road & Transportation Builders Association
Association of American Railroads
National Asphalt Pavement Association
UPS Foundation

---

**America on the Move** has been my constant companion for the past three years in exhibition form, and this book owes its life to that project. I'd like to thank the curatorial team at the museum: Laura Hansen, Michael Harrison, Paula Johnson, Peter Liebhold, Bonnie Lillienfeld, Susan Tolbert, Roger White, and Bill Withuhn for graciously sharing their research and for all their enthusiasm for the history we're getting ready to exhibit. Mike Harrison went beyond the call of duty and was a key part of the image selection process for the book. My biggest professional debt, however, is to Steve Lubar, AOTM's project director. Steve read chapters, helped me create the structure for the book, and provided doses of much-needed encouragement along the way. The folks at National Geographic have also been an integral part of the process—especially Barbara Brownell-Grogan, who has been there since the first meeting we had to discuss the mutual project, and has helped keep the project on track. Much of what is good about this book is good because of her. Mike Sweeney, my excellent co-author, flew from Utah to D.C. to do research in our collections, and has worked diligently and with great verve to write his part of the book. Friends around the country and the world—Susan Larkin, Kathleen Therrien, William Thomas, Alison Buckley, Karin Smyth—all did their part. I'd also like to thank my family—John, John E., Jennie, Xander, Tom, and George (Davidsons all) and my in-laws, Pat and Frank Kerrigan—for knowing when to ask how it was going, and when not to ask. Finally, and most important, I thank my dear friend and husband Brian Kerrigan for sharing the first year of our marriage with this book. He did so with great humour, grace, and kindness, and he didn't seem to mind the constant pile of books and papers that filled our kitchen-office for the duration.
—Janet Davidson

The National Geographic Book Division would like to thank Steven Lubar, Curator and Chair of the Division of the History of Technology at the National Museum of American History, who guided us throughout the project. And Cissy Anklam, who brought the project to us. We also thank Mapping Specialists and XNR Productions for research and production of the map that opens the book.

---

PUBLISHED BY THE NATIONAL GEOGRAPHIC SOCIETY
John M. Fahey, Jr., *President and Chief Executive Officer*
Gilbert M. Grosvenor, *Chairman of the Board*
Nina D. Hoffman, *Executive Vice President*

PREPARED BY THE BOOK DIVISION
Kevin Mulroy, *Vice President and Editor-in-Chief*
Charles Kogod, *Illustrations Director*
Marianne R. Koszorus, *Design Director*
Barbara Brownell Grogan, *Executive Editor*

STAFF FOR THIS BOOK
Susan Tyler Hitchcock, *Editor*
Gerry Greaney, *Art Director*
Marilyn Mofford Gibbons, *Illustrations Editor*
Susan Straight, *Researcher*
Michael R. Harrison, *Illustrations Consultant*
Carl Mehler, *Director of Maps*
Lewis R. Bassford, *Production Project Manager*
Sharon Berry, *Illustrations Assistant*
Margo Browning, *Copy Reader*
Robert Swanson, *Indexer*

MANUFACTURING AND QUALITY CONTROL
Christopher A. Liedel, *Chief Financial Officer*
Phillip L. Schlosser, *Managing Director*
John Dunn, *Technical Director*
Vincent P. Ryan, *Manager*

---